98
VR
3

WHERE
IS HE
NOW?

Where Is He Now?

Sports Heroes of Yesterday --Revisited

by
Jack Drees and James C. Mullen

With a foreword by Bill Veeck

JD| Jonathan David Publishers, Middle Village, New York 11379

Address all inquiries to:

JONATHAN DAVID PUBLISHERS
Middle Village, N. Y. 11379

Library of Congress Catalogue Card No. 71-188243

ISBN 0-8246-0145-9

SECOND PRINTING

PHOTO CREDITS

Cincinnati Reds, Le Bel Negative Co., Pro Football Hall of Fame, New York Yankees, Chicago Cubs, Chicago Bears, World Wide, Detroit Tigers, U.S. Army Photographer, University of Chicago, U.S. Olympic Committee, Lufthansa, Ohio State University, Houston Oilers, U.S. Trotting Association, Arlington Park Race Track, Mickey Owen Baseball School, University of Notre Dame, and Los Angeles Rams.

PRINTED IN THE UNITED STATES OF AMERICA

Foreword

The pendulum has swung, the die is cast. The earth has turned. What once was, is no more. It's a new day, a whole new ball game. And nowhere is this more apparent than in the wondrous world of sports.

Forget Dink Stover, shun Jack Armstrong, spurn Old Siwash and Camelot. Their day is done. They're over the hill, finished, passé, dead as Kelcey's; relegated to limbo by today's spanking new crop of modern, exactly life-size, anti-hero heroes.

So get with it. It's the warts not the exploits that count. Cupidity, venality and violence . . . not heroics are the watchword of today's athletics and athletes. At least that's how it would appear in the most up-to-date, with-it, segments of our current literary efforts. And yet. . . .

Despite the ever increasing importance of athletic contests in our day-to-day life, despite the oft-repeated, trite, well-worn axiom that today's games are but a mirror of the speed, action and violence of our society—still, a nagging doubt remains that maybe in our head-long rush towards fulfillment, we are capriciously interring all the good of the past along with the obvious evil. Despite the present trend, there is much to be learned, admired and enjoyed from what happened before.

Where Is He Now? makes an unusually important and timely contribution to the body of athletic literature. It recalls the days when "hero worship" wasn't arbitrarily a foul epithet; when sports figures living in a simpler age could be somewhat larger than life; when less cynical and less sophisticated (some will substitute naive, idealistic, even innocent) devotees could accept the exploits of athletes for what they were; when it was still believed that athletes, their actions, and careers served as healthy and helpful models for the young.

In recapturing the great moments in the lives of these stars, in recreating, even for a fleeting moment, the glory of their times, the authors have performed a distinct service to every reader. To the young, it brings to life a segment of our recent past; to the old, it recalls memories both pleasant and elusive.

In bringing the careers of these one-time heroes up-to-date in delightful vignettes, the authors provide the answer to the so often repeated, "Whatever happned to. . . ?" No longer does one have to ask: "What's Hank Greenberg doing now?" "Where's Johnny Blood hanging out?" "D'ya ever hear anything about Larry MacPhail?" "Does Althea Gibson still play tennis?" It's all there—highly readable, highly enjoyable.

So hats off, a loud huzzah, and three cheers for Messrs. Drees and Mullen. They've recaptured the past and linked it with the present; reminding us, in the process, that there were some pretty "good ones" around in the past few decades whose moments in the sun are in every way worthy of remembrance.

BILL VEECK

Table of Contents

To Mary—

Who often asks the same question.

To the women in my life:

First to Rita Jane for being understanding.

And then to Donna, Suzy and Brooke—

the beginning of a new generation.

LELAND STANFORD MacPHAIL

The Wizard of Baseball

HE WAS THE PERFECT man for the job. He had a background in law, finance, and baseball, but his most outstanding qualification for rescuing the Brooklyn franchise in 1938 was the fact that he once participated in a plot to kidnap Kaiser Wilhelm of Germany during World War I.

Any man who would take part in such a bizarre scheme, certainly would find putting an artistically sick and financially dying ball club back on its feet a sort of hum-drum task.

And so it was early in 1938 when the Brooklyn Trust Company, which held a half million dollars in notes from the Dodgers, summoned Larry MacPhail from his home in Michigan and put him to work trying to restore the club to some sort of respectability.

The club was a disaster. The front office was a mess. Telephone service had been shut off, employees were openly looking for other jobs and the reception room was populated by people with bills marked "overdue" in their hands, or subpoenas ordering the club to court.

The club was owned by the heirs of Charles H. Ebbets and Stephen McKeever, each holding fifty percent of the stock.

The team had sunk to sixth place in an eight-team league and the usually rabid Brooklyn fans responded by staying away from Ebbets Field in large numbers. Consequently, the listless operation resulted in a sea of red ink and the Brooklyn Trust Company was the biggest creditor.

MacPhail had earlier established himself as an imaginative and successful baseball entrepreneur. By sheer financial wizardry, he had purchased the Columbus franchise in the American Association and turned it into a money maker before selling the club to the St. Louis Cardinals at a handsome profit.

Then Cincinnati called. The Powell Crosley family owned the

Reds, and Crosley Field was sinking into disrepair along with its ball club. MacPhail accepted the challenge, rebuilt the team, cleaned up the ball park and installed lights. And in 1935, history was made when the Reds played the first night game in baseball history. As things turned out, MacPhail not only saved the Cincinnati franchise, but major league baseball as well. He stayed there for three years and left a legacy of back-to-back championship teams that reached its peak in 1939-40.

MacPhail decided that he had done all he could in baseball, and returned to the investment banking business in Michigan with his father and brother. And there he was when the Brooklyn Trust Company decided it needed his help.

After watching its dollars roll perilously away, the bank tried three different times to get MacPhail to take over the ailing club and help it avoid bankruptcy. Ford Frick, president of the National League, and Sam Breadon, who owned the Cardinals then, had advised them that MacPhail was the man who could cure their sickly ball club. On the fourth try MacPhail took the job, making them wait, no doubt, so that he could establish his own authority.

His terms were simple enough. He was to have complete authority, and the bank was to put up a reasonable amount of operating capital. The only moot point was the definition of the term reasonable. To the bank, it meant one thing; to MacPhail another. But in the end MacPhail prevailed.

When he walked into the club's offices at 215 Montague Street in Brooklyn, his first decision was to determine the exact definition of reasonable. He went to the bank's president and simply told him that he needed $200,000 to refurbish Ebbets Field. Curiously enough, he got it. Then, almost as an afterthought, he said he needed an extra $50,000. "What for?" he was asked. "I want to buy an outstanding first baseman," MacPhail replied.

"You mean you want to buy a whole new team, don't you?" was the reply. "No," said McPhail, "I want to buy Dolf Camilli from the Phillies." He got the money and Camilli became a Dodger.

Next, MacPhail went to the General Electric Company and ordered $72,000 worth of equipment to light ancient Ebbets Field. The towers were duly installed, and when the bill was presented to MacPhail, he simply told them to charge it. "I started putting everything on the cuff," he said.

So the first night game in the New York metropolitan area was played June 15, 1938 between the Dodgers and MacPhail's former club, the Cincinnati Reds. MacPhail was equal to the occasion. First there was a monumental fireworks display, followed by footraces between Olympic hero, Jesse Owens, and various ball players.

Then, of course, there was the game itself. And on the mound for the Reds that night was a young left-hander named Johnny Vander Meer, who four days earlier had pitched a 3-0 no-hit victory against the old Boston Braves. Vander Meer responded by becoming the only man in baseball history to pitch consecutive no-hitters when he blanked the Dodgers 6-0. MacPhail accepted the feat as his due. After all, it was an historic occasion in Flatbush and the faithful deserved it.

Burleigh Grimes was managing the Dodgers at the time, and the club fell into its old losing ways and finished seventh, but the fans began to come out. The future looked brighter than at any time in more than a decade. After that finish, MacPhail made another of his gifted decisions.

He appointed shortstop Leo Durocher as the Dodgers' manager, and he could not have made a wiser move. Durocher was the natural candidate for the job for one reason only. He was about as bellicose and belligerent as the Brooklyn fans. In fact, he was then, as he is now, one of the most belligerent men in the game, and his vocal stamina, while considerable, was second only to Mac-Phail's. Thus, the Flatbush faithful, with MacPhail and Durocher running as an entry, knew they weren't going to get jobbed out of anything, particularly by the umpires.

Durocher, who was given the name Lippy Leo years before, had a booming voice and his vocabulary was peppered with a ball player's profanity. It still is. MacPhail was much more accomplished in this regard, and his cursing during moments of self-inflicted stress reached epic proportions.

Larry hit his peak when an officer of the American First Committee wanted to rent his ball park for a rally. MacPhail, who was honorary chairman of the Brooklyn branch of the Committee to Defend America by Aiding the Allies, exploded into a diatribe of profanity that he didn't learn at the University of Michigan, or Beloit College, or George Washington University where he got his law degree. It was just part of him.

In his relentless effort to hypo interest in the Dodgers, Mac-Phail imported radio announcer Red Barber from Cincinnati. He had initially hired Barber for the Reds, bringing him up to that club after hearing him read a report on bovine obstetrics over the radio when Red was a student working his way through the University of Florida. Again it was a master touch.

Much to the chagrin of the Dodgers and Yankees who were against giving away their product, Barber captured Brooklyn in a manner akin to Joe Namath's envelopment of New York three decades later. Meanwhile, MacPhail continued to wheel and deal, hiring 15 full-time talent scouts to beat the hinterlands in the never-ending search for talent. The Dodgers prospered at the gate and on the field, and climbed from seventh to third in 1939, and to second in 1940. A year later, the Brooks won their first pennant in 23 years, but more important, the Beloved Bums became a household word—even if you didn't happen to live in Brooklyn.

When World War II came along, MacPhail didn't want to miss it and he didn't. Although he was 52 years of age at the time, this man, who tried to spirit the Kaiser out of exile in Holland in 1919, returned to active duty as a full colonel in the general staff corps and dreamed about returning to major league baseball after the war. And that's exactly what he did, taking over the New York Yankees as president and general manager.

Slightly over six feet tall, 195 pounds, with red hair to match his flaming temper, MacPhail built a crumbling Yankee franchise into a world championship team in 1947. And just as unpredictably, he sold out, at a $2,000,000 profit, after the final day of the World Series. As he walked to the Yankee clubhouse, baseball writer Hy Turkin was standing under the grandstand with a portable radio to his ear waiting for the last play of the game. It came on a double play, and before poor Hy knew what happened, MacPhail belted him across the face with his open palm: "That's it," MacPhail shouted over the din of the crowd. "I'm through. I retire." Turkin got his scoop the hard way.

Later that night, at the Biltmore Hotel during a victory party, MacPhail slugged John McDonald, his traveling secretary with the Dodgers. He took out after Dan Topping, the millionaire sportsman and one of his partners in the Yankees, wanting to fight, and calling him a "silver spooned slob," he upended tables trying to get at Del Webb, the multi-millionaire contractor who owned the third share of the club.

The next day, MacPhail became an instant millionaire himself when Webb and Topping bought him out. George Weiss, whom MacPhail had fired the night before, was rehired as general manager, and another Yankee dynasty was in the making.

During his career, which spanned 17 years from the time he bought the Columbus team in 1930, MacPhail's method of operation was to always attack, and to hell with the consequences. His life is dotted with famous feuds involving Commissioner Kenesaw Mountain Landis, Commissioner A. B. (Happy) Chandler, who succeeded Landis, Will Harridge, the late president of the American League, Ford Frick, National League president, and later in life, feuds with telephone operators who argued with him, as well as with Maryland state troopers.

Two of MacPhail's most famous rhubarbs were with the late Branch Rickey and Chandler, when he was commissioner. After

Rickey brought Jackie Robinson, the first black, into the majors in 1947, MacPhail said that organized baseball was ready to accept blacks even before Rickey signed Robinson, indicating that the Mahatma of Brooklyn broke an agreement with his brethren in the game's inner councils.

Rickey, of course, denied it, choosing a speech he delivered at Wilberforce College as the showcase. He said that 15 of the 16 major league clubs approved a resolution which stated that the admission of Negroes would endanger baseball's "physical properties."

The battle with Chandler made headlines for weeks, and it involved MacPhail's Yankees signing Charlie Dressen as a coach, and also the year's suspension meted out to Durocher for conduct detrimental to baseball.

Chandler bound all participants to silence, which phased MacPhail not a bit. He talked about the situation as though the commissioner had held the hearings in open court. But the truth of the matter was that Chandler's job was on the line, and MacPhail wasn't about to let that fact go unnoticed. Chandler survived that one, but his position was weakened considerably.

Between the feuds, the pennants and innovations, MacPhail made several major contributions to major league baseball. Not the least of which is the players' pension plan, generally regarded as the best in professional sports. MacPhail force-fed the original plan to his fellow owners, knowing that it would cost him money and also realizing that it was the moral thing to do.

Because of his bombastic personality, the real MacPhail often was shrouded in controversy. But Bill Veeck, who succeeded him as baseball's maverick while operating the Cleveland, White Sox and St. Louis clubs in the American League, remembers him with gratitude and affection. Maybe it was because MacPhail bought a three-toed outfielder named Hal Peck from him when Veeck was trying to keep the Milwaukee franchise afloat.

"He's the most honorable man I ever met in baseball," Veeck says. And coming from the Old Hustler himself, that's quite a compliment.

WHERE IS HE NOW?

Larry MacPhail, born February 3, 1890, lives on his pretentious country estate in Bel Air, Maryland. His first marriage in 1910 to Inez Thompson ended in divorce in 1945, and in May of that year he married Jean Bennett Wanamaker, formerly his secretary in Brooklyn.

There are two sons and a daughter by the first marriage. One son, Leland S. MacPhail Jr., is vice-president and general manager of the New York Yankees. The other, Bill MacPhail, is a top television executive with the Columbia Broadcasting System in New York.

Following his retirement from the Yankees after that wild night at the Biltmore, MacPhail settled down to put his house in order. The Bel Air, originally purchased as a weekend retreat, had become a showcase of Maryland's Eastern Shore with manicured lawns, shrubs, pure-bred cattle and for a time thoroughbred horses.

MacPhail then went into the horse racing business on a grand scale, forming a syndicate that purchased the Bowie track. But the tempestuous redhead didn't linger too long in the racing business. He battled the Maryland Commission for better racing dates, and then got embroiled in a couple of incidents at the track that resulted in his being banned from the grounds, even as a paying customer.

One involved MacPhail's arrest on charges of disorderly conduct and assaulting a state trooper. Police said that MacPhail objected to the way traffic was being handled on one of the roads leading to and from the track.

The other incident was reported to be a loud and profane argument in the clubhouse between MacPhail and two directors of the Horsemen's Benevolent and Protective Association.

In any case, the board of directors at Bowie sacked him, and he returned to Bel Air to raise pure-bred cattle and thoroughbreds. A decade later he sold all of his horses—55 of them for $337,900—and sought new fields to conquer.

At the age of 60, he became a father again—this time of a daughter. And he began another ambitious project, the construction of a $300,000 golf course on his 500-acre farm.

The course was equal to the imagination of its creator, and is regarded as one of the finest in the Middle Atlantic States. After its completion, MachPail sold it to a membership, the Maryland Golf and Country Club, for what it had cost him. The group took the land at its own appraisal and MacPhail holds a 20-year mortgage on the property.

"I have no voice in the operation of the club," MacPhail says. "I'm only a member." But while the course was under construction, he was something else—the old Larry MacPhail. He fought with the architects, and when the members wanted to use it before he thought it was ready, he threatened to get an injunction to keep the golfers off the course.

He never did, and these days, as he summers in Bel Air and winters in Florida, he seems pleased that the course is available to his neighbors.

He is old now. He has fought the good fight against cancer and heart trouble, and the fire in his blue eyes still burns as brightly as it did more than 50 years ago when he tried to whisk the Kaiser out of Holland. He has one of Wilhelm's ashtrays as a memento of that escapade and he looks at it every now and then as if to try and recapture those wonderful moments of youth.

And there were so many wonderful moments for Leland Stanford MacPhail. Noisy, but wonderful.

CHARLES LEO HARTNETT

The Man in the Iron Mask

HE HAD A BIG, RED, round Irish face when he reported to the Cubs in 1922 as a kid catcher out of Milford, Massachusetts. And more than 50 years later, he still has a big, red, round Irish face. Those 50 years in between have been a delight to him, not to mention the Chicago Cubs' faithful as well as the fans in the other National League cities.

His given name is Charles Leo Hartnett, but to the baseball fans of any generation, he is known as Gabby. And from that day in 1922 when he joined the Cubs until he ended his career with· the Giants in 1941, Gabby Hartnett was the National League's top receiver. At least, the baseball writers thought so, for they elected him to the Hall of Fame in July, 1955.

His plaque at Cooperstown reads:

CHARLES LEO (GABBY) HARTNETT

Chicago N.L. 1922-1940

New York N.L. 1941

Caught 100 or more games per season for 12 years, eight in succession, 1930 to 1937, for league record. Set mark for consecutive chances for catcher without an error, 452 in 1933-34. Highest fielding average for catcher in 100 or more games in 7 seasons. Most putouts N.L. 7,292; Most chances accepted N.L., 8,546. Lifetime batting average .297.

From the engraving on the plaque, the inference is that Hartnett is best remembered for his defensive efforts behind the plate. That is true, and for years in Chicago he was called, "The Man in the Iron Mask."

But lest we forget, and before a whole new generation of fans bursts upon us, keep in mind that Charles Leo Hartnett was a hitter, too. Five times during his career he hit over .300, and in 1937 he reached .354 for a career high. His home runs total 236, but like Bobby Thomson who came along 13 years later, only one of them will be remembered for posterity.

That famous home run came near the end of the Great Gabbo's career: on Sept. 28, 1938, to be exact. But there were a lot of years in between.

When this son of a streetcar man reported to the Cubs at Catalina Island for spring training in 1922, Bill Killefer, a catcher himself, was managing the club, and Bill Veeck Sr., was the front-office boss. Jack Doyle, the famous scout for the Cubs, had discovered Gabby playing in Albany, N. Y. and arranged to buy his contract.

Doyle forgot to tell Gabby about it. A hungry young buck of 21 at the time, Gabby approached the manager for a two-dollar touch for meal money and was happily surprised when the man handed him a five dollar bill. "Here take this," he said, "and you can pay me back next spring from the Cubs' training camp."

And that's how Hartnett learned that he had finally made the major leagues. Breaking into the Cubs' lineup was something else. But it was inevitable, and his chance finally came as the Cubs wended their way back east from their island camp. The first stop was in Los Angeles and Veeck Sr., who thrust his son, Bill, on the world of baseball a generation later, was in the stands along with Doyle and John O. Seys, vice president of the Cubs.

Manager Bill Killefer, the club's regular catcher, approached them on the possibility of shipping Hartnett back to the minors or, better yet, returning him to his former avocation of berry picking. But he didn't get very far.

Veeck, Doyle and Seyes figured the kid didn't get much of a chance to show what he could do, and that now was as good a time as any. So Gabby donned his catcher's garb, got behind the plate and made his debut.

What made the occasion even more memorable was that Grover Cleveland Alexander was on the mound for the Cubs. And after the game, Killefer got a first-hand evaluation from the great Alexander. Not known for his verbosity, Old Pete said: "That kid is going to be all right."

He was so right.

And it would be nice to say that Gabby's ascent to the Hall of Fame began that very day like a Cape Kennedy blastoff. But it didn't happen that way. He played in only 31 games the first year and his batting average was an unimposing .194.

Gabby's first National League game was memorable, though. Not only because it was the opening game of the season and Alexander was the pitcher, but because it happened to be the first major league game Hartnett ever saw. It was against the Reds in Cincinnati, and the young catcher was as surprised as any one when Killefer called on him to do the catching.

By 1924, when Red Grange was establishing himself as a legend at the University of Illinois, and Knute Rockne's Four Horsemen were winning their way toward the Rose Bowl, Gabby Hartnett had earned his niche as the greatest Cub catcher of all-time, an honor that was confirmed in a poll of fans by the Chicago *Sun-Times* 45 years later!

There was heartbreak, too. In 1929, the Cubs won the National League pennant under manager Joe McCarthy, who later made the Hall of Fame as manager of the New York Yankees. But Hartnett was unable to contribute much.

His throwing arm deserted him that season and he was limited to pinch-hitting, and in only 25 games at that. Specialists were called in and all sorts of therapy was prescribed, but legend has it that the massages of tobacco juice by Dr. Andy Lotshaw, the Cub trainer, did as much as anything to restore the resiliency to Hartnett's arm in time for the 1930 season.

In any case, Hartnett, who wielded his catcher's glove much like the Reds' Johnny Bench does today, made his comeback, and in 1935 they won another flag. Gabby hit .344 that season, and two seasons later hit his high point at the plate with that .354 mark.

By 1938, late in the season, P. K. Wrigley, the Cubs owner, became disenchanted with the progress being made by manager Charlie Grimm. He searched for a successor, without taking any full page newspaper advertisements, a ploy he was to use three decades later, and settled on Gabby Hartnett. Wrigley never made a wiser or luckier choice. And luck was a factor because, as Hartnett was to reveal years later, Wrigley offered the job to shortstop Billy Jurges first, but he turned it down. Gabby was P.K.'s second choice.

Hartnett had a certain quality of leadership about him which today would be called charisma, and it served the Cubs well. He took a Cub team that was nine games behind the Pirates and on the verge of foundering in late August, and by the last week of the season had it breathing down the necks of the league leaders.

On Sept. 28, 1938 the second place Cubs were only a game back of the Bucs and the showdown game was played at Wrigley Field in Chicago. There weren't any lights then, just as there aren't now, and the two teams battled late into the afternoon. In those bygone days, Chicago games started at 3 P.M., and by the last of the ninth they were locked in a 5-5 tie as darkness settled on the field.

Dizzy Dean had won the series opener the day before to cut the

Pirates lead to a half-game, and Hartnett called on Clay Bryant. The Pirates knocked out Bryant in the eight inning, but the Cubs came to life in their half.

Rip Collins opened with a single and Billy Jurges walked. Pinch hitter Tony Lazzeri doubled to score Collins and Billy Herman brought home Jurges with the tying run on a single.

Veteran Charlie Root pitched the top of the ninth and held off the Bucs, but another factor loomed large. Plate umpire George Barr informed Hartnett that if the Cubs didn't score, he would call the game because of darkness and it would have to be replayed in its entirety.

Tension mounted as the word spread through the crowd of 34,465 that jammed Wrigley Field. Mace Brown was on the mound for Pittsburgh and at this point he was doing all right. Leadoff man Phil Cavarretta flied out to Lloyd Waner in center field. Carl Reynolds brought Hartnett to the plate when he grounded into the second out.

The big, tomato-faced Irishman was the Cubs' last hope as he stepped to the plate in the gathering darkness. He swung and missed Brown's first pitch. He got a piece of the second offering, but fouled it off to make it two strikes.

As the sun dropped behind the third-base side of the grandstand, Brown delivered a breaking pitch and Hartnett sent it on its way to the left field bleachers. Umpire Barr watched in amazement and waited for what seemed like an eternity before raising his right arm to signal home run. Meanwhile, Hartnett, trotting around the bases, couldn't conceal the jubilation that gripped him as he broke into a big grin. The fans went wild. And by the time he reached third base there were as many people on the field as there were in the seats. Still he fought his way to the plate, as the Cub players, equally mad with joy, engulfed him as he touched home. Hartnett had hit the most famous home run in baseball history until Bobby Thomson came along in 1951.

The Pirates were incredulous. Their management had already prepared Forbes Field for a World Series that was never to be played there. The Hartnett blow had touched off the Cubs again, and they clinched the pennant on October 1 by winning the second game of a doubleheader in St. Louis.

Such a feat surely would earn Hartnett a place in the heart of the Cubs forever. Right? Wrong. Two years later Wrigley fired him and signed Jimmy Wilson as manager, and Hartnett drifted off to the Giants as a player-coach where he ended his career in 1941. He later came back with Kansas City as a coach in the 1960s, but despite his more than two decades in the major leagues, no one wanted him as a coach or manager or anything. And for him, that was, and is, a little hard to take.

WHERE IS HE NOW?

Gabby Hartnett turned to bowling after his career came to an end, and for 19 years has owned an establishment in Lincolnwood on the northern reaches of Chicago.

He and his Martha still live on the North Side. That baseball that he hit out of Wrigley Field, and that resulted in a pennant, has a prominent place on the mantle, along with his Hall of Fame Plaque, and his All-Star mementos.

As he looks back at his career he has some misgivings. "Oh, I got along with P. K. Wrigley, all right, but I couldn't see eye-to-eye with some of his so-called experts."

Like who?

"Charles (Boots) Weber and Clarence (Pants) Rowland," Gabby replied. "I couldn't make the deals I wanted because of them and their second guessing," he added.

"I think I did a good job for the Cubs and it would have been a lot better if I had a little co-operation from them."

Hartnett's children, Charles Leo Jr., and Shiela Ann have given Gabby and Martha eight grandchildren, and he's happy about that. But the old longing to be part of the game is still there. "I gave the Cubs 20 years," he says. "You'd think they'd find some place for me."

Would he like to be playing in these lush days?

"You bet," he said. "I'd make a lot of money now. But I think we had more good players in my day, and a lot of them were sitting on the bench. There are some good players now, too, but not as many as we had. I guess it's expansion. Anyway, these guys don't have the desire either. If you have a team with desire, your problems are 80 per cent solved."

Still an avid golfer in his seventies, Gabby takes each day as it comes. "I'm not doing much of anything now," he says. "I play cards a lot in the winter and golf four or five times a week in the summer.

"But I love life and I'm just trying to live as long as I can. I just wish the Cubs would have found a place for me . . . in some capacity."

Gabby Hartnett died on December 20, 1972, his 72nd birthday.

JOHN BLOOD McNALLY

The Joe Namath of the '30s

IT WAS CHRISTMAS NIGHT in 1933 and the tall, dark-haired young man dashed out of Union Station in St. Louis, a beautiful, laughing young lady on his arm.

All they wanted was a cab, and sure enough as they skipped down the steps, hand-in-hand, there was a taxi waiting at the curb. Unfortunately, there was no driver but it really didn't matter. The young man gallantly opened the rear door and helped the lady into the seat, and then he put on his best cab driver's face and drove off down the street.

Eighteen blocks later, a cruising St. Louis police car noticed that the man didn't look like a cab driver at all.

The police were so right. He was John V. McNally, known to followers of professional football the country over as Johnny Blood, a 29-year-old itinerant quarterback. His attractive companion that cold and windy night was Miss Dorcas Cochran, age 24, who told police she was a nightclub dancer.

Charges were not pressed, but the St. Louis cab company did charge Johnny Blood for what was on the meter and it amounted to 35 cents. Johnny paid, and thus another adventure in the life of one of pro football's most colorful players came to a happy conclusion.

If one had to compare Johnny Blood with a player of this era, that player would have to be Joe Namath of the New York Jets. They had that much in common. Physically, they probably could have changed clothes, both being six feet two inches and 193 pounds. Athletically, both were endowed with the natural skills given to only a few, although Namath is one of the game's top passers, and Blood was more renowned as a receiver and a runner.

Life styles? Take your pick and it would be a sleigh ride all the way. Namath's colorful capers are well known to today's "now" generation. They saw him shave off his beard for $10,000 on a television commercial. Johnny Blood had his fun with no help from the electronic media, but he had it no less, and because of it he has become a legend. So much so that when his name is recalled, few remember that he was a great athlete as well as one of the sport's most lovable vagabonds. In short, a likeable scoundrel.

And that was the way he wanted it. No one ever told Johnny Blood how to live and few had to tell him how to play football. He was that good. His freshman coach at Notre Dame, the late George Keogan, tried to make a tackle out of him and lost the decision.

"I am a quarterback," said McNally, as he was then called. "I've always played quarterback."

Keogan, who was to become one of the foremost basketball coaches of his time, told the brash kid to play tackle or turn in his uniform.

Notre Dame regained the uniform it had issued less than an hour before. Johnny stayed in school, though, burning up his excess energy by playing basketball with the South Bend Y.M.C.A. team.

But along came St. Patrick's day and McNally was as Irish as the next, even at Notre Dame. By way of celebrating the grand occasion, he liberated a motorcycle and headed for Richmond, Virginia, with a young lady in the sidecar. After he was found and the incident settled to the satisfaction of all concerned parties, McNally left Notre Dame and headed for other pursuits.

The son of a well-to-do family in New Richmond, Wisconsin, McNally was always precocious. At age 14, he graduated from high school, at the top of his class no less, and had written in the fly leaf of his yearbook:

Dear God, how sweet in spring it is to be a boy.

A year later he tried to join the Navy, but was rejected.

At 16, he entered River Falls State Teachers College, but he lasted only a few months.

Finally, McNally, the pater, put down a strong Hibernian foot, and John spent two years at St. John's College where he played football, basketball and baseball and ran on the track team. He also won the school's poetry and oratory contests, and that served him well many years later in a Pittsburgh bar. There he met the late John Barrymore and the two of them engaged in a Shakespeare-quoting contest until dawn. The famed actor finished second.

Football, though, was Johnny Blood's thing, and after he parted company with St. John's, he headed for Minneapolis and joined a team called the East 26th Street Libertys. And they actually paid a guy money for playing! He was warned, though.

"You fellows can play under assumed names," Blood and a companion were told. "They if you want to go back to school, you'll still be eligible." This created a problem for McNally because he didn't want to be a Smith or Jones, or Anderson or anybody so mundane.

At a movie a couple of nights later, McNally was struck with the inspiration that was to be with him all his life. The picture was "Blood and Sand" starring Rudolf Valentino.

"That's it," McNally said to his friend. "You be Sand, and I'll be Blood." And so Johnny Blood, the legend, was thrust upon an unsuspecting world.

That first season with the East Libertys was only the forerunner of a 15-year career that brought him to such exotic football teams as the Milwaukee Badgers; the Duluth Eskimos; the Pottsville (Pa.) Maroons of the National League; and then to Green Bay. Later he served as a player-coach for Art Rooney's Pittsburgh team.

There were also the Kenosha Cardinals and La Crosse, Chippewa Falls and more than a score of pick-up All-Star teams. And all the while, he kept right on dancing. In 1934, for example, between football seasons, he sailed the Pacific as a deckhand, and from that journey came a 250-page thesis entitled "Spend Yourself Rich." His philosophy was so simple, it was strange no one had ever thought of it before. It was:

Every buck you spend somebody else earns.

That's why money never meant much to Johnny Blood. It was to spend, preferably accompanied by music with a glass well in hand. He thought nothing of a "touch" for his last $100, and conversely would pass an overdraft on a friend in a moment of need. Invariably he made it good.

For Johnny Blood, it was all a big game: football in season, and living the rest of the time. More than once, Curly Lambeau, his coach at Green Bay and one of the pioneers of the National Football League, became distraught at his antics. Like the time he crawled outside a fast moving train after a wet towel fight, and crossed the cars, roof by roof, until he joined the startled engineer.

Then there was the night in Los Angeles when he wanted to get into Lambeau's room without the coach knowing it. So he jumped across the court, window ledge to window ledge, in a driving rain. Curly's room was on the sixth floor.

Blood could play any backfield position, and won his greatest fame as a half back and a pass receiver. Often he made catches that rivaled the ones made by his teammate and fellow member in the Hall of Fame, Don Hutson. Even at age 33, and at the end of the line as a Packer, he was still fast enough to extend the great Hutson, 10 years younger, to the limit in a 100-yard dash.

In those days of 25-man squads, Blood, as well as his teammates, played with injuries. At one stage with Milwaukee, he played the equivalent of a full game with a ruptured kidney before he finally collapsed on the field. Johnny Blood recovered, much to the surprise of the attending physician, and continued his search for fun and football.

As it does for all athletes, the end had to come. So Blood returned to St. John's, and later, at the age of 46, he received his Bachelor of Art degree, and for a year or so he worked toward a Master's at the University of Minnesota while working as a desk clerk in a Minneapolis hotel.

WHERE IS HE NOW?

Johnny Blood and Catherine, his wife of six years, live on Grand Avenue in St. Paul, Minnesota. "Of course, I'd like to be playing today," he says, "who wouldn't, unless he's tired of living, and I'm not that. I was made for this game. Guys like myself, Arnie Herber, Don Hutson—we could go and get them. Then there's the money, excitement and the color. Not that I need the money, because I don't, but it wouldn't hurt me, would it?"

What about the facilities for the players in those early days?

"Rubble, compared to what they have today," he said. "In Pittsburgh, for instance, we played at old, Greenlee Field. There were rocks on the ground, no hot water. It was the place where kids who had no money played.

"Most of the places we played in didn't even have a shower. We'd go to a turkish bath, if the town had one, and dress there so we could take a hot shower. I think we helped create today's game and yet, we don't share in any of it."

Blood and his wife have two employment agencies in the Twin Cities area. "Catherine the Great runs those," he says. "I'm busy trying to form the National Pro Football Alumni and we have 56 paid members in this area. We want to set up chapters in the other league cities around the country. Ernie Nevers is going to try to organize the San Francisco area."

Blood and the rest of the pioneers, as well as anyone who played in the National Football League prior to 1958, do not share in the league's generous pension plan.

"Not that I need the money," he says proudly. "I'm subsidized by a couple of graveyards, so I don't need it." But he has an idea.

"I think the Super Bowl ought to be a three-game series," he said, "with say, a game in Miami, another in New Orleans and the third in one of the new Texas stadiums." His formula is a complicated one, but he has it figured that even if a team loses all three games, they could win most of the money on a total-point scoring arrangement.

"The money could go into a pension fund for those of us who played in earlier times," he says. And so the dream goes on for Johnny Blood McNally. The legend is alive and well in his beloved Northland. And it never will die as long as the game of football is played in America.

JAMES BELL

Cool Papa

"I THINK ABOUT IT, since it's over," the black man said. "There were so many with me, who never got a chance. But I'm glad somebody got up there."

Speaking was James Bell, known as "Cool Papa" to the thousands of fans who watched the Negro leagues during his career which spanned the years from 1920 through the 1951 season. Cool Papa was an outfielder and sometimes pitcher, and is regarded by many as the best baserunner ever to play baseball—and that includes the Dodgers' Maury Wills in his prime. And Bell was talking about the superb black baseball players who never received the opportunity to play in the major leagues, or any part of organized baseball for that matter, because of the so-called "color line."

Branch Rickey, the late Mahatma of the Brooklyn Dodgers, is generally credited with bringing up Jackie Robinson in 1947 as the first black ball played in the big tent. And rightly so. Rickey handpicked the former UCLA athlete from the Kansas City Monarchs and put him on the roster of the Montreal Royals, a Dodger farm club, in 1946.

The 26-year-old Robinson, a superb athlete with a low boiling point, was warned that he would be subjected to all kinds of abuse, verbal and otherwise, in his role as a black pioneer. And that's the way it happened: vicious name calling, threatened strikes by white major league stars, and physical abuse on the field. But Jackie Robinson endured, and he did so because he had a lot going for him including the kind of ability that later earned him a place in the Hall of Fame.

He also had the support of Cool Papa Bell and literally hundreds of black ball players who did their own thing in the cities, towns, hamlets and whistle-stops of the nation for more than half a century. They called them the Negro leagues, and they contained enough talent to stock a major league franchise or two with the best ball players in the world. The only problem was that they were not white, and because of that the doors of the national pastime were closed for what seemed an eternity.

But that didn't stop black men from playing the game. They formed their own teams and leagues, and names like the Monarchs, the American Giants, Pittsburgh Crawfords, Homestead Grays, Birmingham Black Barons, New York Cubans, Indianapolis Clowns and St. Louis Stars became synonymous with excellence on the diamond.

Satchel Paige, of course, became the epitome of the black ball player, pitching smoke for more than forty years in every corner of this country as well as South America, Mexico and the Dominican Republic. And there were others such as Bill Yancey, Dave Malarcher, Judy Johnson, Buck Leonard, Oscar Charleston, and the great Josh Gibson, to name but a few.

Cool Papa Bell was one of these. He belongs in the company of the all-time greats in baseball—black or white. Bell, five feet eleven inches and about 140 pounds in his playing days, is generally regarded as the quickest ever to play the game. The Negro leagues, defunct now for more than two decades, are full of anecdotes and stories that have grown ripe over the years. One of the best concerns Cool Papa.

"He was so fast," they said, "that he could snap off a light and be back in bed under the covers before it got dark."

Chalk that one up as some of the lore that surrounds this man. But not this one:

Cool Papa is on first base with one of his chop singles and the next batter is ordered to sacrifice him to second with a bunt. The pitch is delivered and the hitter lays down a perfect bunt between the mound and third base. Bell, after a long lead, takes off for second and then: "I saw that third base was open because the third baseman had also charged in to field the bunt. Roy Partee, the catcher, saw me going, so he went down the line to cover third and I just came home past him." That was Cool Papa Bell talking and matter-of-factly describing how he went from first to home on a sacrifice bunt, not an uncommon feat for him.

Born May 17, 1905, in Starkville, Mississippi, Bell came up to St. Louis to play with an amateur team along with four of his brothers. Later, he joined an East St. Louis semipro team and then caught on with the St. Louis Stars in 1922 starting a professional career that was to end in 1951.

"I played 29 summers and 21 winters," Bell says proudly. That's 50 seasons." And he is so right. But they weren't easy ones. Today, major leaguers are put up in the best hotels and given $18 in meal money each day, in addition to flying in chartered jets and special aid-conditioned buses from hotel to ball park.

Cool Papa and his compatriots enjoyed no such luxuries. "I played with some teams that let you sign for meals," he said. "But there weren't many of them. In 1942 we were getting 70 cents a day for meals. Later it went to a dollar, then a dollar and a quarter and finally two dollars. Anything over that they'd take out of your salary, know what I mean? So if you had to eat more than the two dollars in one day, you'd pay the rest yourself.

Hotels were something else. "Reservations," Cool Papa says, "were hard to get in some places. We didn't have too much trouble in the big cities or in the South. Down there, there usually was a big colored section and the people would put us up.

"But toward the end of my career, we did a lot of traveling through North Dakota, Iowa, Minnesota, Oregon and places like that. There just aren't many colored people out there, so we got an old bus and fixed it up with 15 bunks. We'd just pull it off the side of the highway and sleep right there, and in the morning go on to the next town for the game."

Following his stint with the St. Louis Stars, where he became a full-time outfielder, Bell played with the Homestead Grays, Detroit Wolves, Kansas City Monarchs, Pittsburgh Crawfords, Memphis Red Sox and the Chicago American Giants. In addition, he played four years in Mexico as well as the Dominican Republic, where, in 1937, President Rafael L. Trujillo drafted Satchel Paige to pitch for his team during an election year. Cool Papa and eight of his teammates on the Crawfords joined the campaign.

Later in his career, Bell managed the Kansas City Monarchs' traveling team and was instrumental in helping to advance Ernie Banks, Elston Howard and Gene Baker to the major leagues. "I was managing Ernie," Bell recalls, "and the Monarchs didn't want to bring him up to the big team. But I told them, this boy could do everything, and it wasn't but a couple years later that he was signed by the Cubs."

As for his denial by the game he loves, Bell is most charitable. "People knew we had good ball players," he says without rancor. "But they just didn't rate us with the big leaguers."

That was baseball's biggest mistake over the years as today's lineups attest. The black man proved long ago that he could have answered Casey Stengel's plaintive lament during a particularly trying day with the early New York Mets. Casey asked: "Can't anybody here play this game?"

Cool Papa Bell and hundreds of others could have answered loudly and clearly. "Yes, I can!"

WHERE IS HE NOW?

Cool Papa Bell, nearing the age of 70, is still in St. Louis where he is a security guard at City Hall. He works the midnight to 8 A.M. shift, and he does it because he wants to.

"It's the daylight," he says. "I've been out in the daylight most of my life, playing ball and all. When I did have to work, I'd leave the house so early in the morning that it would be dark. And when I was through workin' it would be dark again. So I wanted a job where I'd see daylight all year round. I get through work in the morning and have the whole day and then I have the evenings to sleep.

"I like the job. Make the rounds, turn off all the lights, check the doors and things and later on I turn them on again for the people when they come to work."

He and his wife, Clara B., have been married for more than 40 years. "You mean you went off and played ball and left her home alone?" he was asked.

"No, not all the time," Cool Papa answered. "When I had someplace permanent for a while, like in Kansas City or Chicago, she would come and join me."

But if he had it to do all over again, he wouldn't change a thing. Bell would have liked to have had his place in the majors. "If we had a chance to play now, we could prove to the public that we were major leaguers," he says. "If you can play, you can play," he says. "Sure ball players are more intelligent now, college and all, and they know how to meet the public, but we had good ball players, too."

Yes, the Negro League did, scores of them. And James (Cool Papa) Bell was one of them. In fact that's how he got his name. He struck out the great Oscar Charleston as a 19-year-old pitcher with the St. Louis Stars. His teammates, Bell says, started calling him "Cool" after that, and manager Bill Gatewood added the Papa in deference to his tender years.

Cool Papa plans to retire from his security job in 1973. "Those are my plans," he says. "I always plan ahead, you know."

DICK BARTELL

Rowdy Dick

HE WAS BORN TO BE a baseball player. How could it have been any other way?

His father, Harry Bartell, was a big name around the Chicago area at the turn of the century. He had managed the Ferns, the Ping Pongs, the Rock Island Semipros and the Woodstock Olivers. And his uncles, William, Bert and Johnny, all took a shot at playing the game.

William played second base and shortstop for Rogers Park, Elgin, East Chicago and Joliet, and Bert was a catcher with the old Myers' Cubs. Johnny tried out with the White Sox, but the "Old Roman," Charles A. Comiskey, came up a little short when they talked about money. That ended that.

This was the type of heritage Dick Bartell had behind him when he happened into the world in Chicago on November 22, 1907. Five months later, his father landed a job as a county supervisor in Alemeda, California and packed up his family and left for the West Coast.

Baseball was rather a nebulous profession in those days, and a county supervisor, well, that was security. Besides, the climate was temperate enough so young Dick Bartell could grow up with a baseball in his hand. And that's just about the way it happened.

Bartell was gifted in his own way. He didn't have the size or speed in comparison to today's player, but he was good with the glove, and on any given day, he could beat you with his bat. He also had something else.

He was confident, brash, cocky, abrasive and a born hustler. And he carried with him a deep hate, not of his opponents, but of losing. Later in his career, which covered 18 years as a player and a couple more as a coach with Detroit and Cincinnati, he became one of the game's most ardent umpire baiters, surpassing even Leo Durocher in his palmiest days.

He was not above battling with an opponent, a teammate or even a newspaperman. But when he took on the press during an unhappy one-season stint with the Chicago Cubs, his adversaries behind the typewriter virtually rode him out of the league.

It all started in the spring of 1939 at Catalina Island, the Cubs' training base off the coast of California. Bartell had come to the Cubs in the big trade of the previous winter. He, along with Hank Leiber and Gus Mancuso, was traded by the Giants for Chicago's Billy Jurges, Frank Demaree and Ken O'Dea.

He was big news that day in camp, and the writers who enjoy the freedom of the playing field during spring training wandered along the sidelines as Bartell held court for them. But one was not there. He was the late Ed Burns, the veteran baseball chronicler for the *Chicago Tribune.*

Burns arrived on the scene late, along with the Cubs' traveling secretary, Bob Lewis. Both were jolly companions and, as such, were on the corpulent side. As they strode onto the field, the workout was in full swing, and Bartell, noticing the girth of the late-arriving pair, said so that all could hear: "When does the balloon go up?"

According to Warren Brown, the highly respected columnist, sports editor and baseball writer, neither Lewis nor Burns said anything at the time, but Burns never forgot it. And he didn't let Bartell forget it either.

Rowdy Richard, before the training session was over, was sent first to Los Angeles and later to Chicago for treatment of an injured ankle.

Headlines blared the news when he was hospitalized in Chicago for treatment, and the stories hinted darkly that the Giants had palmed off an arthritic shortstop on the unsuspecting Cubs. And to make it worse, from the Chicago viewpoint, Jurges was off to what looked like a banner year. Bartell finally did walk out of the hospital to rejoin his teammates, but all was not well.

In the first 40 games he played, he made 18 errors, most of them throwing. And when the ball sailed into the box seats behind first base, Burns took a particular delight in informing his readers that Dick Bartell did indeed blow another one for the Cubs.

"He had a horrible year," Brown recalls. "Of course he would try to make the impossible plays and they'd give him an error on those, too." In any case, Bartell appeared in 107 games for the Cubs, drove in only 34 runs and hit only .241. His fielding deteriorated so badly that he was replaced at the end of the season by Bobby Mattick, brought up from the Milwaukee farm club.

The crowning blow, though, came at the end of the season

when the Chicago members of the Baseball Writers Association of America held their annual banquet at the Palmer House.

At one stage of the zany proceedings, after Charlie Grimm had played the banjo (left-handed of course), baseball writer Eddie McGuire rushed on to the stage carrying a large boot.

"Boot for Bartell!" he shouted as the fans, well oiled by this time, broke into a wave of laughter. "Boot for Bartell!"

That probably was the low point in Bartell's career, but there were plenty of high spots. Before he had come to the Cubs in the deal with the Giants, Dick had played in the Red Sox system, broke into the majors with the Pirates, and later was traded to the Phillies before the Giants got him. He helped the Giants win pennants in 1936 and 1937.

Later he played with Detroit and, in all, he participated in three World Series and two All-Star games, before his career ended. He managed Sacramento in the Pacific Coast League and Kansas City in the American Association before returning to the Tigers as a coach.

During all those years, there was hardly a dull moment. One of his more memorable altercations was with pitcher Van Lingle Mungo of the Dodgers. They collided on the base path after Mungo brushed Rowdy Richard back. Later, as a coach for the Tigers, Bartell took on bonus catcher Frank House in a bullpen scuffle. According to reports, House, who was paid $75,000 to sign with Detroit, wasn't hustling enough to suit the colorful coach.

In 1949, umpires Ed Hurley and Bill Griebe singled out Bartell as an ump-baiter and ejected him three times before the season was half completed. Bartell defended his actions by announcing, much to the delight of Detroit fans, that "an umpire can be wrong on the close ones. So I figure it's my job sometimes to let him know when he is wrong. I guess they don't like me telling them, though."

He also claimed with typical candor that the umpires "were out to get him," and didn't give him a fair chance to express himself. I guess I do a lot of hollering," he said, "but I've never resorted to profanity to get a point across, which is more than some others can claim."

Controversy followed him throughout his career, and never was it more pronounced than in the final game of the 1940 world Series between Cincinnati and the Tigers. The Tigers picked up Bartell after his fateful year in Chicago.

The series was tied at three games each when they took to the field in Cincinnati for the final game on October 8, 1940. The game was decided in the seventh inning when the Reds put two runs across. Detroit was ahead at the time because of an unearned run in the third. Frank McCormick, who had doubled, was on second when Jimmy Ripple came to the plate. Ripple slashed a fly to right, and the Tigers' Bruce Campbell looked as though he had a good shot at catching the ball. McCormick, not knowing if he would or not, stayed at second in case he had to tag up before taking off for third. Anyway, Campbell couldn't make the catch and the ball hit the fence and bounced and McCormick took off for third.

Manager Bill McKechnie was coaching at third, and according to Hank Greenberg who was playing left for the Tigers that day, the Reds' field boss seemed to be concentrating on seeing that Ripple moved into scoring position at second, rather than paying attention to McCormick.

McCormick, meanwhile, receiving no signal at all from McKechnie, made the turn at third, stopped for an instant and then rushed home with the tying run. Rowdy Dick, meanwhile, took the cutoff and turned to make a play—or not make one, as it turned out. Bartell held the ball as McCormick scored.

Over the years Bartell has defended his decision with typical gusto. "That play didn't lose the series," Bartell maintains. "Four games lost the series . . . four out of seven.

As for the play in question, Bartell explains it this way: "I've had to trust my judgment for a good many years up here. I trusted it that day, and I'd make the same play again—or, rather, not make it. Just before I took the throw-in, I looked around for McCormick. He had turned third. I had no reason to believe he wouldn't be home, before I could do anything about it, so I was watching to see if I couldn't keep Jim Ripple from reaching second. As a matter of fact, Bill McKechnie himself had no idea but that McCormick had scored. He was watching Ripple and the ball."

WHERE IS HE NOW?

Bartell is a gentleman of leisure now, and the only form of athletic endeavor he enjoys these days is golf and he enjoys it so much he plays it four or five times a week.

Dick Bartell and his Olive, who were married in 1928 after having met in high school, still reside in Alameda, California. After Rowdy Dick's playing career ended, he coached for a while at Detroit and Cincinnati, and took a fling at managing in the minors, but then the baseball began to fade out of his life and he entered the world of private business.

First he tried a bay area dairy, and for six and one-half years sold milk on a wholesale basis while waiting for the company to let him do public relations, as he was promised.

Then he went from selling milk to selling liquor in an "Offsale" (package) store, a business which thrived for 10 years before he sold it in the spring of 1972. He was 65 in November of that year, and he and Olive sold their comfortable home and moved into an apartment on Island Drive.

Their children, Richard Jr. and Marylin (Mrs. Jim Chargin) live in the area, and Dick Jr.'s son, Michael, may be as gifted as his grandfather when it comes to baseball. Rowdy Dick can hardly wait to find out.

Bartell still feels badly about his poor year in Chicago and as far as the "balloon" incident goes, he isn't laughing about it even today. "I apologized to Ed Burns many years later," Bartell says. "I really didn't mean anything by it. I was playing pepper on the sidelines with Dizzy Dean when he walked by that day in Catalina. And you know, when you're with Dean you're always clowning around. I didn't even know the man when I said it.

"I understand when he got back to Chicago the guys in the sports department at his paper had the place filled with balloons. That didn't help me any. You know, he (Burns) never let up on me that season.

"They used to say in Chicago that if you wanted a souvenir baseball from Wrigley Field, just sit behind first base and Bartell will throw one there sooner or later. I'm sorry to this day that I couldn't have had a better season for the Chicago fans."

Bartell has no regrets about his major league career, rhubarbs and all. "You know, Olive and I decided to get married when I made the majors. So I finally did in 1928 with the Pirates, and do you know what they paid me? I'll tell you. It was $2,750 for that first season. What's the minimum salary now? "Isn't it $10,000 or something like that?"

When I told him it was $13,500, Bartell whistled in amazement. "Do you know it took me eight years in the majors before I made that kind of money? That's why I thought the strike in 1972 was uncalled for.

"I think the players are given many considerations, good salaries, good working conditions, and if an owner has a bad year, I don't see any of the players offering to take a cut.

"You know, baseball players are not like dock workers and it shouldn't be a union-management arrangement with them. They could have settled everything in a more amicable way."

As for himself, Bartell says, as do many of the other stars in this book, that if he were playing now, he could command a much greater salary.

"But then," he adds softly, "I enjoyed it all. I have no regrets. I do think though with expansion the talent is pretty well thinned out. It wasn't that way when I played."

LON WARNEKE

The Arkansas Hummingbird

IT WAS A WARM SPRING DAY in 1928. The kid was delivering telegrams for Western Union on his bicycle while visiting a sister in Houston, Texas. Farm life in Mount Ida, Arkansas didn't exactly coincide with his plans for the future. He wanted to be a ball player, a first baseman, he thought, because that was the position he played on the high school team.

After he left school, and the farm chores started to drag, he returned to Houston, bought himself a bike and got a job. His name was Lon Warneke. But in those early days, most of the folks around Mount Ida called him Dick.

He was astute enough to realize, as he looked at the big city papers, that professional baseball players had a little something extra going for them. Many of them dressed well, they smoked big cigars, and always seemed to have the price of a good meal. So he got on his "wheel" as he called it, rode to the Houston ball park and announced to the owner that he was ready to try out for the team.

Having no professional experience, and consequently no record, the owner, whose name is lost in antiquity, wasn't exactly elated about having the rawest of rookies infringe upon his time. But he admired the kid's courage, and when Warneke offered to pay his own training expenses, it was decided that he could try out for the team. In other words, the price was right.

Fred Snyder, a former Cardinal and Giant catcher, was managing Houston at the time. He had first basemen. What he was looking for was pitching. "I need a pitcher," Snyder told the tall, skinny Warneke. "Can you pitch?"

"Sure," the kid said. "When do I start?"

"Right now," was the rejoinder. And so, Lon Warneke began a pitching career that was to see him kick around the minors for a few years before joining the Chicago Cubs, Cardinals and Cubs again in a career that was to produce 192 major league victories and 121 losses. Of that total, he won 109 and lost 72 for the Cubs.

He also appeared in three All-Star games, including the first one in 1933, earned his niche in the Hall of Fame with a no-hitter against Cincinnati on August 30, 1941, and had a 2-1 record in two World Series for the Cubs against the Yankees in 1932, and the Tigers in 1935.

A really great record? Maybe not. But Lon Warneke's career as a ball player, an umpire in the Pacific Coast League and National League and, later, his third career as a citizen, has a message there somewhere. Maybe it was best explained when he was asked what made him think he could become a pitcher in the first place.

"A man can do anything he makes up his mind to," Lonnie says. "I've always believed that if you put your mind to something you can do it. I had never pitched, but I knew I had pretty good speed, and I was willing to learn. Besides," he said with the trace of a smile bending the sun-tanned creases in his face, "he asked for a pitcher, didn't he."

Warneke wasn't a pitcher just yet. He could break off a pretty good curve and his speed was more than adequate, but he was merely a thrower and not yet a pitcher. He got by in Houston for a while, but then he was shipped to the Laurel (Mississippi) Club in the Cotton States League and later that same year Laurel sent him to Alexandria in the same league.

The following season Houston tried him again, but once again he didn't make it and was sent back to Alexandria, and he seemed destined for a nondescript career as a minor league pitcher. Still it was better than raising cattle and doing the farm chores, so he kept on trying.

He also broadened his horizons somewhat. The bridge craze was just beginning to sweep the country so he learned how to play that game. "There was nothing else to do," he recalled," except eat, sleep and practice. Lots of rest isn't bad for a pitcher, especially for one who was figuring on coming up in the game. I read a lot, and it was certainly a quiet life, but I had lots of time for baseball."

Late in that 1929 season, just before the market crashed and brokers began jumping out of windows, Patsy Flaherty, a Cub scout, was beating the bushes in baseball's never-ending search for talent, and he came upon Alexandria and Warneke. One look at Lon's record was enough to tell him he had come to the right place. Lon had won 16 and lost 10, indicating that the big hurler had stamina, in addition to his curve and speed.

Patsy liked the look of the raw-boned kid, his looseness and a disposition that seemed unflappable. He recommended him to

Marse Joe McCarthy who was managing the Cubs at the time, and to president Bill Veeck Sr., the sire of baseball's modern day maverick. Veeck paid $10,000 for Warneke's contract—a good price, even for those days.

Warneke went back to Mount Ida, helped his father, Luke, with the 200 feeders they raised, and opined that if the market had gone the way of other material things that fall, they certainly would have enough to eat. "Steak is about all I eat, anyway," Warneke said, and there were millions who would not have a steak on the table for years to come.

Spring finally came to the Ozark Hills, and young Lon took off for Catalina Island, the spring training home of the Chicago Cubs, and an enterprise of the Wrigley family, owners of the club. Despite some occasional fog and a little rain, Catalina was an interesting place to get a ball club in condition. Only goats could climb some of the hills.

The Cubs pitching staff was anchored by Guy Bush, Charlie Root and Pat Malone, and Warneke couldn't break through, so McCarthy sent him to Reading for experience and work.

"I got both in quantity," Warneke recalls. But his record was not conducive to having the Cubs rushing to retrieve his services. He won nine, lost 12, while pitching 185 innings against 841 batters, and his earned run average was slightly over 6.00.

"It wasn't much," Warneke said, "but I was learning." He also began experimenting with a screwball and a change of pace, because he learned that a pitcher cannot survive in the majors on only a curve and good speed.

The following spring, 1931, Warneke again reported to the Cubs, but by this time McCarthy had departed for New York where he was to become one of the winningest managers in the history of the game. Rogers Hornsby, an abrasive man, but a great ball player, was the new Cubs manager, and he liked what he saw—except for one thing.

He told catcher Zach Taylor to take over the kid and see if he could straighten out his control problem. Taylor discovered that Lonnie was not keeping his eyes on the ball after he had delivered it. So he made him follow through on every pitch. It helped some. Lon stuck with the Cubs all that season, but won only two games, both over the Reds. He did reduce his earned run average to 3.23 and that earned him a permanent place on the Cubs' roster.

The following season, the Cubs and Warneke put it all together. The club won the National League pennant with Warneke compiling a fine record of 22 victories against only a half-dozen defeats. Hornsby was gone, and the ebullient Charles J. Grimm managed the club. The World Series was a disaster for the Cubs.

The powerful Yankees, behind Red Ruffing, Lefty Gomez, George Pipgras and Wilcy Moore, bombed the Chicagoans out in four games. Warneke lost the second game to Gomez 5-2, in New York. The next day in Chicago's Wrigley Field, the Yankees, led by Ruth, taunted the Cubs unmercifully for not voting Mark Koenig, an ex-Yankee, a full World Series share. And when Babe Ruth came to bat against Charlie Root, he allegedly called his home run by pointing to center field. At least, legend has it that way.

Grimm brought the Cubs into the 1935 series, and this time Warneke was equal to the occasion. The Tigers represented the American League, and although they won it, Warneke won both games for Chicago in the six-game set. He shut out Detroit and Lynwood (Schoolboy) Rowe 3-0 in the opening game at Detroit, and won the fifth 3-1 in Chicago, again defeating Rowe.

But the high point of his career was to come just a few months before America was plunged into World War II. By this time his fame and reputation had spread and he was known throughout the civilized world of baseball as "The Arkansas Hummingbird." The Cubs, though, fell upon evil days, and P. K. Wrigley traded him to St. Louis for first baseman Rip Collins and pitcher Roy Parmelee. So it was as a Cardinal that Warneke enjoyed his greatest moment in baseball.

It came on August 30, 1941, in old Crosley Field, a structure that just recently was hammered into oblivion by the wrecker's ball. Warneke was near the end of his career, but he never had more stuff than he did that afternoon against the Reds, as he no-hit the National League champions in a 2-0 victory.

One walk and two errors marred what otherwise might have been a perfect performance. Linus Frey drew the only pass, and boots by Frank Crespi and Jimmy Brown put runners on, both of whom were wiped out by double plays.

Less than a year later, the Cubs got him back for the $7,500 waiver price and he stayed with them through the war years, finally ending his career in 1945. As for the no-hitter, he knew he had to have a few things going for him, because four times in his career he had been just one hit away from immortality. One was just a few weeks before the no-hitter when Stan Hack of the Cubs beat him on a slow roller between the mound and first base. Lonnie was a bit slow covering first and Hack beat it out for the only hit the Cubs got that day.

"When you pitch a no-hitter," Warneke says, "first you've got to have all your stuff working, and the team you're playing against has to be hitting below its average that day. That's what happened against the Reds."

Following his playing career, Warneke umpired in the Pacific

Coast League a couple of years before being called up to the National League in 1949. He remained an N.L. arbiter until his retirement in October of 1955, to enter private business in Little Rock, Arkansas. But he wasn't through calling 'em just yet.

WHERE IS HE NOW?

Lon Warnecke first went into the soft water business in Little Rock, Arkansas, and in 1962 he stepped into the political arena and ran for judge in Garland County. His campaign pledge was directly to the point: "Everything for the good of the people." His first election was by a plurality of only 177 votes, and when the incumbent, Henry Murphy, demanded a recount, Lonnie picked up 15 more and took office by a margin of 192 votes.

He was re-elected four times and earned a reputation as a fair and innovative judge, although his background contains no formal legal education. In juvenile cases, for instance, he had a jury of six teenagers who heard the case along with him and then recommended a verdict and punishment. In one case, a youth was being tried for vandalism, and a girl juror confronted the defendant: "You lied to us, didn't you?" she said.

"Yes, I did," the defendant replied without hesitation.

"Your honor, we, the jury, find the defendant guilty. We recommend. . . ."

Since they could only recommend, the final decision was up to the judge and Warneke usually went along. Since the names of juveniles charged or convicted of a crime cannot be published in Arkansas, the teenage jury spread the word in its own way.

"All I can tell you about the system," Warneke said, "is that it reduced juvenile crime in this county."

Lon and his Charlyne have been married since February 12, 1933, and now, after his years in baseball, private business and the courts, he and the Mrs. have turned into nomads, fishing the area in their motorized camper.

The children, Patsy and Charles are married and have families of their own and the Warnekes are grandparents. Lonnie suffered a heart attack in the spring of 1972, but three weeks after, he was on the road again, searching for new lakes and ponds and in the fall he hunts deer in his beloved Arkansas hills.

He's still tall, slender and lean as a buggy-whip . . . just like the old Arkansas Hummingbird was in his days with the Cubs and Cardinals.

BRONKO NAGURSKI

The Indomitable Bronk

THE NAME DRIPS WITH the stuff dreams are made of . . .
Bronko Nagurski. It rolls off the tongue as a symbol of bone-
crushing power even though it has been almost four decades since
he played professional football for the Chicago Bears.

And the Bronk made at least one dream come true. That was
the vision of George Halas, who founded the Bears in Decatur, Illinois, and brought them to Chicago's Wrigley Field in 1921. Harold
(Red) Grange generally is credited with lifting the Bears and professional football from rag-tag status into the exciting and profitable venture it has become over the last half century. And justifi-
ably so, for Grange brought the fans out on Sunday.

But Red had help once they got there. In 1930, fresh out of
the University of Minnesota where he was an All-American at tackle
and fullback, Bronko Nagurski arrived at Halas University. Big,
six feet, two inches and 230 pounds, the Bronk was destined to
become the first and greatest of the big running backs. They didn't
call them that in those early days of professional football, but that's
what he was. A runner, a blocker, a passer and a fine defensive
player.

The Bronk played eight seasons with the Bears, gaining 3,947
yards from scrimmage in 856 attempts; an average of 4.6 yards each
time he handled the football. He also threw 80 passes and completed 38 of them; and his National Football League point total is
236 points. But those are only statistics. Bronko Nagurski, the man,
is something else.

He has been called "painfully shy." Other adjectives describe
his reticence. And it was true to a point. For example, his contract
with the Bears stipulated that the only public appearance he would
be required to make on behalf of the team would be on the football field. And yet, while he was playing for the Bears, and a few

years after his career ended, he appeared in more than 300 wrestling matches. He was even crowned with one of the heavyweight championships—the kind that were being thrown around in those days.

Bronko exerted his personality on the football field, and that's the way the fans knew him and the way they now remember him. He is the criterion of brute force, overwhelming power, and a desire matched only by his strength and ability.

Hardly anyone tackled Nagurski. The trick was to throw a body block around his ankles and hope to upend him. This point was brought to light after Larry Csonka of the Miami Dolphins shook off Bear tacklers with consummate ease in a 1971 game. Halas was incensed at the poor play by more than a ton of defensive linemen Csonka intimidated.

"The opposition used to have the same trouble with Nagurski," Halas said in his Chicago office. "Then they found out that the only way to stop him was to hit him around the ankles." Even that method, though, was living dangerously because Nagurski's calves resembled the trunks of a pair of pine trees from his beloved North country.

Clark Hinkle of the Green Bay Packers recalls one memorable collision with the Bronk. It was in 1934 and the Bears were in Green Bay. The Packers had the ball on their own 20-yard line, third down and 14. Hinkle went back into punt formation, almost a common practice in those days. But the Green Bay fullback, some 30 pounds lighter than Nagurski, had the option to punt, run or pass. And he could do all three. This time he elected to run and burst through a hole at right tackle and headed for the sidelines. As Hinkle tried to make the turn, he found that Nagurski had cornered him.

Bronko was not a tackler in the classic sense. He simply put his magnificent body to work on the ball carrier, applying a shoulder or body block that never failed to send the runner flying. Hinkle, an All-American from Bucknell who joined the Packers in 1932, though, learned one thing from his previous confrontations with Nagurski. That was never to wait for the Bronk to hit you first. "I learned never to stand still and wait for him," Hinkle said. "If I did he would have killed me."

So as he headed for the sidelines, and, with the menacing behemoth closing in on him, Hinkle waited until the last instant, pivoted toward Nagurski, dropped his shoulder and hit him. Hinkle got 30 yards on the play. Bronko received a broken nose and a fractured rib and had to be helped from the field—a rare sight indeed.

Years later, Nagurski recalled the incident. "He hit me so hard, I can feel it yet," Bronko smiled. "That was the time I broke my nose." As big, tough and strong as he was, the Bronk often was injured. But, in the lexicon of pro football, he "played hurt."

The end seemingly came for him in 1938 when Nagurski and Halas couldn't agree on contract terms. The Bronk wanted to pick up extra money wrestling and Halas insisted that his fullback should concentrate solely on football. So Nagurski gave up football and became a touring wrestler.

Then on June 9, 1942, after a wrestling match in Minneapolis, Nagurski called sportswriters into his dressing room and announced his retirement. "I'm all through," he said. "My legs can't stand the gaff. My knees have been injured so many times they can't stand the strain. If I don't quit now, I may end up a cripple. Money doesn't mean that much to me." So after 20 years of competition in football and wrestling, it was all over for Bronko Nagurski, or was it?

A year later, the Bears were beset by wartime manpower short-ages. George Halas, football coach had become Commander George Halas, USNR, and the team was being coached by Heartley (Hunk) Anderson and Luke Johnsos. But, then as now, Halas was not so far away that he couldn't pull a few strings. He issued a call for Nagurski to play one more season. And the 35-year-old Nagurski responded by playing tackle and fullback.

At the time, Nagurski's comeback was viewed by some detrac-tors as a publicity stunt to keep pro football afloat during the wartime season. That is, until September 26, 1943, when at pre-cisely 2:51 P.M. Nagurski trotted on the field to replace his old roommate George Musso at tackle.

On the first play, the Packers decided to find out if the old man still had it. They sent fullback Ted Fritsch, Clark Hinkle's successor, right at him. When Fritsch picked himself off the ground, he knew Bronko still had it, at least for one season.

Later in the schedule, Nagurski was used at fullback and against the Cardinals he gained more than 100 yards as the Bears plowed toward the title game against the Redskins. They won that one, too, and the Bronk scored a touchdown as the Bears won the championship of the world 41-21.

WHERE IS HE NOW?

Bronko Nagurski, father of six, is still living in his beloved International Falls, Minnesota, impervious to the bone-chilling cold. "I'm fine," he says. "I'm doing better than the Bears, not moneywise, but I'm not losing any games."

He sold his fuel oil and gas station business a couple of years ago in preparation for joining America's senior citizens. But he still follows professional football, and has the highest regard for today's players. He also has some advice for them.

"A football player deserves whatever he can get," Bronko says. "It works the other way, too. Whatever an owner or a coach can get out of you, he'll do it. They don't throw much sympathy your way after you're all through and crippled up."

Nagurski says that the players today are better at all levels of competition. "There is better coaching, and there are schools playing now that didn't even have a team when I was a kid. To me that means more players and, consequently, a larger percentage of better players."

Bronko last played football at the age of 50 in a spring game that featured the University of Minnesota alumni against the varsity. That's right: age 50. Greg Larson, a 240-pound linebacker, was captain of that Gopher team. When he tried to tackle Nagurski he bounced off. "Up to then," Larson recalls, "I considered myself a pretty fair linebacker. But after Bronko ran over me, I decided I was better suited for offense."

If Nagurski had his career to start all over again, he says he'd play it the same way—with one exception. "I'd try harder," he said with a laugh, "to get a little more money."

That's kind of a frightening thought—Nagurski trying harder. But he'd make it big in today's game just as he did when George Halas paid him $5,000 a year. The only difference would be a couple more zeroes on that salary, and the playoff money that goes with it.

Surely any team with Bronko Nagurski would have a candidate for the Super Bowl. It would have to be.

He was a super player.

HENRY (HANK) GREENBERG

He Brushed the Babe

IN A WAY, IT WAS very strange. Here was this giant of a kid, virtually raised in the shadows of Yankee Stadium in the Bronx, and he was strictly a Giant fan.

Hank Greenberg was born in New York City, lived in Greenwich Village for a while, but when things picked up in his father's textile business, the family moved to 172nd Street in the Bronx.

Young Henry nurtured a dormant desire to be a baseball player. Nevertheless, he went to work for his father after finishing James Monroe High School. The business was located on 20th Street. His dad paid him $20 a week. Each day, going to and from work on the subway, he passed Yankee Stadium, where, just a few years before, the legendary Babe Ruth had hit 28 of his 60 home runs during the 1927 season.

Hank Greenberg disliked riding the subway almost as much as he disliked the Yankees. He was more interested in manager John McGraw's Giants who played their games at the Polo Grounds on Coogan's Bluff.

"All the kids liked the Giants," Hank said. "I didn't even see a major league game until 1927, and I was 16 years old then. We liked to watch such stars as Art Nehf, George Kelly, Fred Lindstrom, Irish Muesel and Casey Stengel.

"They were the rollicking, fighting type of ball players. We liked that. Then there was John McGraw's personality. McGraw was the spirit of the Giants. No, I seldom went to the Stadium."

Hank Greenberg said that in 1938, and at the time he was the toast of the baseball world. Tall: six feet, four inches; handsome, and always extremely well groomed, Henry was fast closing in on Ruth's record. With five games left in the season, he had hit 58 home runs for the Detroit Tigers. The nation followed his every swing of the bat with a more than perfunctory interest.

Who was this guy, anyway? How could he, a New York-born first baseman, playing for Detroit, threaten to wipe out one of the most sacred records in a sport that lived by its records? Where did he come from? How did he get started anyway?

Well, Hank Greenberg got into baseball when he decided that the $15 a week he made playing first base for a Brooklyn semipro team was more attractive than making $20 for working all week with his father. His grasp of that financial fact was to serve him well in later life. Take the lesser amount and invest it well. The dividends will come.

Greenberg practically backed into baseball immortality. There weren't many places to play baseball in Greenwich Village. The place was crowded with humanity.

When Hank turned seven, the family (three boys and a girl) moved to the Bronx and there, at least, the kids could play in the streets. "We played a game called punch ball, Greenberg says. "You hit a softball with your hands and were put out if somebody hit you with the ball before you got to first base.

"Then in high school they furnished us with equipment, and I took an immediate interest in the game. But I never dreamed I'd get to the big leagues," Henry said. "I was just a tall, skinny kid and never did anything outstanding in high school.

"So after I was graduated, I thought I'd play semipro ball until it was time for me to start classes at New York University," Hank recalls. And he actually went to NYU for a semester, taking a business course, but his mind was on other things, like baseball.

After playing 10 or 12 games with a Brooklyn semipro team, Greenberg got his first break. A Detroit scout, named Gene Dubuc, asked him how he'd like to go to West Douglass, Massachusetts, and play for Walter Schuester's semipros.

"That was in 1929," Hank says. "Jack Barry, who was coach at Holy Cross, was the manager of the team. Because it was a Detroit scout who invited him to play, the Giants and Yankees lost their chance to sign the power hitting youngster. Hank had a good season, and even more important he decided that it was baseball for him.

He went to NYU, but when the semester break came, it was just about time for the major league clubs to take off for spring training in Florida. And who could resist that?

Hank had offers from the Tigers, Yankees, Pirates and Senators. But the Tigers got him. "The Tigers gave me a nice bonus, and besides, I felt somewhat obligated to Dubuc, who had discovered me in Brooklyn."

So in February of 1930, with the nation in chaos because of the market crash, Greenberg reported to the Tigers in Tampa, Florida. "I had signed a contract with them with the understanding that I could go to college for four years, but I just couldn't sit in classrooms studying economics and business when baseball was uppermost in my mind."

Hank made the final cut, played in just one major league game in 1930, and was shipped off to Hartford in the Eastern League. After 17 games, he was off to Raleigh in the Piedmont League and the promise began to flower. He hit .314.

The following season, the home run power began to manifest itself. Still a chattel of the Tigers, Greenberg played with Evansville in the Three Eye League and hit 15 homers. In 1932, his last year in the minors, he belted 39 for Beaumont of the Texas League and led the team to the pennant.

"I knew I was ready for the majors after that season." And he was. By 1935 his powerful bat, along with that of Mickey Cochrane, Goose Goslin and Charlie Gehringer, propelled the Tigers to the pennant and a World Series victory over the Cubs. Greenberg was selected as the American League's Most Valuable Player, hitting .328, 36 home runs and an incredible 170 runs batted in. Five years later, he was again to win it with a .340 mark, 41 home runs and 140 RBI's.

But the 1935 series was Hank's biggest thrill despite the misfortune that struck him. In the second game of the Series he suffered a broken wrist. "I was on second when Pete Fox singled," Hank recalled, "and I tried to score on the hit. Frank Demaree fumbled the ball momentarily, then relayed it to Bill Herman. Herman threw it to Gabby Hartnett, and in sliding into the plate, I jammed my hand against Hartnett."

The Tigers patched up their infield by moving third baseman Marvin Owen over to third base. They took the series from the Cubs in six games. It was a wild one, with the Cubs challenging umpire George Moriarty at every turn. And after it was all over, Cub manager Charlie Grimm, Woody English, Billy Herman and Billy Jurges were fined $200 each for using improper language.

Greenberg's big year was 1938 when he brushed the record of the great Babe Ruth. This established him forever as one of the game's brightest stars. He finished the season with 58 home runs, but had reached that figure with five games to go. The problem was that the opposing pitchers weren't giving him the kind of pitches he liked to hit. Greenberg's power was to center field and he was getting pitches on the fists for the final five games.

On the last day of the season, the Tigers beat the Indians twice with Hank going one-for-four in the first game and three-for-three in the second. But his only extra base hit was a double in the opener. Bob Feller pitched that one, and stole some of the thunder from Greenberg's try at the record by striking out 18 Tigers in a 4-1 loss. It was a major league record.

As late as August 26, 1938, Greenberg was five days and seven games ahead of Ruth's pace, but he accepted the challenge with his usual calm demeanor. "Two factors are against me," he said that day. "First, if I get close to Ruth's mark, everybody will be careful what they throw me, and second, Ruth hit 17 homers in the month of September in 1927. It's going to be impossible for me to do that. I don't know how Ruth ever did it."

Following his MVP year in 1940, Greenberg seemed destined to go on to even greater heights. But on May 7, 1941, he was drafted by the U.S. Army and served 180 days at Fort Custer, Michigan. He was discharged December 5, 1941. Two days later, the Japanese attacked Pearl Harbor, and within a week, Greenberg re-enlisted. It was more than three years before he was to return to the Tigers, probably the best three years of his career. He entered the service a private and came out a captain.

He returned in time to help the Tigers win the flag in 1945 and again beat the Cubs in the World Series. It was not a vintage year artistically in major league baseball, and when Warren Brown, the *Chicago Sun's* sports editor, was asked for his opinion on the outcome of the series, he replied: "I don't think either one of them can win it."

The Tigers did, though, four games to three, and Greenberg was the batting hero of the set. He made seven hits, five of them for extra bases, including three doubles and two home runs. His first homer, with two men on base, won the second game, and his second tied the sixth game, although the Tigers lost it in the 12th inning.

It was a nightmarish game with 38 men in the box score, 19 for each club. The winning run resulted from a freakish hit by Cub third baseman Stan Hack. Hack's drive looked as though it would be an ordinary single to left, but as Greenberg moved to field the ball, it took a crazy bounce over his shoulder and rolled to the wall.

The official scorer gave Hack a single, Greenberg an error, and no run batted in. But a storm of protest followed, and five hours later the decision was changed and Hack was credited with a double and the error removed from Greenberg's record. The Tigers took the deciding seventh game 9-3.

In 1946 Greenberg was waived out of the American League, and was sold to the Pirates for what was believed to be $40,000. He finished his playing career in Pittsburgh. His legacy was a lifetime batting average of .313 and a total of 331 homers, including 25 in his final year with Pittsburgh at the age of 37.

On February 19, 1946, he married Carol Gimble, the brunette heiress of the New York department store millions, but the union ended in divorce. Hank remained in baseball, first buying into the Cleveland Indians, and later the Chicago White Sox, along with Bill Veeck. When Veeck sold out in Cleveland, Hank remained as general manager and a stormy career folowed. The 1954 Indians broke the Yankee stranglehold and won the pennant, only to be swept out of the World Series by the New York Giants, in four games.

Veeck and Greenberg were a strange team, baseball's first front-office "Odd Couple." Veeck was irrepressible, forever thinking up stunts to bring Cleveland fans into the stadium. He succeeded at an astonishing rate, he stole the hearts of the Cleveland fans with his open-collared sportshirt on radio, TV and in the papers.

Greenberg was a direct contrast. Neatly—no, immaculately—attired, the debonaire Hank added the aura of a Wall Street financier to Cleveland's front office. But as different as they were sartorially, they thought alike about baseball: games were too long; the American League ought to expand to California; there ought to be inter-league play; the game had better start thinking about moving with the times or it was headed for trouble, etc. . . .

As usual, they were far ahead of their times, and the establishment, that is, the owners of the other clubs, blocked their innovations at every turn. Walter O'Malley, the guiding genius of the Dodgers, was on the same wave length, though, and he moved his club from Brooklyn to Los Angeles, and put together one ˙of the most successful operations in the history of the game.

After their association in Chicago, which was highlighted by a comic opera court battle with Charles Comiskey, grandson of the club's founder, Veeck sold out to Arthur Allyn Jr., son of one of his long-time financial backers, and went off to his retreat in Easton, Maryland, to become a successful author and sports columnist.

Greenberg went on to success as an investment broker in New York, clipping coupons with the same masterful touch that worked with a baseball bat. He had a new game, and he played it with the same dogged determination and excellence that earned him his niche in baseball's Hall of Fame.

WHERE IS HE NOW?

Hank Greenberg lives the kind of life many of us dream about. He has his own investment office in New York, and spends most of his time there. But he and his wife, Mary Jo, travel a lot, and spend about three months of the year in the Los Angeles area. They've been married since November, 1966.

Hank's three children by his previous marriage are all doing well. The oldest, Glenn, and his wife Judy live in New York where Glenn attended Columbia University, studying engineering.

Stephen is a graduate of Yale University, and taught school for a while, but like his father, the call of baseball overcame his academic inclinations and at this writing was playing with Denver in the American Association as a first and third baseman.

Alva, the youngest, attended Kenyon College, one of the schools that tolerated Bill Veeck in his undergraduate years.

Greenberg has nothing but fond memories of baseball, after spending 35 years in the game. "I got great press as a player," he said, "but it changed when I became an executive with Cleveland. I followed Bill Veeck as the general manager, and he was the only man in the history of the club to get a good press from the Cleveland writers. There were three papers there, the *Plain Dealer,* the *News* and the *Press,* and they used the club to build their circulation," Hank says. "If one paper said something was white, another would say it was green, and the other one would say it was pink. It was constant turmoil and I was pleasantly surprised when we moved to Chicago to take over the White Sox. Of course, we gave them their first pennant in 40 years in 1959. That helped."

Although Greenberg's background shows no formal education in finance, he is most successful in the market place. "I don't trade every day," he says. "Sometimes, I just turn the ticker off and go out and play tennis."

How does he account for his success? He really doesn't. "Any idiot can do it," he says. "Why make money and turn it over to somebody else to invest? If they were any good, they'd be making the money themselves? All it takes is horse sense. Of course, you must do a lot of reading, studying and analyzing. I just trade for myself."

Greenberg plays tennis almost daily, and despite his 60 years, he looks as though he could step out on a baseball field right now. "I used to play handball and squash, but a few years ago I took up tennis. I like to sweat, and I like the people in tennis. It's a nice social game. I guess I play well enough to be considered a Country Club player," he said. "It's a nice life. My work gives me the time to travel and play tennis when I want to, so we come to California a lot because Mary Jo was born and raised in Beverly Hills."

It may not be tennis forever, though. Greenberg and Veeck might try the majors one more time—if the right franchise becomes available at the right price.

That would be something. Baseball's "Odd Couple" back in business.

ARCHIE LEE MOORE

The Magnificent Mongoose Says:
"Any Boy Can"

HE WAS BORN IN December, but the exact date is lost in the mists of many times and many more places. His mother, Lorena, says it was December 16, 1913. But he juggles the dates and says no, it was December 13, 1916.

The place was Benoit, Mississippi. His mother was only 17 at the time, and she had already given birth to a daughter, Rachel, two years before. Life was not easy for a young black couple in those days, and when Archie was 18-months old, his parents, Lorena and Thomas Wright, separated and gave their children to an uncle and an aunt, Cleveland and Willie Pearl Moore, who lived in St. Louis.

So Archie Lee Wright became Archie Lee Moore, and the world in general, and the sport of boxing in particular, had thrust upon it one of the most interesting characters in the annals of fun and games.

For years, it was anything but fun and games for Archie Moore. It was hopping freight trains to get from one town to another for a fight. And the purse might be $3 or it might be $35. It was eating in places that had signs: "For colored only." And it was sleeping on the back of a truck or in an open field with the boxing gear in a little bag his only pillow.

And it was the constant battle to climb what he describes as, the glass mountain. Three steps up to the next precipice and then a setback that knocked him back four. But like all dedicated climbers, when asked why they risk everything to get to the top, his answer was always the same: "Because it's there."

Archie Moore's glass mountain began with a desire to excel, because he learned at an early age that you can't steal the things you want and expect to get away with it. He thought it might be the way for a while, but one day, when he tried to pilfer $7 out of a St. Louis streetcar, while an accomplice stopped the vehicle by pulling the trolley off the power line, he got caught.

Despite the kindly treatment by Uncle Cleveland and Auntie Willie Pearl, he seemed to be going down the wrong side of the road and heading for big trouble. His escapade on the streetcar was a costly one. Archie was sentenced to three years in the reformatory, and the youngster faced a decision that few must make at such an early age. Serve the time and start all over or fight the system with theft and violence and the hell with it.

He chose to do his time, avoiding the stealing and sex problems that permeated the reform school. And at the same time, he decided that his way out of the poverty and prejudice that clouded his life and the lives of his beloved auntie and uncle was with a pair of boxing gloves.

He thought about baseball, but in the 1930s there were no black players in the major leagues, and only a handful of stars in the Negro leagues, as they were called then, made any kind of real money. So when he was paroled after 22 months, he had already learned how to box, and pretty well, too. But the bouts were few and far between and he still had this terrible habit of eating. So he joined the Civilian Conservation Corps, a quasi-military organization, formulated by the Roosevelt Administration to help clean up our forests and national parks.

Later it was the Works Progress Administration, repairing streets and roads and, finally the realization of his unquenchable thirst for combat in the ring on a professional basis. It came on New Year's Eve, 1936, in Hot Springs, Arkansas, and Archie Moore won his first professional fight by knocking out the Poco Kid in the second round.

Thus began a 28-year career in the ring, a career that included 228 professional fights, 140 knockouts (the most in history), eight draws, two lost on fouls, and one no contest. He was the victim of an opponent's knockout punch only seven times.

It was a career that took Archie Moore all over the world, from Keokuk, Iowa, where he KOd Maury Allen in two rounds to both coasts of the United States, a triumphal tour of Australia, and a nine bout tour of Argentina that saw him draw one and win the other eight by knockouts.

Archie was censored by the State Department for being friendly with dictator Juan Peron during the Argentinian tour, but the State Department didn't realize that he wasn't there for politicking. It was the eating money he had on his mind . . . that, and a bout with Joey Maxim, then the lightheavyweight champion of the world.

Maxim, a fine athlete, left a lot to be desired as a crowd-pleasing fighter. Joey was difficult to beat because he had speed and virtually every defensive maneuver known to the sweet science. He was more offended than hurt when an opponent laid a glove on his well proportioned body or face.

But Archie had been fighting for more than 16 years and he knew his record was good enough to earn him a shot at the championship. He also knew that it had cost him personally. His first marriage to Mattie Chapman was ruined when he had to sail for the Australian tour four days after they had been married in January of 1940. When he returned six months later, he and Mattie never were able to put it all back together and, finally, they went their separate ways.

He fought seven times Down Under and came home with a profit of $800, hardly a bonanza, but Archie figured it was worth it for two reasons. One, it gave him an international reputation and, two, he learned the secret of losing weight without loss of strength or agility, two of his more outstanding assets.

Archie sprang his theory on an unsuspecting journalistic fraternity at the same time he was trying to get Maxim into a ring. He said he learned it from the Aborigines while touring the outback of Australia. It was an interesting discovery and came about because he had noticed that the aborigines were slim and strong —not many of them were fat. He asked how they did it, and learned that it was not as difficult as it may seem.

Simply put, it was not to swallow the meat. Chew it, draw all the juices out of it and swallow them. But when the meat was reduced to a pulp, spit it out. He admitted it wasn't a very nice thing to watch, and the crowd at Coconut Grove might not go for it, but it worked.

It also got him publicity the country over. Because of that, and a letter-writing campaign to sports editors, he finally got Maxim to agree to a title bout under the most bizarre terms. Joey got a guarantee of $100,000 and Arch ended up with $800. But he also lifted Maxim's light-heavyweight title by winning a 15-round decision.

He was to fight Maxim twice more, each time taking a 15-round decision. But Archie knew, as any follower of the sweet science does, that the big money, the really big money, was in the heavyweight division. So after he defended his title against Harold Johnson in 1954 (a 14-round knockout) and against Carl (Bobo) Olson (knockout in three) less than a year later, he got a match with the reigning heavyweight, the late Rocky Marciano.

A ruggedly conditioned fighter who swarmed all over his opponents, without much style, but plenty of punches, Marciano almost met his match in Moore. Archie was either 39 or 42 at the time, depending on whether you believed his mother, Lorena, or the Magnificent Mongoose, as he billed himself.

Ordinarily, Marciano was not a cautious fighter. His battle plan was a fairly simple one. He just went after his opponent, and with his uncanny ability to throw punches from any angle, wiped out the opposition with sheer physical force.

So it was rather strange when he stepped into the ring with Archie Moore on September 21, 1955 in New York and gave ground in the first round. Rocky was fighting from a crouch, his shoulder and neck muscles sticking out like pieces of rope. Archie's first few jabs hit the air harmlessly over his head.

In the second round, Moore, in an effort to bring Rocky to a more vertical position and thus become an easier target, feinted and stepped back. Rocky followed, throwing an overhand right at the same time. Moore again stepped back and when Marciano missed a second time, Moore threw an uppercut that sent the heavyweight champion to the deck. He was up at the count of two, and to Moore he looked defenseless.

At this point, according to Moore, the referee stepped between the two fighters, and grabbed Rocky by the arms to wipe off his gloves, jarring him to sensibility. That was all Rocky needed.

His head cleared, he went after Archie relentlessly and Archie let him. To this day, Archie says, that was his big mistake because he now was fighting Rocky Marciano's fight instead of Archie Moore's. But the few seconds that the referee used to clean Rocky's gloves were all the champ needed to recoup, and in those same few seconds Moore blew his cool. He got angry, and professional fighters rarely get angry and win. While Archie put up a game and action-filled fight, Marciano got to him in the ninth and knocked him out.

After Marciano retired, undefeated, and Floyd Patterson assumed the role as a top contender, Moore won another shot at the vacant crown. This one took place in the Chicago Stadium on November 30, 1956, and Archie was either 40 or 43, take your pick.

Patterson, despite some of his critics these days, was a good fighter then. He had speed and he could punch, although his penchant for taking a punch was unknown at the time, the youngster knocked out aging Archie in the fifth round.

So Arch went back to his old division, because there were still a few loose dollars to be made. He successfully defended against Tony Anthony in September of 1957, and 13 months later he was to have one of his toughest fights ever.

It was against Yvon Durelle in Montreal, and by this time Archie was being managed by the inimitable Jack (Doc) Kearns, a man who had a way with money and fighters. After Durelle had Moore on the canvas three times, Kearns implored his stricken warrior to smile and wave to his wife, Joan, and the kids, who were seated behind the Canadian's corner.

Archie did, and only later did he learn that Kearns wasn't the least bit interested in the family at that point. He just wanted to show Durelle that Archie was still alive and well. It worked and Durelle's jaw dropped open when the champion smiled and waved.

Durelle decked Archie again the following round, but the old Mongoose was getting $75,000 for this one, and he wanted the fans to get their money's worth. He floored the Canadian in the seventh and tenth, and finally knocked him out in the eleventh in a bout that was carried on national television. It was rated with the best ever shown on the tube.

A few months later, Moore knocked out Durelle in three rounds and then the Mongoose fought for four more years, the biggest one being against Cassius Clay (Mohammad Ali) in Los Angeles in 1962. Clay knocked him out in three. How old was he then? Either 46 or 49; again take your pick.

Archie Moore retired in 1964 and launched a career in movies and television that saw him in *Huckleberry Finn, The Carpetbaggers, Wagon Train* and *Perry Mason,* among others. He was also working as a job consultant with the Office of Economic Opportunity, but his real place in life was yet to be taken.

He had married Joan Hardy in 1955, and the union with this lovely woman was to bring him the happiest years of his life. There are children; theirs and others who they took into their home.

Others in sports have talked about working for the youth of our country after their stars fade into the night, but few have ever done it. Archie Moore is one of those few, and he's done it well and virtually by himself. Because he followed this one little poem taught to him by Auntie Willie Pearl:

> *When a task is once begun,*
> *Never leave it till it's done.*
> *And if the labor is great or small,*
> *Do it well, or not at all.*

Sound corny? To some maybe, but not to Archie Moore, because it works for him.

WHERE IS HE NOW?

Archie and Joan Moore's home in San Diego's inner city is full of laughter, love and children. The oldest is Billy Daniels, their adopted son; and then there are Hardy, D'Angelo Gregg, Anthony Cleveland, Rena Marie and Joan Marie, and their ages range from Billy, who is in his 20s down to Anthony who is not yet 10. The two girls are in their teens.

Ordinarily, just providing for and taking care of a brood that size would be enough for anyone. But not the Old Mongoose. He promised himself back in that Missouri reformitory that some day, somehow, he would devote his life to the underpriviliged youth of our country. And he's doing it by using his own money and private contributions to finance his program called Any Boy Can. The purpose of the program is to keep the youngsters, be they white, black, red, yellow or brown, from using drugs or perpetrating violence to gain the civil rights they deserve. Only with Archie it isn't just civil rights—it is human rights.

Boxing plays a great part in the program because it fosters discipline and that, in turn, results in self-discipline. Mutual respect for one another and the community also play a large part in Moore's unique venture.

The program, of course, is great, but no method of combating the ills of our society is as good as the man who makes it work. And Moore is as dynamic and dedicated to his new career as he was to the boxing ring.

He demands discipline, and because he does it with empathy, he gets it. After all, what could an oppressed child of the 1970s tell him that he hadn't already experienced in the 1930s? He has been criticized by the black extremists as an Uncle Tom because he censured his black brothers after the fiery Detroit riots.

Although he made his living in the violent world of boxing for 28 years, he abhors violence. There are other ways to gain equality, he teaches, and that is by instilling self-confidence in youngsters.

His program has been so successful that in the spring of 1972 he was invited by General Vincent DePaul Gannon to try his program at Fort Carson, Colorado for eight weeks. The idea was to foster leadership, develop talent and discourage the use of drugs, particularly among the combat veterans of Vietnam who were returning to civilian life.

According to Major General John Bennett, Fort Carson's commander, who approved of the pilot program, it has been a success. Archie is now thinking in terms of an international program, and Any Boy Can is now burgeoning into Any Body Can.

Although he's constantly traveling, Moore's heart is still at the house on East Street in San Diego where the whole thing started. And he fairly twinkles when he talks about his children.

Billy Daniels wants to be a pro football player, but Archie saw to it that he learned to be a plumber first. Young Hardy may be the most motivated, but D'Angelo Gregg is right there with him. Anthony Cleveland is a "beautiful student and shows more fire than any of the others, and already shows signs of having superior boxing ability." Rena Marie is an "excellent student, an absolute wizard," and Joan Marie already "has a stride like Jesse Owens," and runs with the Mickey Missiles, a San Diego track club. Archie and Joan Moore have Archie's mother, Lorena, and Auntie Willie Pearl with them, too. Their lives are full.

DON HUTSON

The First Super End

IT WAS A MATTER of seventeen minutes, but perhaps they were the most important in the long history of the Green Bay Packers. The inexorable tick of the clock had decided many a National Football League game over the years, but that summer day of 1935 was the first time any team had won a legend.

Joe Carr was president of the NFL at that time, a post that is comparable to today's Commissioner, and across his desk came two standard player contracts. One was from Green Bay and the other from the old Brooklyn Dodgers. Both had signed the same player, or better yet, the same player had signed both contracts.

His name was Donald Hutson, and his occupation was listed as "end." He was an inch over six feet, he weighed only 178 pounds and he not only looked skinny, which he was, he actually looked frail. But he could run the 100-yard dash in 9.8; he had moves never before seen on a football field—they called them feints then; and he had a pair of hands that lovingly caressed a football no matter where it was thrown.

Unlike Solomon, President Carr didn't threaten to cut the rangy pass-catching end in half and divide him between the Packers and Dodgers. He used a much subtler method, simply looking at the postmarks on the envelopes that contained the contracts. Green Bay's was posted at 8:30 A.M. and the Brooklyn envelope was mailed at 8:47 A.M. Since the Packers had a seventeen minute jump, he awarded Hutson to them. It took only a couple of years to realize that Carr had made one of the most important decisions in the history of the NFL and Green Bay. That's because Don Hutson developed into such a tremendous pass receiver that he forced the other teams to change the defensive concept of pro football.

Such things as double or triple coverage were unheard of in

those early days. There were no sophisticated zones. It was merely a matter of putting your best defensive back on the other team's top receiver and hope for the best. Don Hutson changed all that the first time he stepped on a pro football field.

It so happened that when Hutson made his unforgettable debut, the Packers were playing the Bears, and the game even then was a bloodbath. Bears' coach, George Halas, knew of Hutson only by reputation. He knew that Don had teamed with Dixie Howell at Alabama, and the two of them had helped the Crimson Tide upset Stanford 29-13 in the Rose Bowl with Howell completing seven of eight passes, two for touchdowns. Hutson caught them both.

So Halas knew he was up against a good receiver, but he didn't know Hutson was a great one. How could he? Anyway, Halas assigned Beattie Feathers, then just about the best back in the league, as Hutson's bird-dog. Arnie Herber was Green Bay's passer and he could hit a gnat's eye at fifty yards. The legendary Johnny Blood was the other receiver and Blood could catch the ball at any distance.

On the first play after the kickoff, the Packers shifted into the old Notre Dame box, and Blood sprinted down the field. Hutson, gifted with sneaky speed, casually began his pattern and Feathers picked him up easily. As Herber faked a run, Blood streaked for the sidelines and picked up a covey of Bear defenders. Meanwhile, Hutson stopped completely and Feathers, meanwhile, took his eyes off Hutson for an instant to watch Herber throw to Blood. That was a mistake.

When the Bear defender returned his attention to Hutson, he found that the Packer end was no longer there. He had turned on his superb speed and an artful Herber pass, almost softly thrown, glided into Hutson's outstretched arms. Hutson scored, of course, the play covering 86 yards. Thus a legend was born on Hutson's first play in professional football and it turned out to be the only touchdown in a 7-0 Green Bay victory.

Halas, always the realist, was one of the first to assign double coverage to Hutson, but he knew that wouldn't always work either. "I just concede him two touchdowns a game," Halas said, "and hope we can score more."

Hutson played with Green Bay for 11 seasons in a total of 117 games. He caught 488 passes for 7,991 yards, an average of 16.4 per reception. One hundred of them were for touchdowns. With five touchdowns scored running, and extra points and field goals kicked, Hutson amassed 823 points during his career. His point total and receptions ranked him seventh on the all-time list, nearly a quarter of a century after his retirement.

The son of a railroad conductor, Hutson was born January 31, 1913, in Pine Bluff, Arkansas. A quiet man, often called a loner, it is said that once he started to go to school he was never known to sit down to a meal or leave the house without a coat and tie.

Only two events over the years have been known to shake him up. One was when his twin brother, Bob, was killed during a paratroop landing in New Guinea during World War II. And the other was a few days later when his father died from the shock and grief over the twin's death.

It was purely by accident that Hutson became a football player. In his formative years, baseball was his game and, before he signed those contracts, he even tried to play professionally. In the summer of 1935, he played with Knoxville and later in his home town of Pine Bluff. Then his contract was assigned to Albany, N. Y., and that club released him in August.

Hutson's high school coach at Pine Bluff, Walter Dunaway, was the first to see the greatness in him. Dunaway saw his speed and finesse on the baseball field and suggested that Hutson try out for the football team in his senior year. He won the starting position at end and also a scholarship to Alabama.

Even after his sensational rookie and sophomore seasons with the Packers, E. L. (Curly) Lambeau, who was coaching then, tried to put a little beef on the bones of his top receiver. Hutson was not married at the time and he and Lambeau lived in the Northland Hotel in Green Bay. "When he was around," Hutson recalled, "he'd always take me into the bar to buy me a bottle of ale. He was quite a believer in diets and prescribed a bottle of ale each night before I went to bed. Even when he wasn't there I'd make it a habit to collect the two bits from him the next day."

In those days, Hutson had to play on defense, too. Since he wasn't big enough to play defensive end, Lambeau used him at safety and assigned another of the backs to play on the line. Lambeau had his reasons. First, of course, was that he didn't want the game's top receiver to get hurt. The second reason was that Hutson, because of his brilliant offensive ability, was almost an equally brilliant pass defender. He knew all the moves.

Hutson claimed that he never wore shoulder pads during his NFL career. "I go without them for two reasons," he said just before his retirement after the 1945 season, "for speed and for freedom of movement in catching high passes. No, I've never been injured seriously without them."

Hutson, who was an All-Pro six times, became a charter member of the Hall of Fame in 1963, but as the legend grew during his playing years at Green Bay, he became sort of a loner. And after

Herber retired and Hutson and Cecil Isbell became the most feared passing combination in the league, he traveled alone and spoke little to Isbell or anyone else.

As the years rolled on the touchdowns mounted, Hutson became a sports page ritual by announcing his retirement at the end of his last four seasons. He had a wife, the former Julia Richards, three daughters, a thriving 20-lane bowling alley in Green Bay and no more worlds to conquer. The fourth time, his annual 'desire to quit became official, and he took off to entertain the soldiers in Europe on the art of professional football.

The years have treated him kindly. The frame is still slender and the golf ball has replaced the football in his athletic life. And that's kind of sad, because in these days of superstars and Super Bowls, Don Hutson would have made it just as big. He had it all.

WHERE IS HE NOW?

For the last two decades, Don Hutson has lived in Racine, Wisconsin, where he operates an automobile agency. He and Julia are the grandparents of two girls and a boy. Their three daughters are all married with Julia living in Salt Lake City, Martha in Philadelphia, and Jane in Las Cruces, New Mexico.

Hutson has kept to his playing weight of about 185 pounds. He is an avid outdoorsman, fishing in Canada, Montana, Colorado and Idaho—always in search of a new trout stream. His hunting takes him to virtually all points of the compass as does his passion for golf. During the hunting season it's Canada or Louisiana or Chesapeake Bay.

His golfing junkets have taken him all over the world as a member of the Senior 200 Club. The group plays the finest courses in the universe and Hutson enjoys them all, especially a month-long golfing vacation in South Africa recently.

He plays the game with the same dedication that he gave football, and his handicap is at seven these days. His best score was a 71, but generally he shoots in the high 70s. As for football, well, the guy who said there's nothing new in the game, may have had something. At least Hutson thinks so in relation to pass receiving. "One thing is definite," he says. "The patterns are just the same. There is nothing new as far as I can see.

"Oh, sure," he says in the soft Arkansas drawl that has never left him. "They throw a lot more passes now and there are a lot of great receivers, real specialists. And they're good, real good, but the patterns they run look the same to me. The defenses are tougher, though, because there are specialists there, too. It wasn't that way when I played. And we didn't throw the ball nearly as much then as they do now."

Larry MacPhail in his younger years.

A recent picture of Larry MacPhail.

Gabby Hartnett donning the "tools of ignorance" for the Cubs in 1929.

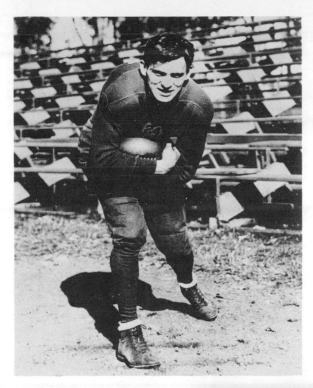

John (Blood) McNally.

James (Cool Papa) Bell as a Kansas City Monarch in the Negro leagues.

Dick Bartell as a New York Giant. He played with the Giants from 1935 to 1938, from 1941 to 1943 and briefly in 1946.

A recent picture of Dick Bartell.

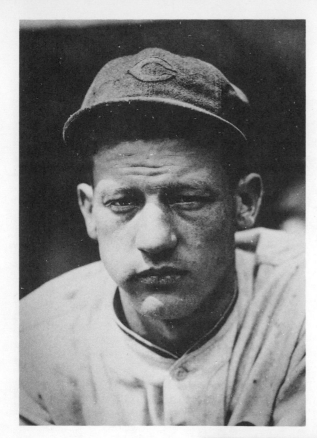

The Arkansas Hummingbird, Lon Warneke.

Lon Warneke as he looks today (right), with Charley Grimm.

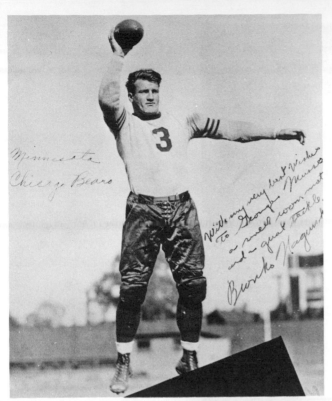

The indomitable Bronko Nagurski.

Bronko Nagurski being honored at the Pro Football Hall of Fame in Canton, Ohio. From left to right: Dick Gallagher, director of the Hall of Fame, Mrs. Marie Lombardi, Nagurski, and Charles L. Andes.

Hank Greenberg as a Detroit Tiger.

Hank Greenberg, today a successful New York stock broker.

Archie Moore still making a difference with San Diego's youth.

The Old Mongoose—Archie Moore.

Don Hutson (14, in white) going up for a pass.

Don Hutson, today, posing with his old number 14.

Jay Berwanger, a dapper young man at the University of Chicago.

Jay Berwanger, left, with Notre Dame football great Johnny Lattner.

Jesse Owens today.

Jesse Owens in the early '50's.

Jesse Owens as an Ohio State trackman in the 1930's.

Enos Slaughter in his prime as a Cardinal.

Enos Slaughter, below, as baseball coach of the Duke University Blue Devils.

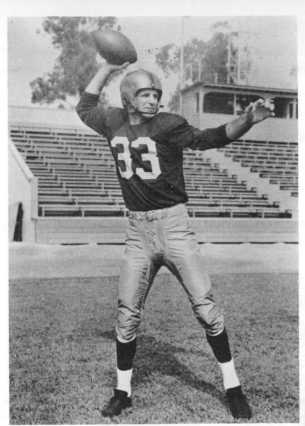

Slingin' Sammy Baugh

Baugh, now a Texas cattle rancher.

Charlie Keller, now a Maryland horse breeder.

Berwanger gained his greatest fame as a running back and is remembered as one of the greatest; and rightly so. But he played in the days when football players had to go both ways, offensively and defensively. And he did that, too. At that time the defenses were rather primitive compared with the sophisticated zones of today.

Seven men played on the line and the other four were deployed in the shape of a diamond with the best tackler playing in the center, the best pass defenders on the wings, and the best kick returner in the back.

Berwanger was the best tackler so he played what could roughly be compared with today's middle linebacker. In one game he made thirteen consecutive tackles, a tremendous feat in any era.

Clark Shaughnessy, who was to become the architect of the T-formation, from which all of today's professional sets are derived, called Berwanger the best in history: "No better halfback ever played football than Jay Berwanger," he said. In Berwanger's last year at Chicago, the Maroons scored one of the big upsets of the 1935 season when they upended a strong Illinois team 7-6.

Or rather, Berwanger did. He returned a punt 50 yards to the Illinois one, and then, after his three backfield teammates failed to gain even an inch, he took the ball in and then kicked the extra point for the one-point victory.

But Chicago's game with Ohio State was Berwanger's finest hour. He burst past the line of scrimmage, into the Buckeye secondary, and finally to the end zone before the game officials could catch up with him. But as he passed the Ohio State bench, his opponents claimed he had stepped out of bounds. Since none of the officials was in a position to see for himself, the referee simply turned to Jay and asked:

"Did you step out of bounds?"

"Yes, I did," Berwanger replied, and the touchdown was nullified.

But, there were other touchdowns and long runs to be remembered, for Jay Berwanger averaged 50 minutes a game during his career at Chicago. There were 22 touchdowns and 20 points after, 1,839 yards gained in 415 attempts and 50 completed passes for 921 yards, and 12 pass receptions for 189 yards. He returned 16 punts for 138 yards and 33 kickoffs for 855 yards, an average of 25.9. His punting average for 213 kicks was a superlative 37.5 and his 31 kickoffs averaged 46.3 yards.

In addition to being the first winner of the Heisman Trophy, Berwanger also was the first player drafted by the National Football League. Because of its abysmal record, Philadelphia won the rights to him. But George Halas, the canny owner of the Chicago

Bears wanted him too, undoubtedly because of the popularity he enjoyed among Chicagoans.

Then, as now, what Halas wants, Halas usually gets. The Bears' owner acquired the rights to Berwanger for a cash payment believed to have been $10,000 and the Bears' first round choice.

All this wheeling and dealing failed to impress Berwanger. After he had left Dubuque High to enter the University of Chicago, at the urging of Ira N. Davenport, who had been captain of the 1912 U of C track team and a member of two football squads at the Midway, Berwanger knew where he was going in life.

Davenport, a half-miler on the U.S. Olympic team of 1912, owned the Dubuque Boat and Boiler Works, and young Berwanger worked in the yards for him during summer vacations. He watched him mature from a 150-pound halfback, who closed his eyes the first time he carried the ball in high school competition, to a 195-pound hard-running halfback who captured the imagination of the country. He wanted Chicago to share in that dream.

"I wanted to go to college," Jay explained. "Secondly, I wanted to play football. But I wanted to take my football at a school where I could balance it with some pretty serious work in the education business. That came first.

"What I learned of Chicago through 'Davvy' and a couple of trips to track meets convinced me I could get what I wanted. I guess maybe I could have done the same at a lot of other colleges, but I felt surer about this one. And I wasn't wrong. If I had to choose again, probably I'd pick it the same way."

That should have been a tip-off for George Halas that he was going to have trouble signing Berwanger. There was no C. C. (Cash & Carry) Pyle flamboyantly negotiating a quarter-million dollar deal for Berwanger as he had done for Grange. That was because Berwanger had set his sights on a career in business. He and Halas negotiated, broke off, tried again for a couple of years and then dropped the whole thing. At the time, reports indicated that Berwanger wanted $1,000 a game, or a $35,000 contract. Bronko Nagurski, the greatest runner in the league, was playing for the Bears at the time, and he swears his top salary at that time was $5,000 a year. So it's not difficult to understand why Berwanger and the Bears couldn't get together. Berwanger had another reason. "What if I play for a couple of years at pretty good money," he said, "then I find out I have to live on $150 a month for the rest of my life?"

Although it was pro football's loss, Jay Berwanger didn't have to live on three 50-dollar bills every pay day.

WHERE IS HE NOW?

Jay Berwanger started his career in the business world following his graduation from the University of Chicago. On Oct. 13, 1940, he married his college sweetheart, Philomela Baker in Bond Chapel in an evening ceremony on the University of Chicago campus. Northwestern was playing Ohio State that afternoon and Jay insisted the wedding be an evening affair so his friends wouldn't have to miss the game.

During World War II Berwanger became a navy pilot and eventually a flight instructor, all the while advancing his career with a company manufacturing sponge rubber products. He is its president now, and that certainly figures.

As for the Heisman Trophy Berwanger had no idea, at the time he received it, that its prestige would grow to match the legend of its first recipient. "The difference between winning the Heisman Trophy today and when I won it is the difference between nothing and a million dollars," he says.

"Back then no one would mention that I won the Heisman Trophy. I've gotten more publicity in the last five or 10 years, simply because I was the first recipient. It was impossible to visualize then how important the award would become."

He credits television with the tremendous growth of pro football interest and for its rise in stature. "When I got out of school, most of the pro clubs were in financial trouble," Berwanger says. "They didn't have TV revenue, pensions and whatnot. I was the first player ever drafted by the pros, but I didn't go because I couldn't make any money at it.

"I think I might have played for $25,000, but he [George Halas] never offered it. There never was a definite salary mentioned."

Berwanger did keep one tie with college football. He was an official in the Big Ten, but was forced to give it up on doctors' orders, along with coffee, because both were too stimulating.

He became involved in a controversial decision in the 1949 Rose Bowl game between the University of California and Northwestern. Northwestern University's Art Murakowski bobbled the ball on a one-yard touchdown dive and the question was, did he have possession of it as he crossed the goal line? Field judge Berwanger said he did, and called it that way. California writers, seeking any angle that would dilute Northwestern University's 20-14 victory, charged that Murakowski had dropped the ball before he crossed into the end zone.

"There is no doubt in my mind that Murakowski scored before he fumbled," Berwanger says. "I'll stand by the call." And he does to this day.

As for the Heisman, it always will have a special meaning for Berwanger, his wife, Phil, and their three children: John, an attorney, Cuyler, a coach and teacher in a junior high school, and Helen, a major in art education.

You see, the trophy shows a football player crossing one leg over the other as he tries to evade a tackler. The ball is securely tucked under one arm and a glance tells you the model must have been something special.

He was. New Yorker Frank Lisou sculpted that first Heisman Trophy from a picture of Jay Berwanger, although a Fordham football player actually modeled for it. The name of the young man from Fordham has been forgotten, but Jay Berwanger's never will be.

He was the first.

JAMES CLEVELAND OWENS

Forty-five Minutes in the
History of Sports

JAMES CLEVELAND OWENS was the son of an Alabama share-cropper who fled the poverty of the South to bring his family to a Cleveland ghetto. His grandfather was a chattel slave, and the Civil War changed his status hardly at all. Instead of being bonded to the plantation owner, he was bound to a small plot of land for sharecropping, and to the local storeowner.

That's why his father came North with his brood only to find a life of destitution in Cleveland. One of his sons was a skinny, weak-lunged kid who was to become, for a time, the best known black man in America. His name: James Cleveland Owens, who became what is now called "the world's fastest human." He ran under the scarlet banner of Ohio State, and the red, white and blue of the U.S. Olympic team. But he was still black and in those depression ridden days of the 1930s, no one let him forget it.

And he didn't let anyone forget it either, because Jesse Owens performed one of the most amazing feats in the annals of track and field, if not in the whole maze of sports, one warm day in May, 1935.

It was the 25th day of the month, to be exact, and the site was Ferry Field at the University of Michigan campus in Ann Arbor. The weather was perfect and an early afternoon whisp of wind tailed off into nothing. The temperature was 82 degrees, and Jesse Owens was a 21-year-old sophomore participating in his first Big Ten meet. A crowd of 10,000 was in the stands, including Jesse's mother, friends, and some of the kids with whom he had gone to high school.

Owens, clad in his scarlet sweatsuit, leaned up against a flag-pole and watched the people file into the stands. He was wondering if he could run at all, when his high school coach, Charley Riley, walked up to shake hands with him and wish him luck.

75

Riley knew. When Jesse was in high school he used to worry about the skinny kid and bring him food from his own home. "Here, eat this, kid, and put some meat on your bones," he would say. Young Jesse did, and before he was finished, he ran a 9.4 hundred-yard dash, and the ears of several colleges and universities pricked up. One offered him a six-room apartment off campus, a six-room apartment off campus, a new car and girls—black of course —but in the end, Riley prevailed.

Jesse wasn't going to go to college at all after his graduation from Cleveland's East Tech High, because the decision of choosing a school was eating his insides out. Finally, though, the old coach persuaded him to go to Ohio State which, ironically, did not give athletic rides for track and field. But Jesse went anyway and worked his way by waiting on tables, stacking books in the library, and running an elevator seven nights a week.

"If I didn't eat on campus," Jesse says, "then I didn't eat. No restaurants or theaters were open to me." Yet there he was at Ann Arbor near the end of his second year, and he had survived. Now he was about to conquer. He strolled from the flagpole and started to take his warmup by jogging 440 yards to wake up sleeping muscles. He couldn't make it because a couple of weeks previously he had slipped and fell down the stairs at his fraternity house and wrenched his back. Then he aggravated the injury in a dual meet against Northwestern when he hit a hurdle.

He sat down on the grass and one of his teammates, Charlie Beetham, a half miler, helped him pull off his sweatshirt. Coach Larry Snyder came over and Jesse told him: "Let me try the hundred. Maybe I'll snap out of this."

His back was still throbbing when he took his mark in the holes he dug for the start. This was in the days before starting blocks were used as launching pads. When the starter gave the "get-set," Owens raised his fanny and the pain subsided. At the gun he was off and 0:9.4 seconds later he broke the tape five yards in front of Illinois' Bobby Grieve. His time tied the world standard then held by Fred Wykoff!

The clock read: 3:15 P.M.

Inside the oval at Ferry Field, the broad jump was already underway. Coach Snyder decided that his aching sophomore would take only one jump because he wanted him to run the 220-yard dash and low hurdles. Owens rested for 10 minutes and then prepared to take his broadjump. He walked over and put down a handkerchief at precisely 26 feet, 2½ inches, the record distance held by Chuhei Namby.

He walked back and took his running jump and the trajectory was perfect. High. And when he leveled off and landed in the pit he looked and there was the handkerchief behind his feet. "I knew I had the record," he said.

Coach Snyder walked over and told Owens: "That's it. No more jumping." And the field announcer, Ted Canty, said to all: "I want to introduce a world champion." Jesse had leaped 26 feet, 8¼ inches, breaking the world standard by more than half a foot.

The clock read: 3:25 P.M.

A few minutes later, the field lined up for the 220-yard dash, and the crowd was beginning to sense that this was no ordinary conference meet. A hush fell upon the stadium as the runners took their marks. The pistol sent them off, and Owens, fluid and graceful, shot into the lead.

"I didn't start pushing until the 100-yard mark," Owens recalls. "But I could feel being all by myself, and I didn't want to look around. I felt I was flowing, and about 50 yards from the finish, I began bringing up my knees, which you do if you're tiring. I guess I finished about 10 yards in front of Andy Dooley of Iowa."

Now there was complete silence as Canty announced: "The winner: Jesse Owens of Ohio State and a new world record of 20.3 seconds." The silence became a roar.

The clock read: 3:34 P.M.

Owens was not the most skillful hurdler in competition, but his tremendous speed compensated for any lack of style. And he knew if he beat the field over the first hurdle he would win the race. So that's what he did. "I got to it first and I just kept running and bobbin' and I finished five yards ahead of Northwestern's Phil Doherty." There it was, another world mark. Time: 22.6; two fifths of a second faster than the record at the time.

The clock read: 4:00 P.M.

Those 45 minutes have gone down in history as the most important in the history of the sport. Owens entered four events, broke three world records and tied a fourth. But world acclaim was to come the following year in Berlin, site of the 1936 Olympic games.

The German capital was no place for a Jew or a black. Adolph Hitler had seized power on the racist theory that the blonde blue-eyed Aryan was supreme. But when the American team came over, there he was, Jesse Owens, black skin, black hair and black eyes wrapped in the red, white and blue of the United States.

Jesse belonged to what the Nazi press sneeringly called the "Black American Auxiliaries." They would not make his task any easier. Neither did the Fuehrer, who became incensed when Jesse ran away with his Aryan theory.

Owens won the 100 and 200 meter dashes, and the relay leg on the 400-meter team for three gold medals. But it was in the broad jump that Jesse was at his incredulous best. Arthur Daley, the *New York Times* columnist who was there wrote years later that Owens was almost jobbed out of his fourth gold medal by German officials. In the qualifying, Owens was assessed fouls on his first two jumps, and he was one try away from being disqualified.

"This reporter," Daley wrote, "binoculars focused on the take-off board, saw no foul." Jesse was ready to panic, and he asked himself: "Did I come 3,000 miles for this? To foul out in the trials and make a fool of myself."

As he walked back from the pit, kicking the dirt and dying a little inside, he felt a hand on his shoulder. He turned and looked into the friendly blue eyes of the Nazi broad jumper, Luz Long, who had qualified on his first jump. Long spoke to him in English, trying to find out why Jesse was having so much trouble trying to qualify for an event in which he had set a world record a year before.

"Look," Long said, "why don't you draw a line a few inches back of the take-off board and aim from there. You'll be sure not to foul and you will be certain to qualify. What does it matter if you're not first in the trials? Tomorrow is what counts, Jesse. Tomorrow."

Owens did, and he made the field, and the next day won his fourth gold medal. Hitler, of course, was furious and hurriedly left the stadium to avoid giving the young, black American his just due. Long was so stunned at Jesse's performance in the finals that he walked back to the starting mark, draped his arm over Owens' shoulder and congratulated him. Owens should have been making a command appearance in Hitler's box, but was not invited.

In any case, the Fuehrer left in a huff and one of sport's greatest legends was born. A black grandson of a slave was helped by one Nazi and snubbed by another in the final amateur event of his life, one that was to forever stamp him as the folk hero of the world.

"Once you reach the top," Owens was to say later, "there's no place else to go. Father Time is no beauty doctor. You learn that as you grow older. It's always better to have people remember you for what you have done. You must accept that some day others are going to take your place, just as you took theirs."

Jesse's records are all gone, now. The last to go was the broad-jump, and he held it for a quarter of a century.

There have been good times and bad, since those fabulous days of the 1930s, and this slim black man, turned from the regimented world of amateurism to the world at large, had to begin hustling for a buck instead of a record.

WHERE IS HE NOW?

The world's fastest human had no professional league or competition to enter after his sensational college and Olympic career. Track and field, then, as now, is strictly an amateur's sport. But Jesse and his wife and daughter had to eat, so he turned pro anyway. He ran against horses at racetracks, and baseball players before important ball games, and then he led a dance band. Later, he lost $25,000 trying to promote Negro baseball, and he played for the Harlem Globetrotters. Then he went into public relations for various companies, and for a time was employed by the Illinois Youth Commission, lending his name and staging athletic events, particularly in track. He also became a disc jockey on a Chicago station.

But it was in public relations that Jesse was to make his mark in the world of business. The money was rolling in at a pretty good pace—so much so, that Jesse got involved with the Internal Revenue Service, which charged that, in the period 1959 to 1961, the former Olympic great had an income of $142,000. The government said that the gross taxable income would have been $59,025 after deductions, and that he owed $29,136 on unreported income. Jesse pleaded no contest and when the case was heard, he was fined $3,000 and given six months to pay the back taxes. He could have received four years in prison plus a $40,000 fine.

Owens' attorney, Bernard Kleinman, had pleaded that Jesse was so busy "running from one place to another, performing good works," that he didn't file returns. "Which one of us is not guilty of a technical error?" Kleinman asked.

In 1970, Jesse co-authored a book, *Blackthink*: *My Life as a Black Man and White Man*. His coauthor was Paul G. Niemark, and the book was published by Morrow. In it, Jesse attacks the black militants, particularly Harry Edwards, the sociology professor who tried to get black athletes to boycott the 1968 Olympics in Mexico City.

Owens opposed the boycott, which failed, and Edwards charged that Jesse was an "Uncle Tom" and labeled a photo of him "Traitor of the Week."

Owens, in his book, defined Blankthink as totalitarian, pro-black, anti-white bigotry. Jesse's theory is that black athletes are in a better position to correct injustices after they compete in the Olympics. "Sports is the wrong battlefield," he says. "It has been the one thing able to achieve the freedom in our nation." While admitting there are injustices, Owens believes that by competing the blacks will gain a greater status in their communities. "I think people judge people by performance more than anything else."

He ought to know. His own life story is the story of Negro life. After all, didn't it all start from a slave? Then, there was sharecropping and, later, the ghetto life in Cleveland. And from there to fame as an athlete, and then the climb to the middle class.

The Owens are grandparents many times over. They gave up their eight-room house years ago for a comfortable apartment on Chicago's South Shore. Later they moved to Phoenix, Arizona. Jesse is still active in business and sports, and he looks back with joy on the life he's led.

He has made mistakes, like the income tax charge, but he faced up to it with honor. And he held an unpopular view on black militancy. But perhaps one of his sons-in-law said it best while talking it over with Jesse. "Where has Rap Brown been, man?" he asked.

Jesse knows where *he* has been and he made it—all the way, and in record time, too.

ENOS BRADHER SLAUGHTER

The Country Boy Who Loved to Run

ONCE HE STEPPED ON a baseball field, he had a compulsion to run. And that's what he did for more than two decades in the major leagues. He ran—to and from the outfield. He thought the basepaths were his own private real estate, and if the opposing infielders trespassed, too bad for them.

They called him "Country," because he came off a tobacco farm in Roxboro, North Carolina. Some say the late Burt Shotton, who was his manager at Columbus, gave him the name. He hit .382 for Shotton during the 1937 season. Others say a Columbus newspaper, realizing that the town had a bona fide superstar on its hands, held a contest and the man himself picked the name because he knew that he was a country boy, and was proud of it.

In any case, Enos Slaughter became "Country" just as surely as Ted Williams became the "Splendid Splinter" and the great DiMaggio was knighted "Joltin' Joe." But unlike Williams, who was an extroverted maverick with unsurpassed gifts in the art of hitting a baseball, and unlike DiMaggio, moody, introverted, alone, Slaughter brought forth a quality of pure joy to those who watched him play for the Cardinals, Yankees, Athletics and Braves during a major league career that began in St. Louis in 1938 and ended in the fall of 1959 in Milwaukee. In the interim, there were 2,295 games, and 2,363 hits, a lifetime batting average of .302, 1,282 runs batted in, and 1,237 runs scored.

One run stands out, though, and it will forever be remembered because Enos Slaughter scored it doing the thing he loved to do best—run. It was in the final game of the 1946 World Series between the Cardinals and the Boston Red Sox, and the teams traded off the first six games in dramatic fashion with Boston taking the opener and St. Louis the second, and so on through to the final contest on October 15 in St. Louis.

There were two out, and Slaughter singled to put the potential winning run on base. Although the Cardinals were a running team, and Country was the best of the runners, nobody, least of all the Red Sox, expected him to score from first base on a routine single. But that's what he did.

While Country hugged first base, manager Eddie Dyer flashed the steal sign, and as Harry Walker hit the ball, Slaughter got a jump and headed down his private driveway, the road between first and second. Walker's hit was one of those soft flies that fell between left and center. Leon Culberson fielded it flawlessly, and routinely threw the ball to Johnny Pesky, the cutoff man who had gone out on the grass to take the ball and relay it to third base. Pesky's back was to the infield and this fact was not lost on Slaughter, so when he rounded second he just kept right on going.

"When I rounded second I knew I was going home," Slaughter recalls. "To this day, I don't know whether or not coach Mike Gonzales gave me the stop or go sign."

Pesky took Culberson's throw, turned toward the plate and immediately went into shock. He cocked his arm to throw, but the incredible scene of Slaughter barking toward the plate, threw him for an instant. He held the ball—not long, but long enough—and Enos slid across the plate with the run that won the World Series for the Cardinals. Not that he needed to slide. Catcher Roy Partee had jumped a few feet in front of the plate in order to receive Pesky's throw, but Slaughter had decided when he rounded third that he would slide and that's what he did.

"When you make up your mind you're going to slide, you might break a leg, if you try to hold up," he said. That run, one of the most famous in major league history, was the highlight of Country's career, and he went on for seven seasons living the life of a folk hero, not only in St. Louis, but the country over.

Although he was honored by the Baseball Writers Association of America as "The Comeback Player of the Year" just a few months previously, and he hit a respectable .291 in 1953, Slaughter no longer fit into the St. Louis game plan.

Eddie Stanky had become manager of the club, and August A. Busch, the multimillionaire beer baron of St. Louis had bought it, and neither was interested in a 37-year-old outfielder even though he still could run like the wind.

The Yankees were working on their sixth straight pennant, and wily Casey Stengel was shopping for a left-handed pinch hitter. So Enos Slaughter, for 13 years a legend in St. Louis, was traded to New York for a minor league pitcher named Mel Wright and two others, Bill Virdon and Emil Tellinger from New York's minor league affiliate clubs.

It was a blow to Slaughter's pride for two reasons. First, the other National League clubs waived him out of the league, and second, he didn't think the Cardinals ever would trade him. So he took the news as any sensitive man who plays a boy's game, would. He wept.

"I didn't think it would ever happen to me," he said as, unabashedly, he wiped away the tears. "It's the greatest shock I ever had in my life. To think that I spent nearly all of my life with this organization and then they trade me after I've given them everything I've got."

Reaction in St. Louis to the Slaughter trade was predictable The fans were incensed. Busch, who in later years was to run a tight ship in relations with his players, showed a little compassion when he announced the trade. But not much. "It was one of the toughest decisions I have ever had to participate in," he said. "Enos has been Mr. Baseball for almost 20 years. The word 'hustle' was practically coined for him," he added as he read from a prepared statement. "The Cardinals are trying to build a young ball club. We must look to the future."

St. Louis was looking for the future, all right, but the word in New York was "now." And Slaughter was ready. "I'll say this," Slaughter said with some bitterness, "I'll be around when a lot of guys they got will be gone. And you can tell Casey Stengel that I'll give him everything just like I gave this club. . . . But I just can't believe it. I wanted to be a Cardinal to the finish."

The Yankees never did win that sixth straight American League pennant. Senor Al Lopez sneaked in with the Cleveland Indians in 1954. But the following season, the Yankees were back up there, and Slaughter wasn't around to enjoy it. He and pitcher Johnny Sain were traded to the Athletics—then in Kansas City—for pitcher Sonny Dixon and cash on May 11, 1955.

Some 15 months later, after he had hit .315, the Athletics released him and again the Yankees picked him up. He helped the New York Club to pennants in 1956, 1957 and 1958 as an outfielder and pinch-hitter, and it looked as though life truly began at age 40 for the country boy from North Carolina.

The Yankees released their great shortstop Phil Rizzuto to make room for the old gentleman and he didn't disappoint them. In 1958, for instance, he hit .304 in 77 games for them as a pinch-hitter, and his contribution was a delight to Stengel who used him as an example to the younger Yankees.

Country's personal life was hardly as stable as his batting average. He went through four marriages before he was wed to Helen Spiker in December of 1955, and his court actions on divorces and separate maintenance suits kept his name in print during the off-season almost as often as his exploits on the field did during the season. The Yankees finally let him go and the Braves picked him up in September of 1959 in hopes that he could give them a lift to a third straight National League pennant.

Stengel broke the news personally to the 43-year-old Slaughter. "I want to thank you for all you've done for us," Casey said in his private office in Yankee Stadium. "And I want to wish you the best of luck in Milwaukee."

That was it. The end came a few weeks later when the Braves released him. He managed in the minors for a while, and at the same time farmed his 240 acres in Roxboro with one eye on the tobacco crop and the other on the telephone. He hoped it would ring, and he hoped the voice at the other end of the line would offer him a coaching job in the major leagues.

It never rang, and Enos Slaughter seemed destined to live out his days at the same place where it all began that day in 1935 when he left home to begin his baseball career with Martinsville of the old Bi-State League. An incredible 24 years had passed, and Slaughter had spent more than 20 of them in the big leagues.

He had seen and done it all, ten times an All-Star, and five World Series, two with the Cardinals and three with the Yankees.

WHERE IS HE NOW?

Country Slaughter is back on the land he loves, the tobacco country of Roxboro, North Carolina. He and his Helen, whom he married in December of 1955, have three daughters: teenagers Gay and Sharon, and little Rhonda.

Slaughter has the life that most former ballplayers dream about. He farms three sections of land in the vicinity of his Roxboro home, growing tobacco and raising cattle. But the love of competition is satisfied, too.

He joined the athletic staff of Duke University in 1971 as baseball coach and spends a couple of weeks in the fall and three months in the spring imparting his vast knowledge of the game to the Blue Devils.

Both Slaughter and Duke seem to be satisfied with the coaching arrangement. "He's a very good coach," says E. M. Cameron, Duke's athletic director. "The kids are crazy about him. And he's very aggressive."

Well, that certainly figures. Enos Slaughter never played the game any other way. And that's the way he teaches it.

"I really enjoy it," he says. "These kids at Duke give me all they got. Some of them don't have the greatest ability, and I haven't any scholarships to give them, although a couple do get some financial aid."

Any bitterness about the present salaries?

"Well, the most I ever made," Country drawled," was $25,000. But the way I played I think I'd be in the $100,000 class now. But one thing you have to remember is that it still takes nine men to play the game."

Slaughter receives a small pension from the Major League Players' Association fund, mostly because the great years of his career took place before the pension was inaugurated.

"Do you know," he said, "that we started the pension back in 1946 and we donated our radio money to get it started?"

Slaughter is more than slightly unhappy that no big league team ever found a spot for him as a coach or even as manager in the minors. He managed Houston of the old American Association to a third place finish and to the seventh game of the playoffs against Denver. But when he searched the minor league meetings the following year he found nothing. "Then I contacted every major league team," he said, "and they were all filled. But I'm happy at Duke and things have worked out fine."

When he said that, Country was celebrating his 56th birthday. Duke was getting ready to wind up its season and Slaughter had spent the morning out at Kerr Lake, 40 miles from his home, where he and Helen have a summer place.

"I've got to get the boat in the water," he said. "It's almost time to go fishin'." Enos and Helen have made a fine life for themselves and the children. And it all came about because of baseball.

They met on an airliner. Helen was a stewardess, based in Kansas City, and Enos spent time shuffling between there and New York in 1955 and 1956. Remember?

Well, he married the gal and they've lived happily ever after.

SAMUEL ADRIAN BAUGH

Football's First Great Passer

IT WAS IN THE NATION'S capital, and Sammy Baugh of the Washington Redskins, the premier passer in all of football, was the guest of honor at the National Press Club banquet. Seated next to him on the dais was Joe DiMaggio, the Yankee centerfielder who had not yet earned his niche in the Hall of Fame. Joe idly picked up a baseball that was lying on the table and said with a grin: "Sammy, I'll bet you wouldn't know what to do with this ball."

Baugh, not known for compound sentences no matter what the occasion, replied: "Just pump a little air into it and I'll show you."

And with that simple declaration, you have Samuel Adrian Baugh, perhaps the best passer who ever lived. Almost forgotten, as his legend has grown over the years, is the fact that he was a fine defensive player and his punting was almost equal to his ability as a passer.

A lanky six feet, two inches and 179 pounds in his playing days, the black-haired, blue-eyed Baugh had the face that matched the rugged Texas land he came from. Tanned, deeply lined from riding the range in the offseasons, Baugh had the look of the Texas Ranger who always gets his man. And he usually did.

A tailback when he first arrived on the National Football League scene from Texas Christian University, Baugh, along with Sid Luckman of the Chicago Bears, became the epitome of the T-formation quarterback during the 1940s. A pocket passer with quick feet, Slingin' Sam, as he became known the country over, was adept at faking the pass-rushers and shooting the gaps with his passes. But even the best of quarterbacks do not always escape unharmed. There was the time that Sammy was sacked by an aggressive rookie tackle who not only decked him, but threw a punch for good measure.

"Take it easy, son," Baugh drawled as he pulled his skinny opponent from horizontal to vertical. On the next play it happened again. So Baugh issued orders in the huddle to let the young man through a third time and he would handle him. At the snap, the power-crazy kid came rushing in, and just as he lunged for the faking Baugh, Sammy pivoted, took aim and uncorked a bullseye. The football, traveling with the speed of a laser beam, struck the tackle squarely between the eyes and the kid dropped to the turf like a felled ox. He was finished for the day, but Sammy Baugh went on and on and on. For 16 years he toiled for the Redskins leading them to five division titles and two world championships. And the records he set tell only part of his story.

He led the NFL six times in passing, four times in punting, in addition to achieving single season and single game punting average records. He also was the leader in interceptions in 1943, and the four he picked off in a game against the Lions set a record at the time.

Sammy was an all-pro four times, but strangely enough only once as a quarterback. The others were as a single-wing tailback. As a matter of fact, he was playing that position in 1937, his first in the league. And he was a smash from the very beginning.

It was December 12th of that year and the Redskins were playing the Bears for the league championship. Cliff Battles put the Skins on the board with a 10-yard touchdown run in the first period, but the Bears countered with two touchdowns by automatic Jack Manders, the first on a 10-yard run and the second on a 37-yard pass from Bernie Masterson, the Bears' T-formation quarterback. That gave the Bears a 14-7 lead at the half. Early in the third period of the game played in icy Wrigley Field, Baugh threw a 55-yard touchdown pass to Wayne Millner, the former Notre Dame great, and the score was tied. But not for long. Eggs Manske caught a three-yard scoring pass from Masterson to put the Bears ahead again but the fourth period belonged to Sammy Baugh. Millner caught the first of the final period touchdowns on a 78-yard play and then Baugh threw a 35-yard pass to Ed Justice, and the Redskins had the championship 28-21.

It was Washington's first. In fact, it was the first year the nation's capital had an NFL team. Owner George Preston Marshall had just moved the club there from Boston where it was singularly unsuccessful. Baugh changed all that. Marshall paid him the unheard of sum of $5,000 to forget about playing baseball for a living and to join his newly-transferred club. It was the best investment Marshall was ever to make in his long association in the NFL.

Despite all his records, Sammy Baugh's contribution to football probably could be summed up as revolutionary. When he came along, the T-formation was still in its incubator and the forward pass, while a potent offensive weapon, was not used with the frequency that is seen today. The game was largely a battle between ground forces, and throwing a pass inside the 30-yard line was only for the desperate or the innovative. Four years previously, Bears' owner George Halas was instrumental in getting a rule passed that legalized passing from anywhere behind the line of scrimmage. Previous to that, the passer had to be five yards behind the line.

Baugh alone was not responsible for changing the concept of the game. But he, and others such as Arnie Herber, Bernie Masterson, Carl Brumbaugh and later Sid Luckman were the biggest factors in opening up the game from its three-yards and a cloud of dust image to the exciting spectacle it is today.

When he had finished, after 16 years of combat, Baugh had played in 165 games, completed 1,693 of 2,995 passes for a 56.5 percentage and gained a total of 21,886 yards. His punting average for 338 kicks was 44.9 and in one year, 1951, he punted four times and averaged 55.3 yards! Over the years he intercepted 28 passes.

Baugh knew how to lose as well as win. He was on the deficit side of that famous 1940 title game when the Bears bombed Washington 73-0. The Bears could do no wrong that day with 10 different players scoring 11 touchdowns and six different men scoring seven conversions.

Early in the first period, after Bill Osmanski had put the Bears in front with a 68-yard run on the second play from scrimmage, Baugh drilled a pass into the end zone for what looked like a sure touchdown. It was dropped.

After the game, in the Washington locker room, Sammy was asked by a not-so-enterprising newsman if the outcome would have been different had the pass been caught.

Baugh thought for a moment and then said in his Texas drawl: "Yeah, I suppose it would have made it 73-7."

WHERE IS HE NOW?

Sammy Baugh is still a lean and leathery 175 pounds. The lines on his face are deeper now from long hours in the saddle on his 34,640 acre cattle ranch near Rotan, Texas. He and his wife Edmonia live a quiet, but comfortable life. And their five sons Todd, David, Bruce, Stephen and Francis have left the nest, but visit often. "I don't like to travel anymore," he says. "I'm out of the house by 4:30 A.M. and I'm usually where I want to be by daylight. Depending on what has to be done, I'm usually back at the house in mid afternoon or early evening."

Sammy tried coaching at Hardin-Simmons for five years after he retired, and later coached the New York Titans in the old American Football League. The Titans, predecessors to the Jets, were owned by former Redskins' radio announcer Harry Wismer, and Harry ran the operation from his New York apartment.

"We got along all right," Baugh recalled with a laugh. "I learned that if you talked to Harry before 10 in the morning it was all right. After that, the chance of getting anything done decreased with each scotch and soda."

Baugh is proud of the fact that he never left a team he coached or played with in anger, and prouder that the money he earned as a pro quarterback and coach enabled him to buy and lease the thousands of acres of land that he now ranches. "I'm satisfied with the way things turned out," he says. "I've always appreciated what football has done for me and I'm well pleased with the way Mr. Marshall treated me."

Baugh says the highest salary he ever received as a player was $21,000 a year, a sum that a rookie lineman commands in these days of high priced talent. "Of course, a dollar was worth more then," he says. "Still I wouldn't mind playing in this age. For the money, I mean. But I have no regrets."

The Baughs ship their calves about four times a year, and when he isn't riding the range, Sam keeps a fairly close eye on today's pro game. He calls Johnny Unitas of the Colts the best he has seen, and has high hopes for the Steelers' Terry Bradshaw and Buffalo's Dennis Shaw.

"Joe Namath of the Jets would have been the greatest if his legs had held up," Baugh says. "I've never seen a better thrower. He sure has a great arm."

He also likes to see the quarterback call his own plays, as he did with the Redskins. "There's something about going to the sidelines, getting the information from the coaches and then going out on the field and calling the play that beats the defense."

The word he reaches for is "challenge." And Sammy Baugh challenged National Football League defenses for 16 years. Sometimes he had the protection, often he did not. Essentially a pocket passer, Baugh had the fakes that sent the rusher to the outside, and that's all he needed. He would pop the ball between the outstretched arms and he completed more than he missed.

But there were times in Washington when the offensive line was not equal to the task. And Baugh eloquently pointed this out in a speech before a group of FBI men. He looked at them and said: "This is the most protection I've had since I came to Washington."

He was kidding, of course, but the records are for real and so is the man. Samuel Adrian Baugh, football's first great passer.

CHARLES ERNEST KELLER

From Batter to Breeder

HE WAS DARK AND HANDSOME and muscular, and he exuded an aura of power when he stepped into the batter's box in Yankee Stadium. The year was 1939 and Charlie Keller was just up from Newark where he had blasted International League pitching for a .365 average.

If he could come anywhere near that in the American League, the Yankees were sure of another pennant. So he took his place in the outfield alongside Joe DiMaggio and Tommy Henrich, and he proceeded to have his best year in a career that was to span 15 years.

Charlie Keller rattled American League pitching for a .334 average that first year and another rookie in Boston by the name of Ted Williams had to settle for .327. "I never hit as well again as I did that first season," he says. "The next season, what with the short right-field fence at Yankee Stadium, the club switched my stance around to get me to pull the ball more. I never felt really comfortable at bat after that."

Comfortable or not, Keller went on to compile a .286 lifetime batting average over his career with the Yankees, and near the end, with Detroit as a pinch-hitter.

How he was able to even swing a bat is a story in itself. Gifted as he was, Charlie was a victim of congenital back trouble that was to plague him all through his career.

There were days when just getting out of bed in the morning was an agonizing experience. But Keller suffered and endured, and the Yankees prospered, winning pennants in 1939, 1941, 1942 and 1943 with Keller. In 1941, for example, he hit a healthy .298 with 33 home runs and 122 runs batted in as the Yankees swept the pennant and went on to face the Dodgers in the World Series.

The 1941 fall classic is one that they still talk about because it contained one of the most bizarre incidents in the history of the game. Going into the fourth game of the set, the Yankees pulled in front two games to one, but the Dodgers appeared to have this one all but in the bag.

It was the ninth inning and Brooklyn was ahead 4-3. Tommy Henrich was hitting against the venerable Hugh Casey. The Brooklyn pitcher had a count of three and two on the powerful Yankee outfielder, and was one pitch away from a series-tying victory. The age-old battle of pitcher against batter started anew as Casey got the sign from catcher Mickey Owen.

Henrich was looking for a fast ball from the portly Brooklyn pitcher, and it looked as though that's just what he was going to get as Casey delivered the ball. Tommy started his swing and at that very instant a funny thing happened. It wasn't a fast ball at all, but a curve. And as the ball started its trajectory, Henrich was so far committed that he didn't have time to check his swing, so he followed through. Then, Mickey Owen, who had accepted 509 chances without an error that season for a National League record, missed the ball! It curved and struck the thumb of his catcher's glove and bounced toward the backstop.

Henrich turned to see what happened and took off for first base. He made it, and the Yankees were still alive. Next hitter in the Yankee order was Joe DiMaggio, followed by Charlie Keller, Bill Dickey and Joe Gordon.

DiMag screamed a liner to left advancing Henrich to second and Keller strode to the plate. Casey got two quick strikes on him with a pair of good curveballs, but when he tried to put a third one past him, Keller smashed a double off the right-field wall. Shaken up, Casey walked Dickey and then Gordon doubled off the left-field barricade and four runs had crossed the plate. The Bronx Bombers went on to win the series and Keller contributed a .389 batting average with five runs batted in.

"The Yankee pride you heard and read so much about was real," Keller says. "Joe McCarthy was the kind of manager whose standards were so high you would run into fences for him just to get a nod. He demanded so much you had to be proud to produce."

As proud as he was to be a Yankee, the life of a ball player was a constant challenge to Keller. He came out of Middletown, Maryland, was graduated from the University at College Park with a Bachelor of Science in Agriculture, and figured some day he would be a dairy farmer. But first he would shoot for the big leagues so that he could make some money and buy land. Although he never made more than $27,500 a year, he did manage to purchase 100 acres of rolling farm land near Frederick.

After the Yankees released him in 1949, he spent a couple of seasons with the Tigers as a pinch-hitter, and he finally went back to the Yanks in 1952 and appeared in two games. Then it was all over.

"I've got nothing against baseball," he was to say in later years. "It gave me all this I've got today. I enjoyed actually playing the game. It's just that the life of a ball player isn't normal. . . . Too much bouncing around and living in hotel rooms and going too long on the road without seeing your family. There isn't a ball player alive who will tell you it's normal. This is normal, what I'm doing now."

WHERE IS HE NOW?

Charlie Keller never did become a dairy farmer, although he retired to those 100 beautiful acres in Frederick, Maryland. He was out of baseball for good, but he wasn't sure what he wanted to do with his life. Having been brought up on a dairy farm, he knew he didn't want that kind of regimentation. So, for a while, he played golf from dawn to dusk—every day. He tried hunting whatever was in season. He took up gin rummy at the local Elks Club and played the game hour after hour. And twice he returned to the Yankees as a coach.

Nothing seemed to work. He followed the horses in Charles Town, West Virginia, and then one day his wanderings took him to the Frederick Fair Grounds where a friend named Joe Eyler was training harness horses.

"I was starting to feel pretty useless," Keller says now. "I was losing pride." So he began jogging trotters, and then it came to him. He decided what he was going to do with the rest of his life, at the same time putting the land he owned to work.

He told Eyler that he had decided to buy some broodmares, and he would breed standardbreds. He began an intensive study of the standardbred blood lines of mares with the thoroughness of a law student. Since Charlie didn't have the capital to purchase the outstanding ones, he selected the best of those who didn't make it because of a minor injury or the like. Strangely, one of his first was a bay named Gay Yankee.

"She was like one of the family," Charlie says. "She put in a blacktop road, she bought some mares and she helped with the remodeling of the farm. She won around $70,000 and did a mile in 2:01.2 as a 3-year-old."

Charlie's place is called Yankeeland because of the pride he still carries from having played with New York. And Gay Yankee was the first of a half dozen mares he trained and raced before putting them into service as broodmares. Over the mantlepiece in the Keller house is a constant reminder of what Gay Yankee did for Charlie Keller and his family. It is an oil portrait of Gay Yankee, a Christmas gift from his wife Martha, whom he married in 1938.

In the years that followed that first purchase in 1956, the Keller breeding operation has become one of the most respected in the sport. One reason is that Keller himself doesn't go for the hard sell. Another is that Keller, being a small operator, couldn't afford a top stallion, so he bought shares in three of the best: Bye Bye Byrd, Hickory Pride and Adios Butler. Charlie sends his mares to them in Mechanicsburg, Pennsylvania, where they are bred, and then they are returned to Yankeeland to foal.

Of the more than 200 horses Keller has bred and sold, all carry the name Yankee. The horse that did the most to catapult Keller's operation into the major leagues of harness racing is a mare named Fresh Yankee. Charlie sold her as a yearling to Duncan MacDonald of Sydney, Nova Scotia for $900. "I must have spent more than that on her vets' fees," Charlie says. "But I have no regrets," he says in that quiet way of his. "It would be silly to do that."

Why should he have regrets? Well, Fresh Yankee has earned her owners well over a million dollars since they purchased her from Charlie Keller. But the former Yankee outfielder remains unruffled.

He begins his day at 6:30 A.M. by feeding the horses. Then he has his own breakfast and prepares for the everyday problems that never fail to arise on a horse farm. His son, Don, and one other person is the entire staff around the place.

In addition to Don, the Kellers have a son, Charlie Jr., who is a Certified Public Accountant in Frederick, and a daughter Jeannie who is married and lives in town with her family. Charlie and Martha Keller are grandparents, and they like it that way.

Keller hasn't changed a great deal. His back problems have been corrected, and there's a shade of gray in his once coal black hair. But, the same strong physique is still there as a result of the daily work around the farm.

Every once in a while someone will remember that he was called "King Kong" during his playing days with the Yankees, and it still rankles him. Hall of Famer Lefty Gomez, a Keller teammate, has fostered the image through the years with such lines as "Keller was the first ball player ever brought back by Frank Buck." Or "Keller wasn't signed. He was trapped."

Funny? Maybe. But to Charlie Keller it isn't funny, because Keller is a quiet, gentle man who is doing his thing and doing it well. After all, he started a whole new career at the age of 39 and became a success because he worked at his job.

He's like the Yankees of old. He's a winner!

GEORGE EDWARD ARCARO

King of the Little Men

"I LIKE BEING A celebrity," Eddie Arcaro said before his retirement in April of 1962. "Once I retire, I'm just another little man."

He was wrong.

George Edward Arcaro never will be just another little man. He won't, because for more than 30 years he ruled the American thoroughbred racing scene as its premier jockey. And he did it when most athletes his age were comfortably settled in the rocking chair of middle age. Those were the brilliant years of Eddie's career, and he was still getting aboard more than 1,000 pounds of headstrong horseflesh as often as nine times a day, taking dangerous turns in heavy traffic at a speed of 30 miles per hour.

Unlike the two-dollar bettor who risks nothing but his money, the jockey risks his life. Yet, in many quarters jockeys are not regarded as athletes in the strictest sense. That is because they are little men. However, there is more skill, talent and courage in a 110-pound jockey than in many of the 280-pound behemoths in the National Football League. "If 100 jocks opened a meeting," he says, "where there wasn't any supervision or rules, only one of them would be alive when the meeting closed. It's the only sport in the world where guys would kill each other to win."

He knows, because in a career that spanned three decades, Eddie Arcaro went to the post 24,092 times, and finished in the winner's circle in 4,779 of those races. Those victories, from Agua Caliente to Aqueduct, earned the staggering total of $30,039,543 in purses. Approximately 10% of that—the standard jockey's share—went into the Arcaro coffers.

Maybe that's why he said, just before his career ended at age 46: "It becomes difficult to get up early once a guy starts wearing silk pajamas." But it wasn't all silk for Arcaro.

Arcaro is unique in the history of racing. He is a man apart,

95

the last of a breed. This is so because of the great changes that have taken place in the supervision of the sport. Arcaro started out in the depression-ridden 1930s where the tricks of the trade had to be learned in order to survive. Hungry kids in Agua Caliente in Mexico would ride a bug-boy off the track just to win eating money.

"We made up our own rules as we went along," Arcaro says. "Besides being able to stay on the horse, we had to know all the tricks, like tugging on the saddlecloths of the other horses, hitting them with the whip, leg-locking the other jockeys, and anything else you could think of to win a race."

He looks back with fondness at places like Windsor, Ontario, "Where they had a steel rail and you could hear a kid's boot sing when you laid him up against the fence." It was at Windsor early in his career that Arcaro was buffaloed by an older jockey during the stretch run of a race. He knew he had to retaliate or get out of the business. Arcaro waited until the last race of the day before he racked the guy up. An experience like that produces either a champion or an also-ran. Arcaro chose to be a champion.

"That's what racing does to you," he says. "I know because racing did it to me. If it wasn't for the film patrol that takes movies of every foot of every race, and for the jobs the stewards and patrol judges do, jockeys would kill one another. I mean that."

Despite the savageness that was instilled in him in order to survive, Arcaro became a mellow, even mild man in his later years. He was held in such esteem by his fellow jockeys that he served as president of the Jockeys' Guild in New York for a dozen years before his retirement. He loves to reminisce about the early hard-riding days, but in the end he abandoned them and developed new skills that enabled him to become the most sought-after rider of his era.

Arcaro won stakes all over the country. Name the track and he has won there: Belmont, Aqueduct, stately Saratoga, Arlington, Hawthorne, Washington Park. Then there were places like Thistle Downs in Ohio and Longacres in Seattle, Woodbine in Ontario, Narragansett and even Europe and the Antipodes, although he didn't win at those foreign tracks.

And Churchill Downs. He won the Kentucky Derby five times: aboard Lawrin in 1938; Whirlaway, 1941; Hoop Jr., 1945; Citation, 1948; and Hill Gail, 1952. He is the last jockey to win the Triple Crown for three-year-olds: the Derby, the Preakness and the Belmont Stakes, and he did it twice—aboard Whirlaway in 1941 and Citation in 1948. Those Derby victories impress everyone but Arcaro. He likes to recall that he lost 16 times at Churchill, and six times he didn't even have a a mount in the celebrated "Run for the Roses." Either he had contractual commitments that required him to ride elsewhere, or he had a low regard for the mounts that were available. "Unless you've got a chance, why bother?" was his attitude for that first Kentucky Derby in 1935.

In the 1942 Derby, Arcaro had a choice between Greentree Stable's Devil Diver and Shut Out. "I worked both horses at Churchill Downs before the Derby," Arcaro recalls, "and trainer John Gaver begged me to ride Shut Out. I thought Devil Diver worked pretty good, though, and decided to ride him. You can guess how I felt when Devil Diver finished sixth, while Wayne Wright won with Shut Out."

Arcaro's career was not without suspensions, or injuries for that matter. In 1933 he went down with Gun Fire in Chicago and was sidelined four months with a skull fracture and a punctured lung. And in the 1959 Belmont Stakes, Eddie was aboard a horse named Black Hills who fell and broke a leg. The horse had to be destroyed, and Arcaro ended up with a face full of mud and a severe neck sprain that kept him off the track for a month.

Despite those injuries, Arcaro never lost his zest for active competition. He was fearless on the track, and often his inclination bordered on the dangerous. Once, he was suspended for a year because he admitted that he tried to ride a rival jockey into the infield at Aqueduct. It happened in the 1942 Cowdin Stakes when jockey Vince Nodarse, riding True Blue, cut in on Arcaro who was aboard Occupation.

The incident happened near the start of the race and Arcaro took off after his Cuban foe. Occupation caught up in the backstretch and Arcaro tried to force True Blue and his cargo over the infield rail. After the race, when the stewards showed the film they asked Arcaro if he had deliberately tried to upset Nodarse. "Yes, I would have killed him if I could," Arcaro replied.

That bit of candor caused him to be suspended from September 28, 1942 through September 19, 1943. Who won the race? Arcaro and Occupation, of course.

Eddie Arcaro made the transition from his rough-riding days to skillful jockey without peer because he knew horses and he was endowed with such native cunning and intelligence that hardly ever was he caught in a jam.

He knew how to make the big move, whether it was a narrow stretch of daylight between horses, or, as in the case of Whirlaway, taking the outside route to victory. He was able to work a horse and reel off the times within a fifth of a second afterward. His brain was described as having a "built-in stopwatch."

Eddie was not without humor. At a party at the Hollywood Mocambo near the end of his career, he demonstrated that the sovereign ruled with a benevolent hand as he passed his scepter on to his successor.

"Meet the new champ," Arcaro said. Then he introduced a bashful little kid by the name of Willie Shoemaker.

WHERE IS HE NOW?

Eddie Arcaro and his Ruth, his bride of 35 years, reside in Miami where Eddie is satisfying his passion for golf. He underwent open-heart surgery in November of 1970 at the Miami Heart Institute after suffering from a blocked coronary artery. Doctors removed part of a vein in his thigh and used it to create a bypass around the blocked area.

After two days in intensive care plus a couple of weeks to regain his strength, Arcaro has returned to a normal, if somewhat quieter, life. The children, Carolyn and Bobby, are on their own now, raising families.

Eddie assaults the golf course virtually every day of the year. Recently at Marco Island, during a celebrity tournament, Eddie teamed with Joe DiMaggio. As their golf cart glided to a stop, television announcer Joe Garagiola called on the former jockey for an interview.

"Can I show my scar?" asked the irrepressible Arcaro as he tugged at his shirt-tail. He does that to his opponents to throw them off their game. After all, looking at a full length scar down the front of his lean and tanned body is not exactly conducive to a sound swing.

"What odds do you think you'd be on the pro tour?" Garagiola asked Arcaro.

"Without a horse?" Arcaro asked.

"No horse," Joe replied.

"I'd say 20-1," Arcaro answered without blinking an eye.

Garagiola went on. "Do you think jockeys are born or made?"

"They're made. No such thing as being born one. I'd never been on a horse until I was 14 years old and went to a race track."

Ask him for an opinion on just about any controversial subject concerning racing and he'll provide an unvarnished opinion. Words like jockette, union and breeding are no strangers to his vocabulary.

He thinks there ought to be more attention paid to the breeding of horses. "Believe me," he says, "when you breed bums to bums, you get bums. And the public doesn't want to bet on trash. The breeding has got to be more selective."

And when anyone asks him about girl jockeys, he's disdainful.

"They couldn't have much confidence in themselves if they are worried about riding against girls. If a girl rider is capable, she'll get a license. I never worry about anybody in a race, boy or girl."

And he never did, because he never had to. That's why they still call him "The Master."

ARNOLD MALCOLM OWEN

The Man Who Dropped the
Third Strike

HE CAME OUT OF Springfield, Missouri, and at the age of 18, he decided that he wanted to be a professional baseball player. So he signed with the St. Louis Cardinals who sent him first to the Arkansas State League.

A year later, in 1935, he moved up to Springfield of the Western Association and the following season he joined Columbus of the American Association. Burt Shotton was managing the club at the time, and he liked what he saw. The kid was a catcher, and he had a great glove for one so young. His name was Arnold Owen, but he didn't go down in baseball lore as Arnie Owen.

Shotton saw to that. "You handle yourself like Mickey Cochrane," he told young Owen. And from that day forward Arnold Malcolm Owen became Mickey Owen, and everybody remembers what happened to him. In fact, that's been the problem for the past three decades.

Mickey Owen was a fine ballplayer, and from that day in 1937 when he reported to the Cardinals, to 1951 when he was released by the Chicago Cubs, he set a standard of excellence behind the plate.

At one stage of his career, from September 22, 1940 to August 29, 1941, Mickey handled 508 consecutive chances without an error to set a fielding record for National League catchers. The record string started with St. Louis and ended in Brooklyn because Owen was traded to the Dodgers over the winter for catcher Gus Mancuso, pitcher John Pintar and $60,000.

It is curious how a man can spend almost two decades in the major leagues, jump to the Mexican League in the great exodus of 1946 and jump back again only to be suspended for five years, be involved in suits and countersuits, and have the public remember him for one split second of his career.

That's what happened to Mickey Owen. And it happened in the 1941 World Series. It was in the fourth game, and Owen and the Dodgers were playing the mighty Yankees.

The New Yorkers were leading the series two games to one, but the beloved Bums of Brooklyn were a pitch away from tying the set. It was the ninth inning and the Brooks led 4-3. Yankee outfielder Tommy Henrich, a fine hitter, was batting against portly Hugh Casey of Brooklyn.

There were two outs, and a count of three balls and two strikes on Henrich. The bases were empty. All Casey had to do was to get one more pitch past Henrich and Brooklyn would have been back in the thick of it. Henrich, poised in the box, was looking for a fast ball and it looked as though that's what he was going to get. Casey delivered the ball and it was right down the middle, so Henrich started his swing, but at the last instant a funny thing happened. The ball started to break. It was a curve ball, but Tommy was too far committed to check his swing, so he followed through.

He missed, but the ball struck the thumb on the glove of catcher Mickey Owen and bounced toward the backstop. Henrich turned, saw what happened and legged it to first base. He was safe and the Yankees, although a run behind, were still alive. Joe DiMaggio stepped to the plate and sent a screaming liner to left, advancing Henrich to second.

Two on, two out and Charlie Keller the hitter. Casey got two strikes on Keller with two good curveballs, but when he tried to put a third one past the husky Yankee left fielder, Keller belted it for a two-base hit.

Catcher Bill Dickey coaxed a walk and Joe Gordon, the next hitter, ended all the suspense when he doubled off the wall in left field. That ended it. The Yankees had put four runs across the plate and from there they went on to win the World Series.

Mickey Owen's National League record for errorless games? Forget it. His career was wrapped in that instant when Casey's curveball hit the thumb of his mitt and rolled to the screen, and he will forever be remembered as the goat of the 1941 World Series.

Henrich was to recall the incident years later. "The pitch looked to me like a good fast ball," he said. "It was right down the middle and I started to swing. Then the ball started to curve, but I was too far committed and I couldn't check my swing. It wasn't a good full swing, but my bat came around.

"Afterwards, they said it was a knuckler, but I don't think so. I think it was a good sharp curve and I was looking back to see how Mickey was handling it. I saw that white thing bouncing and I ran.

"Sometimes you can think in a hurry. It was in my mind that he might have trouble with that ball. It broke so sharply, inside and down. I think maybe it hit the dirt before it got to Owen and the ground was cut around there by left-handed hitters. I wasn't surprised that he didn't handle it cleanly. I just thought, 'I gotta chance,' and I took out.

"As I ran," Henrich continued, "I was very surprised that I didn't hear Earle Combs, who was coaching at first, yelling at me to run faster. Then I passed first and looked around and I saw that the ball had gone clear back to the screen and there was a lot of confusion back there with cops all around. Mickey never had a chance."

Two months after the Series, the Japanese attacked Pearl Harbor and baseball's biggest boner was relegated to limbo for a while. Many of the game's top stars drifted off to military service, and Owen played the next three seasons, alternating between second base, shortstop and catching for the Dodgers.

In 1945, Owen went into the Navy, and following his discharge a year later, the lure of Mexican pesos was heard throughout the land. Jorge Pasqual, the president of the Mexican League, was raiding the American big leagues and was offering what was thought to be big money at the time. Maybe it was, but in the super 70s, his wages wouldn't buy a rookie out of the Midwest League.

Owen succumbed, though. Following his discharge from the Navy on April 1, 1946, Mickey was still the property of the Dodgers. But instead of joining Brooklyn, Owen, Max Lanier and Lou Klein of the Cardinals, and 17 other major leaguers including Danny Gardella of the Giants, listened to the blandishments of the moneyed Mexican.

Pasqual paid Owen $12,500 for signing a five-year contract for $15,000 a year, with the final year also paid in advance. He was to be playing manager of the Vera Cruz team, and the contract also provided room and board for Mickey and his wife, Gloria.

Owen didn't finish the season in Vera Cruz. He and Gloria became disenchanted when they ended up renting their own apartment and buying their own food. So before the season ended, Mickey jumped back into the United States. Instead of finding a sympathetic welcome, he found a five-year suspension awaiting him for being so brash as to challenge baseball's most revered law: the reserve clause.

Mickey returned to his farm in Missouri, raised some sheep, and tried to straighten out his life and his baseball career. He also tried playing softball, caught in some semipro games until the long arm of the commissioner's office put a stop to that. Pasquel sued him for breach of contract, and Owen countersued. The cases dragged on through the courts with Mickey finally losing. In the meantime, Mickey began to repent, but not Gardella, the New York Giant who jumped with him. Gardella sued the commissioner, A. B. (Happy) Chandler, and both major leagues for $300,000 in damages charging that radio and television broadcasts made baseball subject to federal antitrust laws.

"I hope Danny Gardella loses his suit against baseball," Owen said at the time. We went [jumped to Mexico] because of our own weaknesses. Baseball needs the reserve clause, and while I am in the same boat as Gardella, I would not file suit to try to break it [the suspension]," he said.

Mickey put his money and his time where his mouth was. He traveled 8,000 miles in three weeks talking to the other banned jumpers and drafted an appeal to Chandler for reinstatement. "Every one of them except Gardella signed it," Owen said. Then he went to Cincinnati to see Chandler personally.

"He was sympathetic and interested," Mickey said. "I apologized for my actions and we had a long talk. I then decided to get all the players to sign an appeal for immediate reinstatement. We didn't have any lawyers. We worded the appeal ourselves."

Micken then said he was speaking for all the players (except Gardella) and proclaimed:

"I say that we are wholly in sympathy with organized baseball in this fight. We can see our mistakes now. I didn't know I had it so good until I was out of baseball."

Four months later, Chandler issued absolution to the Mexican jumpers and at the ripe old baseball age of 33, Mickey Owen was free to return to the majors. Brooklyn still had the rights to his contract, but they also had a good young catcher named Bruce Edwards, so Mickey was dealt to the Chicago Cubs. He stayed with them for three years, then managed Kansas City in the American Association, scouted for the Cardinals, coached with the Red Sox, managed in the winter leagues and finally drifted off into oblivion.

But each time he made a change, or went to court, or appealed for clemency, the dropped third strike in the 1941 World Series found its way into the story. And so it always will be, but Owen isn't the least thin-skinned about it. Even to this day, he says: "I just kicked it."

Although he never complains, Mickey has found that being a goat is a difficult thing to live with. The very night after it happened, he was standing against a pillar in the hotel lobby in New York and heard a man stage-whisper to his wife: "There he is . . . there's the man who dropped the ball."

But there are good memories, too. After all these years, he still treasures the words of Larry McPhail, who was president of the Dodgers that fateful year. MacPhail, a bombastic, red-faced extrovert, was expected to tear the young catcher apart when he steamed into the clubhouse after the game.

Instead, he told the 25-year-old Owen: "That isn't the first third strike you dropped . . . and it won't be the last . . . you've played great ball for me."

And so he did. MacPhail went off to war, but Mickey stayed on for a while, playing any position he thought would help the club until he went into the Navy himself and then the ill-fated Mexican adventure.

More than three decades have passed and Mickey Owen isn't leaning up against any hotel pillars these days, but the stage whispers are still there and he always will be the man who dropped the ball.

It isn't easy, but that's the way it is.

WHERE IS HE NOW?

Mickey Owen, a portly man in his late 50s, has gone the way of his ancestors. He's back in Greene County, Missouri and like his great-grandfather before him, he's the county's sheriff. A political novice and a Democrat, Owen, at the age of 48, scored a major upset in a traditionally Republican County when he defeated the incumbent by a plurality of 1,900 votes in 1964. He won another four-year term in 1968.

In between there was a huge baseball school for kids he conducted on a 600-acre complex at Miller, Missouri. Mickey Owen's Baseball School became a model for such ventures, but the challenge wasn't there and Mickey Owen thrived on challenges.

So with the idea that law enforcement in his county could be improved, he jumped into the political arena. Greene County isn't exactly like old Dodge City, but Mickey and his 75 deputies have been kept busy. He still dabbles in the baseball school at Miller and he still is dogged by controversy.

In March of 1971, Mickey was forced to auction off some of his personal property to help pay legal expenses for defending himself against lawsuits for more than $15 million. The suits were filed in three federal court cases by prisoners who alleged that they were mistreated while in Owen's custody. Mickey sold his personal handgun, two bird dogs, a pickup truck, an assortment of pistols, rifles and shotguns and a gun cabinet.

His deputies bought the handgun and returned it to Owen and his favorite dog, Old Babe, went for $92.50, but the purchaser accepted her litter of seven pups and returned Babe to Owen.

Mickey says he was offered free legal counsel, but refused to accept it. "It's a matter of principle with me," he says. "I don't put myself in the same category as criminals who go to the judge and scream for free legal help."

The dropped third strike?

It's still around. "I'll still get heckled occasionally," Mickey says. "Sometimes one of my prisoners will say, 'You're the guy that missed that third strike, aren't you?' But you learn to take it as you go. I've pulled some dumber ones than that in law enforcement —but I guess they weren't so spectacular."

Mickey and his Gloria, who were married on Christmas eve, 1937, are grandparents now. Their only son, Charlie, and his wife have three children, and Charlie teaches school in the Springfield area.

"Being a sheriff is a lot tougher by far, than catching," Mickey says, "but I love it."

He loved baseball, too, except for that one instant in 1941 which no one can forget.

CLYDE (BULLDOG) TURNER

The Kid from Sweetwater

HE WAS ONLY 20 YEARS of age when he came to Chicago as the No. 1 draft choice of the Chicago Bears, and the big city was a mystery to him—so much so that the canyons of skyscrapers kept his head tilting upward.

His name was Clyde Douglas Turner, but everyone in sports knew him as Bulldog Turner and he was reputed to be the best center in all of football that year of 1940. It didn't matter that he hadn't played in a National Football League game yet. His reputation had been established during his career at tiny Hardin-Simmons in Texas, where he earned All-America honors and played in the East-West Shrine game as well as the College All-Star game.

Size? He had it: six feet two inches and 235 pounds. Speed? He could run the hundred in 10.8 in full football regalia. Desire? Well, in addition to being one of the top centers in the country, Turner was a terror on defense from his linebacker position, and his ability to defend against the pass was almost uncanny. Because of his speed and ability, despite his beefy appearance, Turner would rate with the great cornerbacks of today on pass defense. And, if a coach needed a pulling guard, Bulldog could do that, too.

So it was no wonder that he became involved in one of football's most vitriolic vendettas when it came time to draft him after the 1939 collegiate season. George Halas, the owner and coach of the Bears, knew about him, of course, but so did the Detroit Lions and their owner George A. Richards and coach Gloomy Gus Henderson. The tugging and pulling between the Bears and the Lions was to become so intense that Gloomy Gus became gloomier when Richards had fired him over the incident, and Richards became so disgusted that he sold the club.

Not only that, it cost the Detroit owner $5,150—no trifling sum in those days. Bert Bell, the Commissioner of the National Football League, had established the player draft four years previously, and one of the rules of the game was not to make any deals with collegiate talent before graduation. The Lions ignored this, and Turner went into his senior season at Hardin-Simmons supposedly all set to play with Detroit following his graduation.

Richards had invited Bulldog to his sumptious home in Beverly Hills, California for frequent visits, and the kindly Detroit owner even financed a rejuvenation of Bulldog's molars at his swank dentist's office, also in Beverly Hills.

Richards laid out $150 in dental bills, and had the word of the 20-year-old Texan that yes, indeed, he would play for the Lions if they drafted him. The Detroit owner was so grateful that, as an NFL investigation showed later, he gave Turner an additional $100 in "walking-around" money. Gloomy Gus was in on all the planning. So, it came as no surprise to him when Richards ordered him to pick Turner on the first round.

The Bears followed the Lions in the order of selection and Halas held in his hand, a standard NFL questionnaire that Bulldog had returned with the notation: "I do not wish to play professional football."

Such a prospect was unthinkable to Halas even though he knew Bulldog had a degree in journalism and might have been engaging in a little fiction writing. There was no way, Halas thought, that this boy would refuse to play in the NFL. He was right, of course, and he got an assist from Gloomy Gus, who made his first mistake when he started thinking for himself instead of following the orders of his owner.

Why waste a No. 1 choice on a guy we've already got in the bag, Henderson's cerebral machinations told him. I need a passer.

So when Detroit's turn to pick came, Gloomy Gus, in a loud and clear voice announced: "The Detroit Lions pick Doyle Nave, Southern California."

Papa Bear Halas almost fell out of his chair. Since the Bears had the next selection, Halas could hardly keep the emotion out of his voice as he selected Bulldog Turner. Then he asked for, and got, a league investigation of the entire incident.

Detroit Owner Richards, enraged at Gloomy Gus's sidestepping of his order, fired the coach on the spot, and the NFL held up the sale of the Lions to Chicagoan Fred Mandel, pending payment of a $5,000 fine for tampering. Richards coughed up the money, then sold the club, and disappeared from the sporting scene leaving behind him one of the most interesting footnotes in the history of the National Football League.

Bulldog Turner, though, was to leave an even larger mark

as his legacy. He arrived in what is now known as the "Second City," a countrified 20-year-old confused by the sights, sounds and routes of the big town.

"I found an apartment," he said, "and I took the L [elevated train] to Wrigley Field for practice every day. I learned that my stop was about eight blocks from my apartment, and I changed to a local each time so I could get that close. What I didn't know," he said in his deep Texas drawl, "was that if I stayed on the express, I could have gotten off about a block from my home. I found that out at the end of the season."

But what a first-season he had. He broke into the lineup as a regular, and in 1941, the Bears were to field one of the all-time great teams in professional history. Bulldog replaced the great Mel Hein of the Giants as the All-League center that season, and during his 13-year career with the Bears he was to win that singular honor eight times.

Bulldog had come a long way from his high school days in Sweetwater, Texas, as a 155-pounder who played almost every position but center. Since scholarships were not forthcoming, he talked his way into Hardin-Simmons on a trial basis and sort of grew with the job. He started out as a 175-pound freshman, then was 185 as a sophomore, 205 as a junior and a healthy 220 pounder in his senior year. He reported to the Bears at 235 pounds, but Halas decided that his weight ought to be at 232 and so it was.

"It was $50 a pound for each pound over Halas's weight," Bulldog says, "and he wasn't about to get any money out of me."

In addition to snapping the ball with split-second timing to Hall of Fame quarterback Sid Luckman, Bulldog was an excellent blocker, particularly on passes; he snapped on all punts and extra points, and with such uncanny accuracy that the punter received the ball with laces up *every* time. He backed up the line on defense and was tremendously adept at pass defense. He picked off 16 during his career, including a league-leading eight in 1942. Two he returned for touchdowns, one for 42 yards and the other for 97 yards, quite a feat for a center.

Following his retirement, Bulldog coached at Baylor for a while, concentrating on centers and linebackers, and later he was a Halas assistant for five years. But as the years went on, he wished to return to his land in Texas and to put his quarter-horse ranch on a paying basis. But in 1962, the call to coach came again, this time for the late Harry Wismer who owned the New York Titans at the time, and ran them zanily out of his New York apartment.

Bulldog took over the team in 1962 when his long-time friend Sammy Baugh and Wismer began trading insults in public, and the one season he had them he won five and lost nine in the

American Football League. Wismer then drowned in a sea of red ink and was forced to sell the club and Turner drifted back to his family and acreage in Texas.

But Bulldog Turner doesn't regret one minute of it all. Compared to today's $100,000-a-year players, the "Dog" as he was known to his teammates, was vastly underpaid. And he thinks about that sometimes now.

He's still proud of the fact that he was the only lineman picked in the first round of the 1940 draft, and that he was the Bears' No. 1 choice. "There were only 10 teams in the league then," he says, "and only 330 players were picked. And if any of those players were in competition today, they would make the grade with a pro team—and don't you think otherwise."

One of them certainly would have been Clyde Douglas Turner.

WHERE IS HE NOW?

Bulldog Turner is back in his beloved Texas, but the hankering to be in the National Football League is still there. He and his wife, Gladys, are grandparents five times over. Their daughter Sandra has three sons, and Patricia has a boy and a girl. "I'm old now," Bulldog says with a laugh, but he really doesn't mean it, because it really isn't true.

"I'm farming and ranching now," he says. "I have about 200 acres of pasture land and I'm raising quarter horses and I do some training, some of my own horses and some for other owners."

A few years ago Bulldog had the second winningest horse at Ruidoso Downs in New Mexico. One of his horses won five overnight races. He's still looking for the big stakes horse, but it hasn't come along yet.

Turner thinks he'd like to get back into coaching, and he believes his long experience as one of the all-time great centers would benefit some team. He admitted that he might have made a mistake when he gravitated back to Texas after his playing days ended.

"I didn't try to capitalize on my name and reputation when I retired," he said, "and I probably should have. The way I was brought up, I thought I was supposed to come back to Texas and get my own piece of land and settle down on my own place. That was my goal all the time I was playing, so that's what I did. I'm just Clyde down here and I'm Bulldog up in Chicago. I didn't realize I could have set myself up for life."

Bulldog has nothing but kind words for George Halas who coached him during his brilliant career with the Bears. "He treated me top shelf," Turner says. "I don't have a complaint about him.

I know others have ridiculed him, but I think, in most cases, it came from players who were cut or traded. I never had that problem. He would always give me the bonus I thought I should get at the end of each season, and as for signing a contract, I wouldn't sign one until I was happy and got what I wanted. And in other dealings he treated me real fine. I think the only people who really talked badly about him were people that weren't helping him. And I can understand that."

Bulldog doesn't see many games in person, but he's an avid follower of football on television. "Some of these announcers have a greater knowledge of what's going on than the radio men when I was playing," he said. "They're good. They tip you off on what to look for. They sure must get the information from the coaching staff. I remember our coaching staff on the Bears wouldn't put out anything to announcers when I was playing. The instant replays are great, and the whole show is very entertaining."

Does he wish he had come along about three decades later?

"Every minute of every day," he drawled with a deep chuckle. "Of course, mostly for the money. They play just a few years now and make big money and get themselves set up for life. I think of that part of it a lot. Still, I'd like to try coaching again."

Turner wouldn't pick an all-time team, but he did have some thoughts on the great ones he played with or against. "Bronko [Nagurski] was the greatest fullback I ever saw," he said. "At halfback George McAfee and Whizzer White [Supreme Court Justice Byron White], and at quarterback I think Sammy Baugh of the Redskins was the greatest passer of all, but Sid Luckman isn't far behind.

"Don Hutson [Green Bay] was the greatest end of them all," he said, "but you know, I always liked Gaynell Tinsley [Cardinals], too, even though he played only a couple of years.

"As for linemen Danny Fortman and Joe Stydahar, my teammates on the Bears were among the greatest. But I wouldn't want to pick a whole team, because I'd be sure to miss some of them."

He left the center position open, and why not? Who would want a man six feet, two inches, 235 pounds who could run like a halfback, tackle with the best middle linebackers of any era, defend against the pass with the top cornerbacks and block with the best offensive linemen in addition to snapping the ball on runs and kicks?

Who would that be? Why, the 20-year-old kid from Sweetwater, Texas who made his place in the Hall of Fame . . . Clyde (Bulldog) Turner, that's who!

JAMES (JIM) MELLO

A Truly Happy Man

LATE IN THE SUMMER of 1941, there was an unusual scene in front of the Sheraton Hotel in Boston. Standing around the entrance were almost a dozen young men, all shapes, sizes and descriptions, but they all had one thing in common. They were all football players.

Originally they were to go to Boston College to further their educations and football careers, but the coach at Boston College had just moved into a position that was to make him one of the most respected, feared, loved and disliked college mentors in the country. His name was Francis William Leahy. Earlier, he had scoured the eastern seaboard for high school football talent in an effort to keep his Boston College team ranked among the top teams in the country. In two years at Boston College Frank Leahy had taken his team from moderate, regional success to the very pinnacle of college football.

In 1939, the Eagles went to the Cotton Bowl, where they lost to Clemson 6-3. But the following season, Boston College went undefeated, won the Lambert Trophy as the best team in the East and, behind the passing of quarterback Charlie O'Rourke, beat General Bob Neyland's Tennessee Vols in the Cotton Bowl, thus establishing Leahy as coach of his first national championship team.

The good Jesuits at Boston College were so happy with Leahy's performance that they gave him a new five-year contract and predicted that the school's football future was now secure.

The day after Leahy signed the document, Elmer Layden quit as head coach at the University of Notre Dame.

So it was that day in 1941 in Boston. Leahy was allowed to abrogate the newly signed contract at Boston College so that he could return to Notre Dame as a successor to his mentor, Knute Rockne. But there were problems.

111

He had promised scholarships to a score of high school players in the New England area, but they were scholarships to Boston College, not Notre Dame. But this was easily resolved. Those who wished to accompany him to the hinterlands of South Bend, Indiana, were free to do so. Indeed, they were most welcome.

Leahy had preceded his New England recruits to Notre Dame, but D-Day was arranged by letter, and, at the appointed day and hour, six used Fords, piloted by Notre Dame students and managers, pulled up in front of the Sheraton in Boston, and the New England brigade of the Fighting Irish piled aboard. Among them was a kid named Jim Mello.

Also in the group were: John Yonakor, who was to become an All-American end; Jack Zilly, also an end, later to become an outstanding player with the Rams as well as a successful college and pro assistant; and Gerry Cowhig, a bruising running back, who was to become an outstanding pro with the Rams, Cardinals and Eagles. It was a veritable bonanza of talent.

And when they got to Notre Dame, they were joined by the likes of George Connor, Johnny Lujack, Bob Dove, Lou Rymkus, Ziggy Czarobski, Angelo Bertilli, Terry Brennan and Bill Fischer. Leahy, the master, had chosen well.

This was the kind of competition that Jim Mello faced at Notre Dame, and he found that making the varsity and then becoming one of its starters was more difficult than facing the opposition on Saturdays. But, by the time he was a sophomore, he was the starting fullback, and by the time he had finished, he could say that he had played with some of Notre Dame's greatest teams.

He played in 1942-43, and after two years in military service, he returned to star on the 1946 national championship team. In the three years that Mello was in the Irish backfield, Notre Dame won 24 games, lost three and tied three, including the memorable scoreless tie with Army in Yankee Stadium in his last year. That season the Irish scored 271 points while limiting nine opponents to 24.

Jim Mello enjoyed the success and so did his father. When he saw his son's name emblazoned in the headlines of the sports pages, the old gentleman even mellowed a bit. Frank Mello really didn't care much about sports when young Jim was growing up in a house that included six brothers and three sisters.

When Pater Mello stepped off the boat from the Azores, he had spotted a fifty cent piece lying in the gutter. He picked it up, put it in his pocket and learned that America, indeed, was the land of opportunity.

As the Mello family increased, so did Frank Mello's fortunes. He began as a laborer and farmer, then went into the grocery business, and later in life opened a bar and dabbled in real estate. All the while the children were expected to pitch in. And nine of them did. Jim Mello took his chances with the paternal wrath each day he stayed after school for football or basketball practice. And when he arrived home, he not only got the back of his father's hand, he was made to do the chores he had so cleverly escaped.

"My father was all work," Jim said with a smile. "I was the only one who escaped him, because I was determined to become an athlete. Sometimes I took a worse beating from him than I did at practice. Then he made me clean the chicken coop or deliver groceries or something. But later, when the headlines came, he was philosophical about it."

Leahy, too, was to become a formulating influence on Mello's life. "I have always been inspired by the man," Mello says. "He started me as a sophomore, too, which was unusual for him, and I'll always be grateful for that. To me, he will always be a commanding figure."

Mello, like so many others from Leahy's teams at Notre Dame, went to the pros following his graduation. In 1947, he joined the Boston Yanks, a team owned by singer Kate Smith and her business manager, Ted Collins. But he was hurt in the second game of the season and stayed with them for just one season.

During the summer he was traded to the Rams, but after the second game of the 1948 season, he jumped to the rival All-America Conference to play for the Chicago Rockets, joining Ed McKeever, who was his backfield coach at Notre Dame.

"Ziggy Czarobski was a tackle on that team," Mello said, "and he didn't make a block all year!" The following season, after his contract with Chicago expired, he joined the Detroit Lions, then coached by Bo McMillin. McMillin switched the hard-running Mello to defensive halfback and linebacker.

At five feet, eleven inches and 195 pounds, Mello didn't consider himself too small to back up the line. "If you've got that blow torch inside," he said, "you can play anywhere.'

Now his real career was ready to begin. Mello returned to South Bend and for five years he worked for the Bendix Corporation. "The money was good," he said. "In fact, it was terrific, but after five years I said to myself one day: 'What am I doing here working with cold steel and production and things, when what I really want is to be working with people?"

So he gave up the money, the security, the good life as it is often called, sold his house and started on a new career. He joined the faculty of the Joseph H. Ladd School for the Retarded in Rhode Island as a physical education instructor.

"I didn't know the retarded from the insane," he said. "But I knew that this was the kind of work I wanted to do. And I've never regretted it."

Then, in 1963, he took a job as physical education director at the State Training School for Retarded Children in Mansfield, Connecticut. He's a coach, too, but instead of fleet flankers and 260-pound tackles, his players are the unwanted children of our society.

WHERE IS HE NOW?

Jim Mello is still at the Mansfield School, and if ever there was a truly happy man, it is he. He will say, "I hate normal kids," and after the listener is properly outraged, he adds with a smile, "I don't really mean that, but I get so much pleasure out of my work. I have found the meaning of true charity. It is really the truest test life has to offer.

"These children don't say thank you to me. They don't have to. I can see it in their eyes. I've been here 10 years and I wouldn't do anything else—even if I could. You want to know why? Because every time I give them something they give me more in return."

Jim and his wife Jacquie have four children of their own. Jim Jr., Debra, Tim and Pam, all in their 20s. Jim Jr. has made the Mellos grandparents, and Debra is married to law student Mark Seigle. Tim is also teaching retarded children.

Mello's job is still athletics, although not in the strictest sense of the word. He has a staff of six instructors and he tells them: "If you don't get a belly laugh each day on this job, you ought to find yourself another job."

Mello divides the Mansfield children into two classes: profound and severe. "But strangely enough," he says, "it is not difficult to communicate with them. It can't always be done verbally, but you can express yourself in other ways, by motions and signs, for example. In other words, you've got to set an example and they'll follow it. They know. And they also know the honest and good teachers from the bad ones. It is strange, but they do."

Mello contends that sports is an outlet for the retarded child. "Anybody with a handicap can, and frequently does, become overly aggressive and frustrated," he says. Sports provide a good way to blow off steam. They also teach kids self-reliance and responsibility."

At one time, Mansfield had a football team. In those days delinquent children were sent there, but they are now institutionalized elsewhere, and football has been done away with. Now, there is basketball, soccer, baseball and track for the children.

And one of Jim's boys, Warren Snowden, won the first gold

medal in the Special Olympics for Retarded Children, the fund-raising event started by the Joseph P. Kennedy Foundation.

He's proud of that. "Some are blind, others are palsied, some have different problems, but they're all handicapped," Mello said.

He is grateful for his Notre Dame experience. "I suppose every kid in America wanted to go there at that time," he said. But that is all over now, and although he has passed the half-century mark in age, Mello looks to the future with hope.

"Someday, I hope there won't be any institutions like this," he said. "These children belong at home with their families. I'll probably never see it in my lifetime, but that is what we are working for."

In the meantime, Jim Mellow keeps learning from his children —things like patience, tolerance and understanding . . . and love, and charity . . . true charity.

EWELL (THE WHIP) BLACKWELL

Pitching by Way of Third Base

ONCE IN EVERY GENERATION, an athlete comes along who is destined for greatness, the kind of achievement that means the Hall of Fame, or a $100,000 salary, or even having his name become a household word.

Then along about the middle of his career, something happens. The star, which was once shooting across the heavens in a blaze of glory and lighting up the universe, suddenly explodes and then disappears over the horizon, never to be seen again. Often it is not even remembered.

Ewell Blackwell's star was something like that. It blazed across the National League in post-World War II days, illuminating the skies of baseball brilliantly, and then, because of physical problems, it faded into oblivion. But those few brief shining years were something to remember because Ewell Blackwell had it all, and he knew what to do with it.

He didn't have the classic physical attributes of the truly great baseball player. He was too tall: six feet, six inches, and too skinny: about 185 pounds. But he had something else. He could pitch a baseball with such speed and deception that in 1947, when all the war heroes were back at work in the majors, he won 16 consecutive games for the Cincinnati Reds, a modern major league record.

Included in that remarkable string was a no-hit, no-run game against the Boston Braves on June 18, 1947. And he very nearly got a second one next time out against the Dodgers, which would have equalled the astonishing feat of teammate Johnny Vander Meer a decade earlier. In this second game there was one out in the ninth when the Dodgers' Eddie Stanky came to the plate in the ninth inning. Stanky stroked a groundball to Blackwell's left that rolled to a stop on the outfield grass behind second base. Jackie Robinson touched him for another single before he retired the side.

The no-hitter, though, was a masterpiece since Blackwell faced only 25 official batters in a 6-0 victory that knocked the Braves out of first place in the National League. It was Blackie's tenth victory of the season, surpassing his victory total of nine the year before.

In facing the Braves, Blackwell walked four and fanned three and three Braves were left on base. Braves' runners reached second base only once. That was in the eighth inning when Blackwell walked Phil Masi and Sibbi Sisti with only one out. But he retired the next two to preserve his no-hitter.

It was his first start under the lights at Cincinnati. That was because the kid hadn't been around too long. He had only had one year of experience, that was in 1946, when he won nine and lost 13 for the Reds. But his future was filled with promise because of those nine victories. Six were shutouts; tops in the league that season.

That Blackwell was a pitcher at all was merely a quirk of fate or better yet, the decision of his high school coach. Blackie's father, a semipro player of note around Laverne, California, wanted his son to be a third baseman. His reasoning was sound, the kid could hit and he wanted him to play every day, not every fourth day as a pitcher usually does.

The coach at Bonita High School, the same school that sent Glenn Davis to football immortality at West Point, had other ideas and decided that father doesn't always know best. He converted his gangling third sacker into a pitcher for his last two years in high school. He also pitched one semester at LaVerne College before he quit to go into defense work at Vultee Aircraft.

Blackie was pitching for Vultee, and losing a 2-1 game against Anaheim, when Pat Patterson, a discerning Cincinnati scout spotted him and persuaded him to sign with Ogden (Utah), a Cincinnati farm club in the Pioneer League.

Other clubs were interested, too. Brooklyn, Cleveland, the Yankees, the Browns, the Cubs' farm club in Los Angeles, and Hollywood of the Pacific Coast League were after him during his high school days. But Blackwell resisted them because he wanted to graduate before trying his luck in baseball.

That was in 1941.

Cincinnati finally got him because Patterson promised to take him to spring training the following year in Tampa, Florida. "I figured it this way," Blackwell says. "If I was sent down to a Class C club, I might waste a lot of years in the sticks before anybody noticed me. I thought, if I went to a major league training camp, some men who really knew baseball would at least look at me and give me some notion as to whether I had the makings of a big leaguer."

Blackwell never went near Ogden. The Reds liked his side-wheeling delivery and kept him around until the last cut. He was sent to Syracuse of the International League where he won 15 and lost 10. He really sparkled in the playoffs, winning four games in the title series, pitching three shutouts and three scoreless relief innings. His earned run average was 0.00.

Cincinnati had a star in the wings, but before the Reds could bring him to center stage, the Army drafted Blackwell. And it was a couple of years before he made it to the big club.

Blackwell joined the 84th Infantry Division and took his basic training in Texas. In January of 1945, he went to Fort Benning, Georgia, to join the 71st Infantry Division with which he went to the European theater.

Because he had been taught to cook by his sister, Mary Ellen, the army was quick to make Blackie a mess sergeant, despite the fact that his physical appearance suggested malnutrition, rather than a well-fed GI. In any case, he was a success in the kitchen.

He played baseball, too, along with Al Brazle, Ken Heinzelman, Benny Zientara, Johnny Wyrostek and Bob Ramazzotti.

He won 16 and lost only two in the European Theater of Operations competition, and was selected as a member of an All-Star team that played in Leghorn, Italy.

Zientara remembers Blackwell's culinary talents well. Benny made a habit of sneaking into Blackwell's army kitchen from his own outfit "to get some decent chow."

Blackwell's recollection of his days in the army kitchen was one of mixed emotions. "The biggest headache was," he said, "that if you threw away any food, the brass would howl. If you skimped, the men howled. We never had much left but scraps, so I guess the guys liked what we put out."

Blackie got his Army discharge in March of 1946 and immediately took off for spring training in Tampa. But by the time he arrived there the Reds were ready to move northward, so he remained in Florida for 10 days and worked out with the Syracuse club.

He had a hard time getting started, because he was suffering from acute tonsilitis. "There were many games I pitched," he says, "when the trainer had to paint my throat between innings so that I could go on." Still he topped the league in shutouts, registering nine victories and 13 defeats, and was on the verge of his greatest year.

It came in 1947.

The tonsils came out during the off season, and Blackwell began to feel much better. His appetite picked up, and he added about 20 pounds to his emaciated frame. And when he reported to the Reds the following spring, the veteran Bucky Walters took him aside and helped him perfect his amazing delivery.

Blackie never did have too much trouble with right-handed hitters because of his unorthodox side-arm delivery. In describing him, Stan Hack, the great Cubs' third baseman, said: "When he throws it looks like the ball is coming from third base."

Others were more descriptive.

Both Phil Masi and Bob Elliott of the Braves are credited with this one: "When Blackwell pitches, he looks like a man falling out of a tree."

Anyway, Walters suggested he come overhand more when a lefty was batting so as to hide the ball. Blackie tried it and it worked. "If this guy doesn't win 20 games, I don't know who will," Walters predicted that spring. How right he was!

Blackwell won 22 games that very season, and 16 of them came in succession. In the middle of that sensational string was the no-hitter against the Braves and the near-miss against the Dodgers. The New York Giants shattered the string on July 30th when Buddy Kerr lined a single to center to score Buddy Blattner with the winning run in the tenth inning.

Blackwell was the most "fragrant" pitcher in either league all during the six weeks of his streak. After he pitched the no-hitter against Boston, the photographers crowded into the clubhouse. They had a hard time getting near him.

"Even his best friends tell him," third baseman Grady Hatton said, that night. "But he won't change shirts in the middle of a winning streak."

"Can I help it if I'm superstitious?" Blackwell said. "Besides, what's wrong with honest perspiration?"

Fate then took charge of Blackwell's future. In January of 1949, he underwent emergency surgery for the removal of a kidney in Glendale, California and he beat that one. He won 17 that season for the Reds, despite a late start due to the operation. He followed it with a 16-victory season in 1950.

Late in September of 1950, he suffered an appendicitis attack and underwent emergency surgery in Cincinnati. Two years later, he was waived out of the National League, and the Yankees picked him up for pennant insurance. He helped a little, but after that it was a brief fling in the Pacific Coast before he was forced into retirement.

It wasn't the surgery that precipitated his decision to step down, but rather his arm. His major league totals show only 87 victories and 77 defeats, and all but three of those triumphs were for Cincinnati. He won three for New York.

Like all men who throw a baseball for their daily bread, Blackwell knew about pain. He lived with it all through his major league career, mostly because of his sidearm delivery, which constantly strained his shoulder. But great record or not, Ewell Blackwell deserves a place in baseball's memory book. He came along when the nation was involved in the most devastating war in its history, and he gave up two years of his baseball career to take part in it. As an ex-GI he pitched his way to prominence, and maybe he did look "like a guy falling out of a tree" when he pitched. But he was a lot more than that, even though his record may never place him among the galaxy of stars in the Hall of Fame at Cooperstown, N. Y.

He will be remembered, though, and he deserves it.

WHERE IS HE NOW?

Ewell Blackwell moved from the world of sports into the world of business with the same excellence that he demonstrated on the baseball field.

At the end of his baseball career, Ewell opened a package liquor store in Tampa, Florida, the spring training home of the Reds. He sold it a year later, in 1955, to join the sales force of National Distilleries and Chemical Corporation, and is now the state manager for that firm in Columbia, South Carolina.

He and his wife, Dotty, have two children, Linda, who is married to Sam McDowell (not the pitcher) and Debbie, an assistant buyer for a Columbia department store. Blackie, who turned 50 in October of 1972, began collecting his pension from the Major League Players' Association. It amounts to $258 a month.

"Just think," he says. "If I were finishing now it would be something like $700 monthly. That's how much it has been improved."

He seems uniniterested in major league baseball today. No bitterness, or anything like that, just unconcerned. "When they expanded the leagues," he says, "they spread the talent too thin. There are too many minor leaguers playing today. I can't help it, that's just the way I feel about it."

At one point, before he got into the liquor business, he thought about becoming a professional golfer, and it looked as though he had the ability. He played around the Tampa area and got his score into the 70s and once a 66. "But because of my family," he says, "I just couldn't see myself doing all that traveling. George Zaharias wanted to help me get started, but I just couldn't."

Occasionally he watches a baseball game on television, and although he wouldn't say it, there must be a twinge in his right shoulder once in a while.

"Sometimes," he says, "I wish I'd have come along 30 years later because the money is a lot better now. But really, I have no regrets. We had some great ones in may day, too."

And Ewell Blackwell was one of them!

ROBERT BROWN THOMSON

The Home Run Heard
'Round-the-World

THE YEAR WAS 1942 and the 19-year-old kid had just signed a contract with the New York Giants for $100 a month. He was assigned to the Bristol (Virginia) club of the Appalachian League because Bill Terry, General manager of the Giants, thought the youngster might make it at third base.

The problem was, though, that Hal Gruber, who was managing Bristol, was satisfied with the third baseman he had, and since the club was involved in a fight for the pennant, he didn't feel like experimenting with a kid named Bobby Thomson, fresh out of Curtis High School on Staten Island, N. Y.

So he shipped the kid to Rocky Mount, North Carolina of the Bi-State League and young Bobby made his debut in Organized Baseball in a night game playing third base against Danville, Virginia.

The Rocky Mounts lost and Bobby Thomson didn't particularly distinguish himself for a guy who had a budding reputation as a hitter. He went "0 for 4" and in the parlance of the national pastime, that was no hits in four times at bat. After the game, George Ferrell, who was managing the club as well as baby-sitting them, took the team to a cafe for sandwiches and milk. When the players had finished eating, Ferrell got behind the wheel of the team bus and the Rocky Mount team departed for another town and another game.

As Ferrell drove off, he didn't even bother to call roll. Defeat does that to managers even in the minor leagues. So he didn't know that his new third baseman, distraught over his inauspicious debut, was still sitting at the lunch counter, twisting his half-full milk glass as he watched the condensation make circles on the marble top.

A few moments after the bus pulled away, a local police officer wandered in and began to question the young and dejected stranger. Bobby Thomson told his sad story and the officer came to the rescue. "Don't worry," he told the kid, "we'll catch them." Bobby Thomson got on back of the police motorcycle and a few miles out of town caught up with the team. They hadn't even realized that he was missing.

"I was sick at heart," Thomson said later, "realizing that no one knew or cared that I was missing. Still I tried to sound as if it didn't matter. I said to the manager, 'Gee, do you forget a guy just because he goes 0 for 4 the first time out.' Then I laughed."

Bobby Thomson played only 29 games for Rocky Mount, and then his country called and he became a lieutenant and bombadier in the Air Force. Following his discharge in 1945, the Giants showed little interest in his future. But Thomson thought he had one, and he turned to semi-pro baseball, playing for a team sponsored by a brewery and another company that advertised California wines.

In 1946, he finally got the call. The Giants wanted him back and assigned him to their Jersey City club in the International League where he played outfield and third base. In 151 games he hit a creditable .280 and, more importantly, 26 home runs. He was on his way. Late that season, the big club waved the flag and the kid who had missed the bus reported to the Polo Grounds.

Bobby flourished under Mel Ott, who was managing the club. He hit .283 and 29 home runs his first full season with the Giants in 1947. But then, volatile Leo Durocher defected from Brooklyn and took over the Giants the following season. Speculation immediately arose that Durocher would trade Thomson, a soft-spoken mild-mannered man in comparison with the verbose and often rude Durocher. The darling of the New York writers, Leo wasn't known for his diplomacy even in those days. Nor is he now, for that matter.

In any case, he was quoted in a newspaper interview as saying: "Thomson? He's certainly no good as an outfielder. I don't know where he can play."

"My morale dropped to its lowest ebb after reading that," Thomson says. Bobby's hitting fell off, and Mel Ott, who stayed with the club in a front office capacity, noticed it and advised Bobby to change his stance. Thomson did and managed to salvage a .248, batting average his first year under the abrasive Durocher, but his home run production fell off to 16.

After the season, Thomson was still bothered by Durocher's attitude, so he went to see him. Bobby wanted a steady job at one position, preferably the outfield. "If you let me go to center and stay there," he told Durocher, "I promise, you won't regret it."

Durocher, a hunch player, no matter if the game is baseball or gin rummy, was impressed. "O.K., you're my centerfielder as long as you can hold the job," Leo told him. Thomson responded by hitting .309 the following season. He hit 52 homers over the next two seasons, and then it all fell into place. The year was 1951.

Charlie Dressen had taken over the Brooklyn club that season and in his own zaney way had the club running away with the National League pennant. By August 11th the talented Bums were 13½ games in front. But the Giants, propelled by the instincts of the crafty Durocher, began to chip away at their lead. Dusty Rhodes put down his cup of cheer often enough to become a miraculous pinch hitter. And pitcher Sal Maglie, known as the Barber, was shaving the opposition so close that even Durocher was satisfied.

On September 1, the Giants were riding a 16-game winning streak as they opened a two-game set with the Dodgers. The irrepressible New Yorkers won them both behind Maglie and Jim Hearn. Later in the month, they split a pair and both hit the road. The Giants picked up another game, and by the final week of the season the Dodgers were a half-game ahead with three games to play, all against the Phillies. New York had two left against the old Boston Braves.

The Giants had to win two and hope for a Dodger swoon. It didn't happen. They won their two all right. Brooklyn lost the first to the Phils, but Don Newcombe shut them out in the second game 5-0. In the finale, it was all Jackie Robinson. The Dodgers' great, black infielder who had broken the color line in 1947, saved the game with an amazing catch on the Phillies' Eddie Waitkus and then, in the top of the 14th inning, Robinson homered for a 7-6 Brooklyn victory and a tie with the Giants for the National League pennant.

The three-game playoff series opened in Ebbets Field, and the Giants, on the strength of Bobby Thomson's two-run homer off Ralph Branca, won the opener 3-1. Clem Labine shut out the New Yorkers 10-0 in the second game and suddenly all the money was on the table.

The date was October 3, 1951 and 34,320 fans jammed the Polo Grounds. The place was seething with excitement. Big Don Newcombe was on the mound again for the Dodgers and he was trying to protect a 4-1 lead in the bottom of the ninth. Alvin Dark and Don Mueller were on base for the Giants and Newcombe was two outs away from winning the pennant for the Dodgers.

Bobby Thomson remembers it well. "All of a sudden it dawned on me that we had a chance to pull it out," he recalled. Carroll (Whitey) Lockman, the Giants' first baseman, doubled and Dark scored while Mueller moved to third. Mueller turned his ankle sliding, and while the Giants huddled around him, Dressen waved in right-hander Branca from the bullpen. Bobby Thomson was the next hitter and he wanted another right-hander in there. Anyway, lightning couldn't strike twice.

In those days, Leo Durocher didn't hide in the corner of the dugout. He was coaching at third base and as Thomson strode to the plate, the Giants manager said in that basso profundo voice of his: "One little Chinee homer, Bobby. Please, just one little Chinee homer."

Since the left-field line at the Polo Grounds was only 279 feet away from the plate, Durocher was telling him to pull one down the foul line for a "cheap" homer.

But let Thomson tell it now:

"I got mad at myself," Thomson, who was 28 years of age at the time, recalls. "I don't know why . . . maybe it was a form of self-discipline.

"I kept saying to myself, 'Now don't swing at a bad one . . . wait for your pitch.'" Branca finished his warm-up throws and delivered a fastball inside for a strike.

Branca took the return throw, rubbed up the ball, touched the resin bag, tugged at his cap, hitched his belt and did all those nonsensical things that pitchers do, and then reared back and threw. It was Thomson's pitch all right, high and inside. Bobby lofted it into the left-field seats, about 30 feet fair and the Giants had an amazing 5-4 comeback victory. More important they had the pennant.

The Polo Grounds immediately became a madhouse and 10 million Americans watching on television, looked on in amazement. Thomson was so unhinged he started to hop with happiness as he ran the bases. "I didn't run, I rode around them on a cloud. I just couldn't believe that was happening to me. I felt as if I were living one of those middle-of-the-night dreams. Everything was hazy."

The scene quickly developed into one of the happiest moments in the history of sports. Leo Durocher ran amuk, and Eddie Stanky, the Giants' second baseman, cut across the diamond and wrestled the manager to the ground in a gesture of pure animal joy.

Sportswriters covering the game were as stunned as everyone else, and there was enough paper torn out of typewriters that day to recycle a newspaper. The superlatives flowed commensurate with the champagne in the club house as Bobby Thomson earned his niche in the history of American sports.

The kid, whose father brought him to this country from his native Glasgow when he was two years old, became a genuine folk hero. He spent 10 more years in the big tent, playing with Milwaukee, the Cubs, and Orioles before he decided to hang them up in 1961. And over the years, the Thomson legend has persisted, although there was talk for a time that the Giants had a spy in the scoreboard flashing the pitches to the bench. No one ever denied it, but what difference does it make anyway?

Ralph Branca pitched the ball, and Thomson hit it. It cost Branca his career in the majors and it gave Bobby Thomson the immortality few players receive.

WHERE IS HE NOW?

Bobby Thomson and his wife Winkie are the parents of three children. They live in Watchung, N. J., a rural community of some 5,000 about an hour and a half from New York City. Daughter Nancy studies oral hygiene at the University of Pennsylvania. Young Bobby is quickly advancing on his teens, and little Megan was born in March of 1964. "I guess you could say we have two families," Bobby says, "because we had kind of a dry spell for a while after Nancy was born."

After he left the Giants, Bobby played with the Braves, Cubs and Red Sox, in addition to a second tour with the Giants, but that playoff home run in 1951 is, and always will be, the high point of his career.

Thomson looks back on his life in baseball with affection, but he never regrets having left it. And no wonder. He has become a success in the business world and holds the title of National Accounts Representative for Westvaco Corporation, of New York City.

Bobby calls it an "integrated company" which produces paper all the way from the timberlands to the finished product. He specializes in the New York area, although he is responsible for orders from Chicago, New Orleans and Atlanta.

And how he got that far with just a high school education is almost a story in itself. "I knew that when I was finished with baseball, I would be finished, so I wanted to get out and find out what I could do outside the game," he says. So he went to a testing firm called Stevens Institute and took 15 hours of tests to determine his aptitude. "It was the slow, hard way of doing it," Bobby says, "but I had to find out how much gray matter was up there."

Apparently there was plenty, because he is an executive with a company that does almost $500,000,000 a year in sales. And the old determination is still there, too.

Bobby still reads about baseball and follows the exploits of his former manager Leo Durocher with interest. "I read a lot, watch games on television and see a game in person now and then," he says. "It's a fun thing for me now."

As for Branca, Thomson sees him occasionally. "I understand he's in the insurance business and very successful. As for the home run, he has learned to accept it and live with it."

"You know," he says, "people still talk about it."

Bobby's game is tennis now, and he still is in better condition than most men who have just turned 50 years of age.

How about Leo Durocher?

"I've got my own thoughts about him," Bobby said.

Always the gentleman, he didn't want to say what they were. Maybe it's just as well.

ROBERT LAWRENCE LAYNE

The Built-in Timepiece

HE LIVED BY THE clock, but it wasn't the standard American timepiece. He had his own special chronometer, embedded somewhere deep in his psyche and it told him that when it was midnight for mere mortals, it was only high noon for him.

For 15 years in the National Football League, Bobby Layne fought this phenomenon, playing by night, toiling by day, but always attending to the joys of living.

He was a paradox in a world of jocks, crew-cuts, curfews and coaches, and from 1948, when he was drafted by the Chicago Bears, until he retired from the Pittsburgh Steelers in 1962, he wandered through 175 NFL games in the daylight hours, and sipped the nectar of the Gods at night.

Curfews were not his bag, not that he wanted to be disobedient. He didn't. He just wanted to be different, and he was. "Anyone can be ordinary," his credo says. "Be different, but be better." But the comparative degree does not describe the man. The superlative is needed, because he was the best—he was one of a kind.

There have been better passers than Bobby Layne in the history of the National Football League. And there have been better runners and kickers and men who played longer in a game that demands so much physically.

But there was no one who possessed Layne's ability as a mover and a shaker. No one who could take a football team from its own 20, and cross the enemy's goal line in the shortest period of time. There was no one, because nobody, before or since, had the clock.

There are lots of descriptions for this unique ability. Coaches call it leadership, direction, determination, guts, and even *esprit de corps*. But coaches are masters of the cliche, and many of them are trying to sell the same old product with methods they learned from their coaches who learned it from their coaches, *ad infinitum*.

Nobody could coach into Bobby Layne his unparalleled ability to get things moving. He was born with it, just as surely as he was born with blue eyes and blonde hair in Dallas, Texas on December 10, 1926.

Layne played in an era of great quarterbacks—Bob Waterfield, Sid Luckman, Sammy Baugh, Norm Van Brocklin, Otto Graham, Bart Starr, Y. A. Tittle and Johnny Unitas were his contemporaries. Great as they were and are, Layne was more fun to watch because he made time stand still. They call it the "two-minute" drill in the NFL and they work on it. The offensive team takes the ball on its own 20 and tries to score within the next two minutes.

It is an essential part of the modern pro game and it originated, or rather evolved, from the mind and ability of Bobby Layne. When he did it, so often and so well from Pittsburgh and Detroit, every other team in the NFL incorporated the tactic into their playbooks.

Layne's accomplishments on the playing fields of the NFL are legendary and place him among the top quarterbacks who played the game. He completed 49% of 3,700 passes during his 15-year career, gaining 26,768 yards for 196 touchdowns. He rushed for 25 others, gaining an additional 2,451 yards on 611 attempts in a day when the only sane way to play the game was to stay in the protective pocket.

The Bobby Layne the fans saw on the field was not the same Bobby Layne who defied the clock during the nocturnal hours. "I'm just a born night owl," he says. "Maybe I'm a better player, because I start having fun at midnight, get to bed when everybody else is waking and sleep all morning. It makes me fresh as a daisy for the game."

That sort of reverse logic sent many a coach up the wall on Saturday night, but by late Sunday afternoon most of them had to admit it worked. "I'm one of those people who can get along on five to seven hours of sleep," he explained at the height of his career. "If I go to bed at 11:00 the night before a game, I'll get up by 5:00 A.M. By kickoff time, I've already played one game in my head with the real one still to come.

"But if I get to bed at one, I'll sleep until eight. Then I won't have so much time to fret before the game starts." He meant it, too, although he may have been stretching the hands on the clock to Pacific Coast time instead of Eastern Standard.

But he was as forthright about his habits off the field as he was barking signals on the field behind the Lions, Steelers, New York Bulldogs and Chicago Bears.

"If I feel like a beer or two, I'm not going to sneak around some alley joint. I'm going to the best place in town and walk in the front door." He walked out the front door, too, when he was good and ready, and, if the party was still moving along at a good pace, it was not unusual for him to toss a hundred dollar bill on the table and demand:

"Here, keep it going."

Just as surely as he knew his ability on the field, he pretty much knew his capacity off it. Steeler running back Tom (The Bomb) Tracy, found that out one night before a game in New York.

Tracy, a tough and rugged competitor, joined Bobby on a tour of Layne's favorite Manhattan haunts until the wee hours of the morning. The next day against the Giants, Bobby showed Tracy no mercy, calling his signal no fewer than 18 times.

Toward the end, Tracy was virtually immobile from fatigue and as he collapsed on the bench for a brief respite from combat, Layne jogged over and said, "Bomb, you just haven't been training."

Despite his meanderings, the game was the thing with Layne. He never used a face mask, the better to spot his receivers, and he came on strong when television discovered that there were millions out there in the vast wasteland ready for pro football after a diet of Kukla, Fran and Ollie.

Close-up shots reveal a fiery Layne, blasting an official, wagging his index finger under the nose of one of his teammates for missing an assignment, or frantically waving his arms while sitting on the bench. "Move the ball" was his mission, move it because "I've got the clock."

And that inborn desire went for everyone and for practice sessions as well as games. He simply would not stand for anything less than an all-out effort. The Layne Law was simple: "Sloppy preparation brings a miserable conclusion." So his rather unorthodox training methods really didn't mean a thing. They wouldn't have worked for anyone else, but they suited Layne.

Buddy Parker, another Texan, who coached him at Detroit and Pittsburgh explains it this way: "They don't make them like Bobby anymore. He's a case of don't-do-as-I-do, but do-as-I-tell-you. Sure, he's a man who goes against all the rules, but, by golly, it works."

The Layne-Parker partnership at Detroit was a profitable one for the Lions. They won divisional championships in 1952, 1953, and 1954 and the World Championship, as it was then called, the first two years. And they beat the Cleveland Browns, the dominant power in that decade, both times.

Detroit slipped past the Browns 17-7 for the 1952 crown, but a year later the same two teams met in the title game at Detroit's Briggs Stadium. The matchup, of course, was Layne against the great Otto Graham of the Browns. Bobby won it hands down and once again he beat the clock to do it.

Three field goals by Lou Groza helped the Browns forge into a 16-10 lead in the game's waning moments. But the unshakeable Layne was equal to the task. With three minutes to play, the Lions got the ball at their own 20.

Back in the huddle before he called the first play, Bobby told the Lions: "Awright, fellers. Ya all block and ol' Bobby'll pass you right to the championship. Ol' Bobby'll get you six big ones."

And with his clock ticking with Swiss-like precision, Bobby completed four of six passes including a 33-yard touchdown pass to seldom-used Jim Doran. The Lions won it 17-16 and it took Layne just 60 seconds to drive the Lions from their own 20 to the championship.

Doak Walker, a Texan and a teammate of Layne's on the Lions, zeroed in on the secret of Bobby's fabulous success. "Bobby never lost a game," he said. "Sometimes, the clock just ran out on him." But that frigid day in Detroit against the Browns, the man with the built-in timepiece beat the clock. He made time stand still for him.

The 1957 Lions won a world title, too, but Layne wasn't around to share in the glory. He had broken his leg, and the following season Parker traded him to the Steelers for Earl Morrall.

Layne reported immediately and announced he would hang around until he brought the Steelers a championship. Bobby played five years with the Steelers, and, although he turned the team around for a while, he never was able to bring them the title he promised. Time finally caught up with him and he retired after the 1962 season.

Looking back, it would be easy to say that Bears' owner George Halas made a terrible mistake when, in 1948, he sold Layne to Ted Collins and the newly-formed New York Bulldogs.

But Halas' logic seemed sound at the time. He had Hall of Famer Sid Luckman, who was to play for two more years, and Johnny Lujack, the All-American from Notre Dame, who had joined the club the same year as Layne. Nevertheless, now, more than a quarter of a century later, Halas must wake up in the middle of the night and sadly ponder what might have happened had he kept Layne and sold Lujack.

One thing is certain, the Grand Old Man of football would have gotten a lot less sleep over the years. Bobby Layne would have seen to that. His clock would have worked the same way on Central Standard time.

WHERE IS HE NOW?

After Bobby Layne married Carol Ann Krueger on August 17, 1946, he began to spend all his off-season time in Lubbock, Texas, Carol's home town. "I not only liked the town," he says, "but I really began to like the people of West Texas."

The union has brought forth two sons, Robert Lawrence Jr., who was to be married as this was written and was drilling oil wells in Ecuador.

Tommy Alan recently graduated from Texas Christian University.

As for Bobby, he still is a quarterback, but not on a football field. Instead, his arena is the world of business. "I don't really have a position," he says. "I'm involved in all sorts of things. I drill some wells, I own two bowling alleys, and I make any kind of deal I think will be profitable, like operating farms, things like that."

As for his ability to beat the sands of time on a football field, Bobby's explanation was that it was just the way he was. "It was my makeup," he said in that hoarse voice of his. "It was just the way I thought."

Layne then used former teammate Doak Walker as an example. "When we were winning 49-0 Doak was just another player," Bobby said. "But, when the score was 7-7, Doak was nothing short of fantastic. He did things when he had to do them, because he was born to be like that."

Bobby rates Buddy Parker as the greatest coach he has ever been associated with, and he said Parker taught him the advantages of living by the clock.

He taught me," Layne said, "that the two minutes before the half, and the two minutes before the end of the game were the most important four minutes of the game. He also believed that winning solved a lot of problems. It's just like this war [Viet Nam]. If we are going to be in it, let's win it and get out of there. Don't you think that's right?"

Bobby and some of his friends lease 11,000 acres of land about 90 miles from Lubbock and the group uses it to hunt doves and quail. "We have dogs and there's no telephone there," he said. "I love it and try to get over there every chance I get."

Layne completed 1,814 passes in his 15-year NFL career and he rates Doak Walker, a fellow Texan, Cloyce Box and Dorne Dibble, the former Michigan State star, as his favorite receivers. Dorne Dibble?

"That Dibble was something. He had all the natural ability, but I'd have to say that Doak was the smartest."

How about Jimmy Orr?

"He was great, too," Bobby said. "But he was different from the others. He was a dedicated man and we worked together for hours after practice. I mean it, hours and hours. Jimmy made himself a great receiver."

Layne is fighting the weight problems of middle age, but he attacks them with the same flair that brought him so much success on the football field. And the clock is still working for him.

And it still isn't the one the rest of us live by. Bobby Layne still has his own and it keeps telling him—the time is now.

DUKE SNIDER

The Duke of Brooklyn

WARD SNIDER HAD HIS son learning to swing a bat and shag fly balls as soon as the little guy could run.

The year 'round baseball weather in the Los Angeles, California, area could accelerate the development of a budding baseball player, but they rarely start as young, and there is no question the senior Snider played an integral part in what was to come.

He hung the nickname of "Duke" on his little boy when the youngster was four years of age, a name that was to reach the proportions of legend in Brooklyn, New York, with the Dodgers.

The father-son sports relationship didn't confine itself to baseball. Young Duke Snider grew to be an almost incredible high school athlete.

Duke won 20 letters in all and was a genuine star in football, baseball, basketball and track. His forward passes rocketed regularly for 65-yard distances.

But baseball was his game, and Snider's prowess was such that several major league scouts included his performance as a regular stop on their beat.

With high school finished, they moved in . . . but cautiously. World War II was at its height in 1943 and the blandishments of the big league clubs were not heavily upholstered with dollar bills.

Duke Snider signed a Brooklyn Dodger contract not so much for the money (the Dodger scout got him signed for $750), but more because of Red Barber.

The famed sports announcer was at the microphone for the Dodgers in their drive to the 1941 pennant and he had a no more avid listener than young Snider. "I gave Red Barber a lot of credit," says Duke. "He made it sound terrific on the radio."

When he reported to the Dodger camp in 1944, Snider was just 17 years old. A left-handed batter, his swing was a picture. His fluid, lashing motion was to set him off with Ted Williams as the epitome of a perfect swing.

He wasn't ready for the Dodgers at age 17, and Snider's first port of call was Newport News, Class B. His anxiety to hit cost him $25 when he popped up a three-and-one pitch he had been ordered to take, but the year was otherwise uneventful.

The physical skills of Duke Snider were called for by the United States Navy in 1945 and as the war was grinding to its halt, Duke was out of uniform by June of 1946 and back in baseball.

This time the Dodgers sent him to Ft. Worth, and the maturing Snider began to bloom. His batting average in that abbreviated season wasn't all that high at .250, but Branch Rickey, major domo of the parent club, looked at him and publicly pronounced, "This is potentially the greatest hitter I have ever seen."

Results started showing in St. Paul in 1947 with a .316 average, and Duke spent the end of the season with the Dodgers. Big league pitching cut him down to .241.

At Montreal in the triple-A International League he slashed through a .327 season, but again found Ebbets Feld too much for him in September.

But that picture swing and the steady minor league production of over .300 brought the big decision. Duke Snider was in the big leagues. Brooklyn brought him up to stay in 1949.

It was a turning point all around. Although those brief September appearances had over-matched him, Duke compiled a highly respectable .292 in his first full season . . . and smashed 23 home runs.

Another little turning point for Snider that year came in the World Series, a disastrous series for the Dodgers. They found their bats strangely silent and were wiped out by the New York Yankees four games to one. The Dodger batting average as a team in the series was a meager .210. Snider managed only three hits in 21 at bats for a .143. More embarrassing, he struck out eight times to tie a series record held by Rogers Hornsby.

"I was an extremely moody ball player," Snider recalled. "When things weren't going right I would really get down in the dumps. I figured I was a cinch to be an ulcer case sooner or later because I kept everything bottled up inside me.

"But, after striking out eight times in that series, I always had that as a low point to look back on, and it helped when I would have one of those O-for-four days. I had to fight that moodiness and I did conquer it, but it took quite a bit of time. And it made me a much better ball player."

It was the last time Duke Snider was to have a poor World Series. In 1952, again against the Yankees, Snider hit .345, with four home runs and two doubles. Unfortunately for the Brooklyns, the Yankees won it again, four games to three.

It was the fourth straight World Championship for New York, and when the same two teams met the following year, Casey Stengel guided the Bronx Bombers to their historic fifth straight series victory. The first time in the history of the game any team had put together such a string.

In the losing cause, Snider rattled Yankee pitching for eight hits in 25 at bats, one homer, three doubles and a .320 average.

For the Brooklyn Dodgers, it was their seventh straight World Series disappointment, a frustrating statistic which was finally to end in 1955, the next time the Dodgers were to make it to the big show. It was the Yankees and the Dodgers once again. This time Brooklyn came through to win the championship four games to three.

Snider was a terror in the field and at the plate, although his game-saving catches in center field in the fourth game were to be eclipsed in memory by the spectacular grab of Yogi Berra's looper in the final game by Sandy Amoros. The unexpected grab made an easy double play on Gil McDougald and it meant the ball game.

Snider again hit .320 in the Series, this time with four home runs.

1956 found the same two teams continuing their habit pattern, again series opponents, with the Yankees returning to the top of the heap, in another seven-game battle, four games to three.

It was the last World Series for Snider and this time he hit at a .304 clip.

In his five World Series, Snider put together a .293 batting average and hammered out 10 home runs.

Snider was a left-handed hitter who didn't have to be platooned. Southpaw or right-hander, he smashed anybody's pitching.

1954 was the year in which he proved himself against lefties, hitting .308 against them. Duke remembered the year well: "I think we saw more of them that year. We had a predominantly right-handed hitting club and I was about the only left-handed hitter in the lineup most of the time.

"Gosh, we went a year and a half without seeing Warren Spahn. That's how strong our club was against left-handed pitchers.

"I remember once in Milwaukee that year we faced five straight left-handers. In the first game I think I struck out two or three times. Then in the second game of the double-header I hit a home run and the next day I hit another home run off another left-hander. Joe Nuxhall pitched the next day and I hit a grand slam off him."

Pitchers on his club were the biggest help to the hitting of Duke Snider. He felt a pitcher, facing batters, would be the quickest to spot him doing something different that was hurting his swing.

"Ralph Branca started it," said Duke. "He told me one day, 'I've got a mental picture of you now while you're going good. If I see you changing or doing anything wrong I'll holler at you.'

"The dugouts at Ebbets Field were very close and he used to shout things quite often and it helped a lot."

After Branca left the club, Snider relied on his roommate, Carl Erskine. After Erskine, observer duty was taken up by Pee Wee Reese when he became the third-base coach with the Dodgers.

"He worked out a sign system that showed me what I was doing wrong at the plate," Duke said. "Maybe I would be taking my head off the ball, or moving my feet around too much.

"The biggest problem I had was with my head. I'd get to letting it fly up a little too quick and take my eye off the ball.

Snider's favorite manager remains Charlie Dressen. "Every manager I played under was a good baseball man," Duke recalled, "but Dressen was a good psychologist. He discovered that when he got me upset or embarrassed I dug in and tried harder. He'd criticize me in front of the other players, and I'd go out to show him I could do the things he was embarrassing me about."

Snider turned gray at an early age, and that crop of silver hair led to one of the best remembered episodes in his life. He became a testimonial for hair coloring.

It must be remembered that, at the time, any great concern by a man over his hair was looked upon as something less than masculine. To color his hair left a man open to ridicule.

Obviously it was good business to change this attitude, and the hair-coloring firm sought out Duke Snider to do the job. They were memorable commercials, augmented by equally memorable magazine ads. Snider's hair parted in the middle, with half his head left gray, and the other half colored a dark brown.

"I can remember doing that commercial in New York," laughed Snider. "Walking down the street with my hair half gray and half brown, almost black. People would look at me and wonder what was going on.

"But it was a lot of fun and I enjoyed doing the commercial. Matter of fact, it won an award that year.

"I still color my hair," Duke went on. "I'm still connected with Clairol—the firm that makes it. My wife likes it and it makes me look a little bit younger. I'm only 45 and what the heck, there's no use looking 60 when you can look 45."

WHERE IS HE NOW?

For three years Snider worked as an announcer on the San Diego Padres baseball broadcasts. Now they have prevailed upon him to manage in their farm system and bring his very valuable skills to developing young players. His first stop: the Texas League, at Alexandria, Louisiana.

Married in 1947, his family includes his wife, Beverly, and four children. The two oldest, Kevin and Pamela, are through with school and are working. Sixteen-year-old Kurt is echoing his father's high school athletic success in three sports: football, basketball and baseball.

Donna is the youngest at eleven years old, and is carving out a sports reputation of her own in swimming. She has won a few ribbons in AAU competition, notably in the backstroke and free-style.

The Duke looks kindly on today's ball players. "Expansion has watered down the talent in the major leagues a little bit, but most of the guys are still basically about the same type of players that we had. They're a little more mod, but what the heck, you and I are a little more mod, aren't we?

"I remember back in the early fifties when I got an award as one of the ten best-dressed men in America. The only reason I got it was I took to wearing bright red and yellow slacks. That was as far out then as some of the clothes are today."

Snider singled out Joe Pepitone as one of his favorites today, hair pieces and all. "He's a colorful guy and I think it's great that he can take a little ribbing and hand a little back and stand up for his convictions."

About the only thing Duke Snider is still waiting for is election to baseball's Hall of Fame. It would seem inevitable, but Duke is not optimistic about it happening soon.

"To me, it appears the voting is a little more of a popularity contest than on some of the years a guy had. I'm not particularly happy with that, but how else are you going to do it? If someone comes up with a better idea of deciding, I'd be all for it.

"I know these guys vote from their hearts sometimes instead of their minds, but you can't blame them. I think I'd probably do the same thing.

"My votes have been increasing by about twenty a year, so I'll be ready for the old timers by the time I finally get in."

If there are any regrets over the career of Duke Snider, they come, not from Snider, but from the pro football commissioner, Pete Rozelle.

Rozelle and Snider were classmates in high school, and played on the same basketball team. Rozelle can still remember those soaring, 60-yard passes right on target. The NFL commissioner is convinced Duke would have been a great pro quarterback.

JACK FLECK

It Started with Hogan's Clubs

HE HAD SNEAKED INTO a golf tournament as a teenager. Watching the pros in action ignited his interest in the game. He announced himself a golf professional at 17 years of age, after having just graduated from high school. He worked at menial jobs on golf courses around Davenport, Iowa, finally becoming the "pro" at the two municipal courses. He played infrequently in the tour events and never finished better than fifth. He shot an 87 in a practice round, then went out and won the United States Open Golf Championship. And he beat Ben Hogan in a playoff to do it.

His name is Jack Fleck. And, as he looks back on this most unlikely of golf careers, he remembers Ralph Guldahl as the man who unwittingly got him started.

They were playing the Western Open in Fleck's home town of Davenport. He, and two companions, eluded the watchful marshalls to sneak in and catch the action. They were soon apprehended, but as they were ushered out they were asked if they would like to work as fore-caddies during the remaining rounds of play. The response was a quick "yes" from young Fleck, and he became fore-caddy for the man who eventually won it, Ralph Guldahl. "Here," thought Fleck, "is a game I can play."

Jack was too small for football, and had displayed no special skill in anything else. Yet, he dreamed of a life in sports, and this appeared to be a way.

Fleck became a caddy at the local country club. Kindly members would give permission to the boys to use their clubs on "caddy days" each Monday morning, when the course was closed and caddies could play. Jack began to develop a skill at the game.

When Fleck finished high school, he wanted no part of amateur golf. Mainly, he couldn't afford it. Instead, he simply announced himself a professional.

"That's all it took in those days," says Jack.

He started working in the golf shop at the country club. When winter came, he hitch-hiked to San Antonio, Texas, the scene of the Texas Open. For Fleck, it was not to play in the tournament, but to hit up the assembled professionals, many of whom were club pros in the summer, for a job. He got one, too, as an assistant pro in the capital city of his home state, Des Moines.

The following year he made his way south again, this time to play in the Texas Open. The tournament was played in a steady rain and Fleck was forced to withdraw. He didn't have rain gear, and didn't have enough in the way of shoes and clothing to just go out and play in it.

The process of north in the summer, south in the winter, was to continue for several years. The tour was vastly different in those early and middle 1940's. There were few touring professionals, and playing in a tournament was no more involved than entering it.

"I would save a couple hundred dollars from my summer work, and that was enough to get me through two or three tournaments," said Fleck. "There weren't any motels around then, and most everyone stayed in a private home. You'd get a nice room in somebody's home for a dollar a night.

"Around 1948, when Fred Corcoran was running the tour, one of his big jobs was lining up places for the golfers to stay. I remember once in Tucson, he got us in the old Pioneer Hotel there. Seventeen of us were up on the mezzanine floor, sleeping on cots. It was the only place we could stay."

Jack was beginning to pick up a little prize money now, augmenting his slim savings bankroll, and each year his tournament activity would stretch out a little more.

The job as professional at Davenport's two municipal courses had come along, and a young lady who brought a broken club into the shop for repairs wound up marrying him in 1950.

His wife, Lynn, encouraged Jack to extend his winter competition as long as possible. He also began to find time to play in some summer events as Lynn and her brother would remain in Davenport to handle the pro shop business. There was no such thing as a sponsor, nor any affiliation with a manufacturer.

That was the progression of Jack Fleck, from fore-caddy to professional as he came to that fateful year of 1955.

An intriguing bit of irony developed in the weeks before the U.S. Open. Ben Hogan had embarked upon the manufacture of his own line of golf clubs. The process of getting them into production was troublesome. Hogan would not allow an imperfect club to leave the factory, and would not put them on the market until quality of production was assured. Hogan had a virtually hand-crafted set for his own use and ordered another set made for his good friend, Tommy Bolt.

Before the clubs arrived, Bolt had agreed to terms with another manufacturer and, as an endorsing professional, could not accept the set from Hogan. They caught up with Bolt at the St. Petersburg Open, where Fleck was also playing, and Jack asked if he could take a look at them.

For Fleck, they seemed ideal! good feel, big blade on the irons. He promptly, but with little hope, wrote a letter to Hogan inquiring if he could get a set.

To Jack's surprise, he shortly received a letter from Hogan's factory manager, Charlie Barnett, saying Bantam Ben had passed the letter along with instructions to make up the set.

So it came to pass that many weeks later, when Hogan and Fleck finished the regulation four rounds of the United States Open tied for the championship, they were the only two players in the entire tournament using Hogan clubs. Quite an endorsement for a new line!

The clubs came to Fleck piecemeal. He got the irons in time for the Colonial Invitational at Ft. Worth. (He feels, because of the clubs, Hogan was instrumental in getting him invited.) The woods arrived at Kansas City. Just a week before the U.S. Open, Fleck got the last of the set—the two wedges.

The scene of the U.S. Open Championship in 1955 was the Olympic Club in San Francisco. To begin with, the course is carved through a stand of magnificent trees. The "narrow" feeling a golfer has as he stood on the tee was accentuated by a devilish rough that further confined the acceptable area of the tee shot.

The cries of anguish could be heard in Oakland as the first round of play saw less than half the field hardly able to break 80.

Fleck shot a 76, Hogan a 73—against a par of 70.

Jack Fleck's 69 in the second round brought him even with Hogan who had a 72, but there was no one who thought seriously about the part-time Iowa tourist at that point.

On the final day, with 36 holes to play, the guess was that either Hogan would become the first man in history to win five Opens, or the jinx-ridden Sam Snead would win his first. There were others through the long day who created flurries of excitement, but they all faded.

Snead had pulled to within two shots of Hogan when Ben faded his drive into the rough on 14, a long four-par that had the green still 210 yards away from his tee shot.

The rough was a breed of rye brass imported from Italy with

heavy blades some three-eights of an inch wide. It was cropped to two inches in height along the fairways, then up to five inches for another ten to twelve feet. Beyond that, a golfer was fortunate to find his ball, for the dense grass flourished a foot high.

It was here that Hogan had hit the shot he felt had won the tournament. He was in the five-inch rough, and the gallery gasped as he drew a four wood to hit it out. With the precision that was his hallmark, Hogan came into the ball with a slight cutting action and laced it to the green 210 yards away. He got it down for a birdie as Snead made bogey on 16 and 17 ahead of him.

Hogan scored a birdie and three pars through the four finishing holes for an even par 70 and, to all appearances, the championship. Then along came Fleck.

He found a putting touch he himself couldn't quite believe. Beginning on the fifth hole in the second round, Fleck did not record a single three-putt green for the rest of the tournament.

Now, at 18, he needed a birdie to tie. The hole was a short but demanding par four with a small, slick, well-trapped green.

Hogan, whose knee was still troubling him after a near-fatal automobile accident, had sunk heavily into a locker-room chair, savoring a scotch and water.

Fleck pulled his tee shot just a shade as he began 18, and it made the rough on the left edge of the fairway. In the locker room, Cary Middlecoff walked over to congratulate Hogan.

Jack came to his ball and found it sitting up high on the short, dense rough. He was 117 yards from the pin.

"It was a nine-iron shot," Fleck reminisced, "but the green was slick, and I figured you couldn't hit something as hard as you'd have to hit a nine and hold that green.

The ball was sitting up high, and I decided I would try and cut a real high seven iron in there instead. It was a shot I had practiced a lot, and it's real good in a situation like that.

"Actually, I could hit it higher than a nine-iron and what I wanted to do was have it just kind of die over the green and fall almost straight down. The fact it would kind of fade to the right would help."

Fleck's seven-iron snipped through the grass as the ball soared in a high floating arc. Dropping almost straight down, it landed hole high some seven feet to the right of the cup; and held there.

The putt was downhill, breaking to the left. It was a tempting putt to baby, but Fleck stroked it firmly and put it right in the center of the hole. Hogan was tied.

In the locker room, Ben Hogan muttered a soft curse. "I was wishing he'd either make a two or a five. . . . I was wishing it was over."

Fleck won the 18-hole playoff with a 69 to Hogan's 72, principally by ramming home a startling string of long putts on six, eight, nine and ten.

"There were a lot of complaints about the course," Jack recalled, "so much so that I don't believe they've ever had rough that tough in any Open since.

"The course was ideal for me, because I hit it straight. The course was fair in the sense that it rewarded a good shot and penalized a bad one almost exactly in accordance to how far off line it was. If you got in that deep rough, you were lucky just to get back on the fairway.

"I never was a good putter, but the small greens helped me there. If you could hit the fairways and hit the greens, you were in good shape."

Asked about that practice round 87, he replied: "I never shot well in practice, mainly because I was trying to figure out the golf course and not worrying about a score. I've always discounted practice rounds, good ones or bad ones. You gotta do it when it counts."

Jack did very poorly after the Open victory. He got involved in the many business activities that go with that win, and made a lot of banquet appearances and the travel that went with them. He wasn't accustomed to it, and just couldn't cope with it.

It was to be, for Jack Fleck, just one fleeting nod from fame, but it came in the biggest championship there was.

WHERE IS HE NOW?

Jack Fleck is the club professional at the Plumas Lake Golf and Country Club at Marysville, California. Marysville is about 55 miles due north of Sacramento.

He and Lynn have had one child, a son named Craig. Craig is an army sergeant, and a newly-wed.

"I'd like to play again," he says, "but financially it kills you, the expenses are up so high.

"I enjoy teaching, but once the competition gets in your blood anything else seems sort of pale. I told Jack Nicklaus a year or so ago: 'Don't ever quit. Don't ever quit playing competitive golf. Don't ever quit till you can't walk. You can ask all the ones that don't play, and every time they regret giving it up.' Most of them quit too soon."

With the growing number of pros today, Jack feels there should be two tournament circuits, but not satellites.

"Satellites will never make it," he insists. "They all flop and the only way the PGA can get one going is to have the major tournament underwrite it. Nobody will come out and watch unknowns play. They can't draw enough to sustain themselves."

Fleck's notion is to have an Eastern and Western circuit, with a twelve-man team picked from each to finish it up with a national championship match.

"It might be the way to get some kind of a pension plan going," he opined. "Like the Super Bowl and World Series set things up for football and baseball.

"Golf is the greatest game there is, even though I think it was a lot tougher when I started. The money was so low, and it was so difficult to get from one tournament to the next."

Jack still remembers back to the words of an old-timer who came upon him whaling away on the practice tee.

"You're gonna make it, Jack," he said. "But I'll tell you something. When you make it, and you look back . . . all the struggles . . . and the time coming up . . . you'll remember those as really the good times."

"He was right," says Jack.

"Coming down is the hard part."

TONY TRABERT

The Cincinnati Kid

THE SKINNY, TOW-HEADED kid, all knees and elbows, was laboriously belting a tennis ball against a wall. It was a hot, summer day in Cincinnati, Ohio, and he had obviously been at it for quite a while.

The young man stopped to watch him. He was not impressed with the boy's ability, but with his apparent dedication.

"Would you like a couple of pointers on that game?" he asked the youngster.

A grin split the boy's face. "I sure would, sir!" he shot back.

The two spent about twenty minutes in discussion and demonstration and, as the young man left, the boy began batting them again with a fresh fervor and a slightly altered technique.

It was a chance meeting that was to make a great star. The young man was a ranking tennis star of his day, Billy Talbert. Talbert was in Cincinnati for the Tri State Tennis Championships.

The boy was Tony Trabert.

When Talbert's route took him by the same spot the next day, he was impressed to see little Tony again hard at work and especially concentrating on the tips the star had passed along. From that point, Talbert pretty much took young Tony under his wing.

Tony Trabert, born in Cincinnati, August 16, 1930, began swinging a tennis racquet at six years of age. He enjoyed baseball, too, and his summers were filled with playing one and the other.

As his teen years approached, it became apparent Tony had considerable, natural athletic ability. His dad sat him down one day and said, "son, if you want to become good at either of these games, you'll have to concentrate on one and give up the other. Around here, anyway, they're both played at the same time of the year . . . in the summer."

143

There certainly wasn't any winter tennis or baseball in Cincinnati. Tony thought the matter through, and decided on tennis. He played in his first tournament at ten years of age. From boys' competition he moved steadily into the junior tournaments, and it was there that he recorded his first important victory.

In the development of any tennis player, there are milestones along the way—triumphs that add confidence to skill and lead to greater glories.

"The first big one for me was the National Junior Indoor Championship," Tony recalled. "I was favored to win it the year before and, when I didn't, it was quite a mental setback." The setback was wiped away when Tony took the crown in 1948, his first important championship; the first real title he had ever won.

The second milestone, and the one that really triggered Tony toward the high atmosphere of world class competition, came two years later. Tony's mentor, Billy Talbert, was back for Cincinnati's Tri State Championships. This time, the pupil beat the teacher. In a gruelling final match that went the full five sets, Tony took the championship from a man regarded as one of the best players of his time.

"It was quite a moment," Tony reminisced. "I know Billy gave it everything he had, but I honestly believe he was as happy as I was over my winning.

"I can't give Bill Talbert enough credit for what he did for me over a long period of time. As a friend, and in life in general. I don't think there is anyone short of my own family to whom I owe more than Bill."

Indeed, it was Talbert's strong continuing interest that made that 1950 Tri-State title arrive as soon as it did.

In 1949, Trabert had not yet made the top twenty in American tennis rankings. Talbert was instrumental in getting Tony included among United States players in a European tennis tour in the spring of 1950. The experience sharpened his game tremendously, the triumph of Talbert in the Tri-State being just a part of it. When the year 1950 ended, Tony Trabert was the number three ranked player in the United States.

By now Tony was also playing collegiate tennis for the University of Cincinnati, and added the 1951 National Intercollegiate title to his growing cupboard of trophies. The peak years of Tony Trabert's tennis career were at hand.

In 1953 he became the number one player in the United States, winning the coveted National Championship at Forest Hills, New York. Two years later he became the best in the world, roaring through the venerated Wimbledon Championship, beating Denmark's Kurt Nielsen in the finals, without the loss of a set. His game plan for that final match was intriguing. It underlined the analytical ability which had joined up with his booming serve and flawless shot-making.

Nielsen used a continental grip, which gave him a vulnerable forehand. He compensated with aggressiveness, charging to the net at the earliest opportunity. The Trabert plan was to direct his attack to the unimpressive forehand of the Dane. He would also take something off the speed of his service, hitting his first serve in most of the time with accurate placement, and keep Nielsen from coming to the net on the return. Tony would take the net away from him by charging to it on his own serve, as well as on his return of Nielsen's service.

Two psychological ploys were also used. One was to play in very close on Nielsen's serve, saying without words that Nielsen couldn't hit the ball hard enough to move him back. The other was to hit the ball very high on lobs: Give him time to think about it, while he's waiting for it to come down. It worked. Nielsen missed many overhead smashes that ordinarily would have been put away.

The thinking paid off handsomely. Tony Trabert became the first player in 17 years to win the Wimbledon crown without the loss of a set.

Now Trabert was much in demand and his tournament commitments were almost without interruption. A shoulder went lame just three weeks before the United States team, with Tony and Vic Seixas the key members, was due to defend the Davis Cup against Australia that it had won 1954.

There was some feeling that enforced rest caused by the injury was the best thing that could have happened to him, but it was not to be. The shoulder trouble disappeared, but the absence from play and practice took the sharpness from his game. Australia won the first two singles matches and needed only the doubles win to wrap up the cup and take it back to Australia.

Lew Hoad and Rex Hartwig teamed against Trabert and Seixas. Hoad's blazing, flat serve had become the talk of the competition. His first was an explosive blur that only Trabert had any consistency in even returning. For this reason, Tony played the key left side.

In the final set, the Australians needed one more game to win. The game had moved from deuce to advantage, Australia. Hoad was serving, and the expectation was that he would ease off to get the first serve in. Hoad gambled instead. The serve was pure flame, and it was in. Probably no one but Trabert could have gotten a racquet on it, but it wasn't enough. Hoad followed with a perfect drop volley, and the match was over.

The disheartening loss of the Davis Cup didn't stall Tony. He went back to work on his interrupted game, got it back to the top for the Nationals at Forest Hills . . . and won, beating both Lew Hoad and Ken Rosewall along the way, without losing a set.

There was nothing left to achieve in the amateur tennis game. Tony Trabert was the best. Jack Kramer had started his touring professional troupe, and Tony was his next target.

The offer was a $75,000 guarantee, and Trabert turned pro.

This was the only area of higher achievement available. If Tony failed, he was out of the game. And fail he did.

Tony Trabert versus Pancho Gonzales was the headline attraction of the barnstorming troupe. Trabert couldn't acquire in weeks, the years of experience Gonzales had in the accelerated bounce of the indoor court. At one time, Pancho had a lead over Trabert of 32 victories to nine.

When the year finished up with the 1956 Professional Tennis Championship, Trabert lost to Pancho Segura. And it was over.

A vanquished Trabert was no longer a drawing card. While he still had championship ability, he had cut his amateur ties, and, as his mentor, Billy Talbert, wrote for *Sports Illustrated,* "He had no place to go."

WHERE IS HE NOW?

Tony Trabert has made a circuitous tour through the world of business to get back into tennis. It has been a year and a half since he left Burlington Industries to open the Tony Trabert Tennis Camp, in Ojai, California. Tony leases the Thatcher School there, and runs three-week sessions during the summer for boys and girls nine to 18 years old, teaching beginners and advanced players the fine points of tennis.

"I've wanted to get back into tennis, and I'm glad to be back," says Tony. "I went into business so I could get a better understanding of it, so when I got into a tennis business of my own I'd know something about running it."

Tony is married for the second time. His wife, Emeryl, is an accomplished airplane pilot. They met when Tony began taking flying lessons. It was quite a fortuitous meeting at that.

Emeryl had one try at the famed Powder Puff Derby and wound up in the harrowing position of running out of gas in mid-air, one minute from the Tucson airport. She swooped her dead airplane under some low hanging power lines and got it safely landed on a dirt road.

There are two Trabert children by his previous marriage. Michael, 15 years old, and Brooke, 13, live with their mother in Salt Lake City.

As Tony scans back over his tennis career, his great regret is the late arrival of open tennis. The opportunity for professionals to play now in tournament tennis along with amateurs is something he wishes had been around when he wrapped it up.

There are many who look upon the advent of the professional as a threat to the importance of the Davis Cup competition, to which Tony replies: "The thinking has to change. When Dwight Davis established the Cup, it was meant to establish tennis supremacy by a nation. He did not specify amateur or professional, since there was no professional tennis then. It was meant to match the best players of a country, and it still should."

Trabert went on: "In the last couple of years, they have permitted non-contract professionals to play in the Davis Cup. To me this is a farce. Arthur Ashe was making as much money as some of the guys under contract. He was permitted to play and Rod Laver was not.

"I think this was done because it permitted certain countries, and the U.S. was one of them, to have their better players participate. Perhaps they shouldn't be paid to play in it, but the best players should be allowed to play."

Tony Trabert today is 41 years old. His tennis now is for fun, although he did come back for the first National Open at Forest Hills. He teamed up in doubles with old partner Vic Seixas, just to say he had played in it.

DUSTY RHODES

Four Games in 1954

IN 1954 THE CLEVELAND Indians had won more games than any American League team in history and were a prohibitive 22-1 favorite to whip Leo Durocher's New York Giants in the World Series.

What resulted was as shattering an upset as World Series history has ever seen. The Giants not only won it; they won it in four straight, laughing along through scores of 5 to 2, 3 to 1, 6 to 2 and 7 to 4.

Durocher has never been accused of being a push-button manager, but he had the button to push that brought it off.

The name on the button was Dusty Rhodes.

Dusty Rhodes was a fun-loving, hard-drinking, curfew-violating, itinerant ball player who wandered in and out of the minor leagues, and who cared little where he played, as long as the game was on.

He was Leo's pinch hitter, and, as a pinch hitter, the 1954 Series turned him into one of America's genuine folk heroes.

During the seven game series, Durocher pushed that button seven times in the quick dispatch of the so-called unbeatable Indians. Once, Dusty Rhodes drew a walk.

In his six official at-bats, Rhodes hammered our four clutch hits, two of them home runs, and drove in seven runs. The entire Cleveland entourage was to score only two more than that in the series.

The "book" on Rhodes was that he was a good fast-ball hitter. Throw him the change-up.

A year earlier, the Giants had made an exhibition tour to Japan. On his first turn at bat, Rhodes struck out. The Japanese pitcher got him on a change.

Rhodes came back to the bench muttering: "Godammit, if I was playin' at the North Pole some stinkin' Eskimo would pop his head out of an igloo and say, 'Can't hit the change.' "

Apparently an Indian sticking his head out of the wigwam was something else. In the first game against Cleveland, Rhodes won it with a three-run homer off Bob Lemon. He hit a change-of-pace.

In the second game, Dusty singled in the tying run in the fifth inning, then clinched it with a home run in the seventh. The homer came off a knuckle ball, which is a change-up of sorts.

The clubhouse quotes were many following that fourth game that ended the series, but there was only one from Dusty Rhodes: "Where's the champagne?"

The New York Giants owner, Horace Stoneham, has established some notable marks in the area of conviviality and he discovered in Rhodes someone who could go the route. It resulted in an edict to the manager unheard of in baseball. There was never to be a curfew imposed on Rhodes, or his kindred spirit, roommate Bobby Hofman.

"We were on that trip to Japan," remembered Dusty. "We stopped over in Manila. I had been out with some battle-axe and got back to the hotel about 4:30 in the morning. There's about 20 messages waitin' for me from Stoneham saying he wanted to see me. So I go up to see him. There's this big room with a big long table. There must be 99 bottles half full of scotch sittin' on it and there is Stoneham in a corner all by himself."

" 'Where you been?' he says."

"I figured he wouldn't know what time it was so I told him I just got up."

Stoneham suggested Dusty join him in a drink. "I'll have a VO and Seven-Up," said Rhodes.

"VO and Seven-Up?" the owner shouted. "If you're going to play on this club you'll drink scotch."

"In that case," replied Rhodes, "just fix me a double."

A bond was formed.

"You know that hacienda he's got out in Phoenix?" Dusty tells. "He's got a house there all to hisself where he can invite people and do his drinkin', which he can do far into the evening. The only way you could get away from Stoneham was to pass out.

"Got so we'd wait until he went to the bathroom, and we'd all pile out the windows and the doors, and when Stoneham came out, there would be nobody there.

"He solved that . . . he took the door off the bathroom. When he's drinkin', *no*body leaves. Oh, I tell you. I've had two or three good days with him."

Dusty's square name is James Lamar Rhodes. He was born in Mathews, Alabama, May 13, 1927.

His serious baseball, as serious as it ever got, began in the Kitty League with Hopkinsville in 1947. He became instantly established as a hitter (.326) and a blithe spirit.

His hitting intrigued the Chicago Cubs and they bought his contract. The association was a short one, the Cubs feeling his after-hours escapades were the greater of his skills.

Rhodes rattled around from team to team. He recalls stopping briefly in Des Moines, where Charley Root was managing.

"Charley had three rules for his club. Never drinkin' in the hotel you're stayin' in; no women in the hotel; and if he says twelve o'clock curfew, he means it.

"So there I am with another guy, and we're about 40 miles from the hotel and it's one o'clock in the morning. Ain't no way we're gonna make that twelve o'clock curfew; so I says, why don't we just stay out the rest of the night and we'll walk in about 9:30 in the morning?

"So about that time we get out of a cab in front of the hotel and look around there's not a soul in the lobby . . . I thought. We kind of eased over to the elevator and I hear a guy holler, 'Hey, Rhodes!' It is Root.

"So I says, 'Why hello there Skip, how are you this mornin'?'

"He says, 'Where in hell were you?'

"I popped back real quick, 'Why, we was just comin' back from early Mass,' forgettin' it wasn't Sunday."

Two days later Dusty was on his way to Grand Rapids, Michigan. "I made five clubs that year," Rhodes said with a chuckle. "I would have made the sixth, but the time ran out."

In 1952, Rhodes spent the season batting .347 for Nashville. The New York Giants had a working agreement with Nashville, and paid $25,000 for Dusty's contract.

When he reported to the Giants in 1953, either by the rarest of understanding or most remarkable bit of luck, Rhodes was assigned a roommate named Bobby Hofman, now a coach with the Cleveland Indians. They were two of a kind and the curfew exemption coming down from Horace Stoneham made them historic.

Dusty laughed remembering it. "Called us the Gold Dust Twins. . . . We was always together. We used to have some balls, I tell you. He'd hit 'em right; I'd hit 'em left.

"When I first came up I was a country boy, and we were in Philadelphia at the Warwick Hotel. You know that place. You order food up, and a hamburger costs you a couple of dollars.

"So Bobby says, 'Roomie, there's no need for us going out tonight. Let's have dinner sent up to the room.'

"So I think this boy is all right. Here I am a country boy playing 'B' ball all my life and all of a sudden I'm in the big time. I says, 'What the hell, roomie, why not?'

"So he called down and asked the *chef* to come up and I think this kid's all right. First thing I know he's ordering all the stuff I can't even pronounce, let alone know what it was.

"Just about the time the guy walks in with the food, Bobby runs in the outhouse and it costs me forty-seven dollars. I don't want the guy to think I was cheap so I tipped him two dollars.

"I got back at him about a month later in St. Louis. This time I did the ordering and when Bobby started to pull the same trick I stepped in front of him and said, 'Oh no, roomie . . . this time it's my turn to go!'

"Bobby used to say, 'You know, if we had done it at the Waldorf it woulda cost us a hundred dollars.' I made it a point never to stay at the Waldorf."

Thoughts rolled back to Dusty's dramatic domination of that '54 World Series. Came the obvious query of it being his biggest thrill.

"To be honest with you," said Dusty, "I wasn't all that excited about it. You know, the hardest job was tryin' to get there. It's tough ridin' those buses, you know."

He was to ride them again. "It's not so bad when you're going up, but it's hell goin' down.

"I was sent down in 1958 to Phoenix. We won the pennant there and I went back to the Giants in '59. We almost won another one, but we missed by a couple of games, and that was the end for me. I played three more years in the minors, then I quit."

Does he ever see Leo Durocher any more?

"No," answered Dusty. "I went out to the ball park once, but Leo was home sick and I missed him.

"That old sonuvabitch, he's the best manager I ever played for. I think he's the best manager in baseball. I understand he talks quite a bit about me once in a while.

"I would have liked to see that big ad Mr. Wrigley put in the papers when they was trying to get Leo fired. You got to realize Wrigley is nobody's fool, and the Cubs didn't draw a million people, till Leo got there, for how many years? Twenty-five?

"Wrigley's a business man. If Leo had had a couple of relief pitchers, he might have won it all the way.

"We've had our differences, Leo and I, but deep down I still say he's the greatest manager that ever lived."

WHERE IS HE NOW?

For Dusty Rhodes, home port is New York. He has a son, Jeffrey Lamar, who is 11, a daughter, Helene, aged 13, and his often sorely-tested wife, Mildred.

"Believe it or not, I'm on the tug boats. That's quite a switch, ain't it?

"Stoneham brought me out to San Francisco a couple years ago for an old-timers game," Dusty recalled with a smile. "Sent me and Millie a couple of round trip tickets and got us a suite in a hotel."

Dusty laughed harder now. "I got out with Stoneham and his son Pete, who is also a good friend of mine, and, you know, I forgot all about my wife being in the hotel. When I got back the next morning she was gone. Went back to New York."

The laughter grew to a guffaw. "You know, I was so shook up I stayed another week."

When the rambling Rhodes finally did make it back to New York and walked in the door, his opening line was a classic!

"Well. . . . How'd it go, dear?"

Dusty is still quick to respond to any suggestion that sounds like it can carry a little fun with it. It's how he wound up working on the tug boats.

A friend of his knew a man who owned five or six tugs, and also a motel in Florida. They were heading down there for a week or so and asked Dusty if he'd like to go along.

"Well, yes indeed," was the quick reply. And off they went.

The pleasure-seeking became marred with a business crisis. Franklin Reinauer, the tugboat owner, was getting some flack from the union about putting oilers on his tugs. He asked Dusty if he'd like a job.

Dusty surveyed the invitation to steady work. "I told him, 'Hell-l-l-l no.' But he said, 'Dusty you won't have to *do* anything.' And I said, 'I'll take it.' "

A week later they were back in New York and Rhodes was an oiler on a tug.

Dusty doesn't get around to the ball parks much anymore. When Bobby Hofman, or Marv Grissom, or Alvin Dark get to town, he'll search them out and for a while the old times are the best times once again.

Dusty Rhodes passed through the waters of baseball without leaving much of a wake, but for that one brief four-game span of the 1954 World Series, he was the biggest name in the game.

ALTHEA GIBSON

"I Was Born to Be a Female Athlete"

THE YEAR WAS 1950. The color barrier in the truly lily-white game of tennis was broken. It was broken, resoundingly and finally, by an invitation to the first black player in history to compete in the National Championships at Forest Hills, in Long Island, New York, the prestigious mecca for all that is tennis in the United States.

The pressure-laden responsibility of being the "first" to break the racial barrier in sports fell not on the stalwart shoulders of a Jackie Robinson, but on those of a tall, skinny, scared and nervous girl. She was 23 years old and her name was Althea Gibson.

Her arrival at Forest Hills was the end result of compassionate and dedicated efforts by the American Tennis Association, the black players' governing body, and the United States Lawn Tennis Association.

Now it had come, and on August 28, 1950, just three days after Althea Gibson's 23rd birthday, Miss Gibson was the winner in her first match at Forest Hills. She disposed of Great Britain's Barbara Knapp in straight sets, 6-2 and 6-2.

Here, the competition level accelerated sharply. Althea's second match was against the great Californian, Louise Brough. Miss Brough, winner of both Wimbledon and U.S. National titles, was eons ahead of Althea in competitive experience at the highest levels.

It was a moment of high drama. The magnitude of a possible Gibson victory here, against an opponent of this stature, was almost shattering to the senses. Althea was visibly nervous as the match began, and Miss Brough quickly ran through the first set, an easy 6-1 victory. Then the competitive class of Althea surfaced. The tennis qualities that had brought the tennis Fathers to her as the player to make this historic break-through began to show through.

The Gibson game was power. Her height and strength combined in a booming service. She could volley brilliantly and with power. The low bounces off the grass at Forest Hills were not suited to her ground strokes. To win, she had to force the attack.

Althea settled down in the second set and unleashed a brand of power tennis the Nationals hadn't seen since Alice Marble. She almost blew Louise off the court with an over-powering 6-3 triumph to square the match.

They were playing on a side court just outside the main stadium at Forest Hills. The Pinkerton guards had to close off the area as more than 2,000 spectators overflowed into every possible vantage point as the word spread of this fabulous upset in the making.

Miss Brough regained her composure sufficiently to win the first three games of the final set before Althea turned on her devastating power to break the California's service three times and take a 7-6 lead.

But the Lord, in His wisdom, blunts the hopes of black and white alike. In the crackling excitement of this remarkable turning point in the match, the skies, which had been growing progressively blacker, opened up. A violent thunderstorm, fingered by frightening bolts of lightning, delivered a deluge that forced the match to be called.

Louise Brough appeared clearly beaten. The courage and power of this unknown Negro girl had left her obviously tired and bereft of any appearance of poise. As the match was halted, the press descended upon the shelter Althea sought and here again the newness of the situation worked to her disadvantage.

Self-appointed "protectors" attempted to keep the reporters at a distance. Loud and bitter words were exchanged, and the unfettered acrimony of the incident reduced Miss Gibson to a state of near shock.

The resumption of the match on the following day was anticlimactic. The near accomplishment of beating so famed a player as Louise Brough made for a sleepless night for Althea. A well-rested Louise had regained her strength and poise, and she ran out the set and the match with three straight winning games.

It was to be seven years before Althea was to win her nation's tennis crown at Forest Hills and, by remarkable coincidence, it would be this same Louise Brough who would be her opponent in the finals. That it took that long was surprising to the game's experts and, at times, a maddening frustration to Althea.

Althea Gibson was born August 25, 1927 in what could only be a dot on a very large map. Silver, South Carolina, had a listed population of only fifty, and number 51 was not to remain there long. The Gibson family moved north, to the teeming Harlem district of New York when Althea was two. Her father was a garage mechanic. Along with three sisters and a brother, she called home a walk-up tenement on 143rd Street.

In Harlem, playing is done in the streets, and some of the lesser thoroughfares are blocked off to provide recreational areas.

Althea's first game was basketball and she was good at it. With a little urging, she will confide it is still the favorite of her childhood games. But along the way she came upon paddle tennis, played with a rubber ball and paddles. The important advantage in that locale was that it required much less space than tennis courts.

It was her excellence in this game that caught the eye of Buddy Walker, a Police Athletic League supervisor. Walker got her a tennis racquet, set her to practicing against the wall of a handball court, and arranged for her to join Harlem's tennis center, the Cosmopolitan Club. Here, she got instruction on the finer points of the game, entered her first tournament at the age of 16, and won it. As a result she became New York State champion of the Negro American Tennis Association.

It was clear that here was a talent that would go far beyond the limited activities of the NATA. The color line was already breaking down in tennis by 1950, but it was a nibbling at the fringes. There could never be a thorough breakthrough until a black player appeared on the symbolic grass of Forest Hills.

The American Tennis Association was the body which supplied the United States Lawn Tennis Association with the names of players deemed deserving of invitation to the National Championships. Said Arthur E. Francis of the ATA: "The USLTA does not know the quality of our players. They depend on us and our recommendations. We wanted to be sure we could offer a player who would be worthy of competing."

The heads of the ATA and USLTA, both understanding of, and sympathetic to the need for the breakthrough, began secret discussions on its manner of achievement, one that would be fair to the stature of the championships and to the player.

When it was decided that Althea Gibson would be the one to be the Jackie Robinson of tennis, the USLTA took over the role of carefully mapping the tournament schedule that would get her there.

The National Clay Courts championships at River Forest, Illinois, was the first breakthrough in Althea's movement outside Negro tennis. They accepted her entry, helped by the strong recommendation of former British tennis star Charles Hare, and Althea reached the quarter-finals where she lost to Doris Hart.

The next big step, and one filled with misgivings, was to request an invitation to the Eastern grass court championships. There was understandably an expectation of opposition here and there along the way. When Althea's entry was accepted by the Eastern Lawn Tennis Association, Arthur Francis was moved to write:

"In these days of racial and religious restrictions it is very difficult to get people to think in terms of fairness, much more to act fairly, and your outstanding contribution of justice and fairness, your unafraid declaration that merit be recognized as one of the most important qualifications for an opportunity to play in your tournament, inspires us with the belief in the doctrine of the fatherhood of God and the brotherhood of man.

"Believe me when I say that members of my racial group, and of all groups who believe in fair play, will be everlastingly grateful to you and your colleagues who thought as you did. . . ."

Althea was now under the guidance of former tennis star Sarah Palfrey Danzig. To the teacher, for a player to reach the Eastern grass courts was a milestone development. Althea had never played on grass, and with her acceptance in this tournament Miss Danzig was able to call upon the president of the West Side Tennis Club at Forest Hills, Mr. Ralph Gatcomb, and request an apportunity for Althea to utilize their facilities for practice.

"We'll be glad to have her," was his response.

The first practice session with Mrs. Danzig was an eye opener. Althea's big serve, her good volley and smash were ideally suited to the grass surface. Her still developing ground strokes were not quite so vulnerable as on clay. The lower bounces on the grass were somewhat troublesome to a player of her height, but her ability to power her way to the net seemed likely to more than offset them.

She reached the second round in the Eastern grass tournament before losing to Helen Perez, but by now she had clearly demonstrated her ability, and that she was worthy of national competition.

She received her entry blank for Forest Hills.

Then came the long, lonely, frustrating seven years. Seven years to achieve the qualities and dexterity to become a winner.

It was not totally depressing; not without its moments of reward. Althea's tennis won her a scholarship to Florida A & M, where she majored in health and physical education and graduated with top honors.

In 1955, under State Department sponsorship, Althea was sent on an international tour, a scheduled junket of tennis competition that, in perspective, provided the needed turning point.

In that summer of 1955, Althea was ready to quit tennis. For five years she hadn't improved to the extent that people thought she would. She had achieved ranking in the country's top ten, but never in the upper reaches of the list.

She was growing deep into her twenties. The years were slipping by all too fast. She began to feel it was time to start thinking of a reliable way of earning a living.

Althea was a singer of ability. Her PAL mentor from her paddle tennis days was a band leader, and she often sat in with his band in their Harlem night club engagements. Perhaps this talent, embellished by her tennis name, was a way to go. Then again, her college degree could possibly move her into teaching or recreational work.

She was, admittedly, a bit frightened when she could not properly deliver on the promise many recognized in that memorable near-triumph against Louise Brough.

The State Department tour seemed to settle things down, to bring on the realization that she was not just another player, but a star. It is a special confidence that comes only from an inner belief that one is better and more important, that the others know it.

The new Althea was proclaimed at Wimbledon in July of 1957. The previous year, fresh from a string of 16 tournament victories from India to England, on the afore-mentioned government-sponsored tour, she had gotten to the quarter-finals before losing to Shirley Fry. Despite the loss, Althea's new-found confidence was surfacing. "I will be back here next year," she said.

Now it was next year—1957. Althea's toughest hurdle came in her semi-final match.

Periodically, women's tennis produces the sensational schoolgirl, a youngster who explodes on the scene with dramatic victories over the older, veteran players. Such a one had arrived at Wimbledon.

Christine Truman had become the special darling of the Wimbledon crowds. A British 16-year-old making her first appearance at the famed Centre Court, she had electrified the pundits by knocking out England's top-seeded Shirley Bloomer to get to the semi-finals.

Despite the partisan crowd, the 16-year-old Miss Truman never had a chance against Althea. The Gibson power attack was overwhelming and terminal. The center court crowd found nothing to cheer for, and watched the slaughter in near total silence.

It was more of the same in the finals against Darlene Hard; and Althea was finally to walk to the center of the court and receive the Wimbledon trophy from Elizabeth, Queen of England.

Small wonder that this time she had no qualms about Forest

Hills. "I felt no fear of any of the players there. I knew if I played my game the way I should, I could beat anybody."

Althea had come home from her Wimbledon triumph to a Manhattan ticker tape parade. She had moved on to win the National Clay Courts Championship. She came to the National Championships as the top seed.

She slashed past Karol Fageros, Elizabeth Lester, Shiela Armstrong, Mary Hawton and Dorothy Knode to get to the finals.

Her opponent for the crown was the same who eliminated Althea in her historic Forest Hills debut seven years earlier, former U.S. and Wimbledon champion, Louise Brough. Althea ran her off 6-3, 6-2 and in doing so had gone through the entire tournament without losing a set.

At Forest Hills, Althea received her National Championship Trophy from the Vice-President of the United States, Richard Nixon.

WHERE IS SHE NOW?

Althea Gibson is now Mrs. William A. Darben, wife of a New Jersey businessman.

Althea moved from tennis into professional golf, where she is a sporadic player on the women's professional tour. She has yet to win, although she tied for first at Columbus, Ohio, in 1971 before losing in a playoff.

What is remarkable is that she could move so effortlessly into professional golf. "I had not played golf during my tennis career more than maybe four or five times before I began taking it up seriously," she once remarked. Yet, she was, and is, good enough to compete on the tour.

Until recently, Althea had been employed by the Essex County, New Jersey, Park Commission in charge of recreational work. In this, she was not involved with tennis, or any specific sport, but in overseeing a general program of women's and girls' activities.

"It was very interesting work, but other opportunities presented themselves and I am finally getting back to tennis," she tells. "I am now the Director of Programs for the Valley View Racquet Club in North Vale, New Jersey.

"We are building six new indoor courts and I will be the director and head professional. Actually, this may be an opportunity to enable me to play more golf. Since ours is an indoor operation, I expect it will be more active in winter than in summer, and once I have installed my staff of assistants, I hope to have a little more time during the golf tour to play in more tournaments.

"I like golf very much, but I would like to win. Being a winner and a champion made tennis much more enjoyable and I hope that through natural ability plus some diligent work and practice I may be able to win a tournament before I put the clubs down."

With her thoughts turned back to tennis, a rueful observation on the timing of life is of interest:

"It has been said many times that I was born too soon, and I agree. It is just too bad that open tennis didn't come along while I was reigning as champion.

"Now tennis has become like professional golf, and I think it is wonderful. I have always said that any athlete who has devoted all his life to a particular sport should be able to make a living out of it, after they have accomplished the skills and the attitudes and put so much devotion into it.

"It certainly would have made things much simpler for me had I been able to make a living playing tennis."

With the new opportunities open tennis is providing, Althea is enthusiastically contemplating a junior development program at the Valley View club. "We hope to develop a youth tennis program and try and stimulate interest in young people to come in and learn to play the game of tennis," she exudes. "I will be instructing, because I want to see the development of young players coming up.

"Not only in tennis, I like to see them develop in any sport that is now in existence at a professional level. They need a good amateur program first to sort of prepare themselves and I think if we have a good clinic going and same some kind of stimulation for the young people it could possibly develop some future champions.

"I am a real believer in sports. I love it. I think I was born to be a female athlete."

If Althea Gibson can instill some of her devotion and skill into the youngsters of New Jersey, tennis won't have to worry about the quality of future champions.

CARMEN BASILIO

The Canastota Onion Farmer

IN BOXING'S TELEVISION heyday of the 1950's, no boxer was more in demand than the unsinkable Carmen Basilio, who reached for and won both the welterweight and middleweight crowns.

Basilio came wading in through every round, the epitome of the battler who loved to fight. He would hit and be hit. He was short on finesse, long on courage, and devastating with either hand.

His scarred and craggy features looked like they should be cast in bronze and titled "The Gladiator."

Carmen was of a family of ten children. His father was an onion farmer in Canastota, New York. As a boy of nine or ten, Carmen prevailed upon his father to allow him to stay up and listen to the broadcast of the fight in which Joe Louis challenged Jimmy Braddock for the world's heavyweight championship.

Braddock was the idol of young Carmen, and when Louis knocked him out for the championship, "I cried," says Basilio. "I vowed then I was going to grow up to be a boxer and win the championship from Joe Louis."

Basilio was never to become a heavyweight, but he was to become a champion.

Boxing began for Carmen as a member of his high school boxing team, continuing through a tour of duty in the Marine Corps. He came out of the service in 1947, had a brief fling as an amateur and in 1948 turned professional.

These were dramatic times for boxing. It was well along on its decline already, though few yet realized it. The vast array of depression-spawned boxers hadn't aged enough yet to depart the scene. There were sufficient numbers to people the rings of three weekly television shows. But new faces were scant. The post-war prosperity had sharply depleted the ranks of those youngsters who would accept the ordeal of training for the low financial rewards of the beginning boxer.

Thus it was that any crowd-pleasing boxer who could win was likely to advance quickly to the highly profitable television appearances.

Carmen Basilio moved well in these times. He was the totally honest fighter who gave completely of himself. He was a man of deep character. He was devoted to his wife, Kay, who had solved a difficult family situation by bringing her sister's two sons into his home, adopting them, and raising them as their own.

Boxing was his life. He loved it. He loved the hours in the gym; he loved the miles on the road. He never stepped into the ring in less than perfect condition.

Carmen was dissatisfied with his first management relationship, and once that agreement expired, he hooked on with Joe Netro and John DeJohn. With these as co-managers, Basilio stormed the heights.

DeJohn was from a boxing family. His brothers, Ralph, Carmen and Mike were all notable fighters. John never went into the ring himself, but was a superb instructor and exactly what Basilio needed.

Joe Netro handled the business end of the team, and had the connections to get meaningful opponents.

The three moved quickly up the rungs of boxing's ladder and, in 1953, they secured a welterweight title shot against the champion, Kid Gavilan.

It was the rapier against the broadsword, and the smooth and skillful Gavilan felt little cause for concern against the "Canastota Onion Farmer" who would take so many punches in his effort to land one.

It was so tough a showing against the seemingly invincible Gavilan that Basilio was to wait two long years before another shot at the title would open up. Two years of fighting anyone he could, wherever he could.

When Tony DeMarco slipped past him and won the welterweight championship by beating Johnny Saxton in a date Basilio should have had, the press started labeling Carmen the uncrowned champion.

Where Gavilan, then Saxton both had ducked Basilio, DeMarco wouldn't, and he accepted the Basilio challenge for June 10, 1955 in Syracuse.

They were to fight twice, these two, and those so fortunate as to witness the encounters saw two of the most savage and thrilling bouts the ring has ever known.

These were two hitters. They didn't clinch, they didn't hold, they didn't stall. Each round was a full three minutes of furious punching.

Now, on this June night in Syracuse, DeMarco was out to prove his championship was no arrangement. He slammed into Basilio with either hand, drawing blood around the eyes and mouth. Basilio was relentless. Taking two to give one, he plodded on after his man.

The crowd, which crushed into the municipal auditorium in what had become Carmen's hometown, were on their feet through every round.

For nine rounds the two fought on practically even terms. In the tenth, Basilio powered a shot that knocked DeMarco senseless. Even when the bell interrupted the count, there were none who could believe that the game Boston Italian would answer the bell for the eleventh.

Somehow he did, and stayed on his feet through an onslaught that defies description. Now DeMarco's nose was broken, his puffed eyes peering out through slits. He hooked and crossed and jabbed at a target he scarcely could see, while his head swiveled and snapped as Basilio raked him with every punch he could throw.

Into the twelfth round they went, but halfway through it referee Harry Kessler stepped between the fighters to halt what was now, for Tony DeMarco, a lost cause.

Carmen Basilio was the Welterweight Champion of the World.

This was a time of scandal headlines in boxing. Mob figures and International Boxing Club head James D. Norris were labeled a curious and unholy alliance. Frankie Carbo and Blinky Palermo were men to reckon with in landing the important and lucrative TV dates. Blinky managed a fighter named Johnny Saxton.

Palermo's unsavory reputation was such that the New York Boxing Commission would not issue him a license to manage a fighter in the state.

Illinois was something else. This was Jim Norris' home state, his control over all of boxing reaching out from his home base of the Chicago Stadium in a manner that earned the IBC the press sobriquet of "Octopus, Inc."

Illinois would okay Palermo and the IBC matched Saxton against Basilio in Chicago for the welterweight championship. It was set for March of 1956.

In the third round, Basilio landed flush with a devastating hook and Saxton crashed senseless to the canvas. He was saved by the bell and draped over the stool. His corner man, Whitey Bimstein, worked furiously to revive him. Then a curious thing happened.

"I don't know just what they did in his corner," says Basilio, "but when he came out for the fourth round he had a nice slit in his glove."

The slashed glove soon split open and the padding began to drop to the ring floor. The referee held up the fight and ordered a new glove brought out.

Again, curiously, it took fifteen minutes to locate a glove and bring it to the ring. By now Saxton was fully recovered.

For the rest of the fight, Saxton was on the run. He ran and Carmen chased, but Saxton could not be caught again.

There was no question as to the winner except, apparently, to the officials. They announced the decision to Johnny Saxton.

It was a blatantly bad decision and the crowd erupted in a cacophony of boos and catcalls. The days that followed brought a storm of editorial protest. But Johnny Saxton, with the help of a razor blade on his glove, was the welterweight champion.

For Carmen Basilio, it was a shattering moment. No matter how purely and honestly inept the decision may have been, to Carmen it was convincing evidence that the mob had moved in. All the things he had heard and read about Palermo were now the focal point in that unfair defeat.

All that remained of his hopes was the return match that had been made a part of the Saxton contract.

This time, with an assist from the New York Commission, the fight would be in Syracuse. Commission Chairman Julius Helfand, anxious to see justice get its chance, agreed to rescind the ban on Palermo in order that the fight could be staged under his jurisdiction.

"This was the most important fight of my life," said Basilio. "If I didn't win this one, I knew I would never have another chance for the championship. To me and my wife and family, this fight was everything."

The pre-fight publicity played heavily on the runaway tactics of Saxton in Chicago. The question of Johnny's courage was a daily issue and it apparently touched his pride.

Whatever the reason, Saxton stood and fought for the first two rounds. It was a mistake. Not that he didn't do well, for he did indeed, holding Basilio even in the first round and clearly winning the second. But, in the process he had taken some punishing body blows, and, from the third round on, both his zest and a good bit of his speed were gone.

He was once again the back-pedalling fighter of Chicago, now with his reflexes dulled and Basilio landing.

In the seventh round a Basilio smash almost tore Saxton's upper lip off, the blood draining into his mouth and sickening him in his stomach.

Basilio figured he would try to protect the cut, so Carmen ignored it, raining blows to the body and the head.

Somehow, he made it through the eighth round, but not the ninth. Staggering, out on his feet, Saxton was a punch away from oblivion when the referee stepped in and stopped it.

Carmen wept almost hysterically, so much had been riding on this fight. He reached through the ropes to embrace Kay, dashed across the ring to thank Commissioner Helfand, dropped on one knee and thanked God.

They were to fight again, rematches being a standard in a championship fight agreement. This time the fight was made for a more or less neutral setting, Cleveland, Ohio.

It didn't last two rounds. Basilio stormed through Saxton's attempts to jab and run, to belabor him with what was described as perhaps the most damaging body attack the ring has seen.

A sweeping left hook found Johnny's jaw and Saxton was counted out in 2:42 of the second round.

Now Basilio set his sights on bigger game. The middleweights looked vulnerable, with an aging Sugar Ray Robinson holding forth as champion for the third time.

Carmen's timing was right. In September of 1957 he defeated Robinson in Yankee Stadium for the 160-pound crown.

Rematch again. The fight was scheduled for Chicago on March 25, 1958. Sugar Ray looked upon Chicago as a lucky town. Basilio remembered it as something else.

For Robinson, it was a chance to regain the title for an unprecedented fourth time. But he was 37 years old and Basilio had clearly been the best in New York.

But age or no, Robinson was still a truly remarkable fighter, and the luck he had found in Chicago surfaced again.

In the early rounds, Sugar Ray landed a punch to Basilio's left eye with a 100-1 shot result. It hit and ruptured a small vein and the eye almost instantly puffed up and closed. From the sixth round on, it was a one-eyed fighter against the darting fists of Sugar Ray Robinson.

As the fight moved along its course, there was no longer a question of its outcome. Robinson steadily circled to his right, out of range of vision of Carmen's one good eye, pot-shotting to the blind side.

Basilio returned the championship to the man from whom he had won it.

WHERE IS HE NOW?

Carmen Basilio fought his last fight in April of 1961, a last challenge for the middleweight championship, then held by Paul Pender.

When Carmen emerged the loser, he called it a career.

Basilio had become good friends with Tommy Niland, athletic director and basketball coach at Syracuse's Le Moyne College.

The school had just completed an athletic center building, and was moving into a dedicated program for physical fitness for the students.

Niland asked Carmen if he would consider a post with Le Moyne as a physical instructor. Basilio accepted and has been there ever since.

He finds his boxing memories completely pleasurable. "I loved boxing. I loved every minute of it, the training, the roadwork, the people I met, and, of course, the fact I realized my ambition, to be a champion.

"I miss it."

He looked at the sport today: "There are some good boxers, but there aren't enough to make a division competitive. Boxing's decline is just a case of economics. When times are tough and jobs are scarce, a lot of kids show up in the gym to see if they can make a buck as a fighter. But they just don't feel it's worth the sacrifice when times are good. We had a lot of good fighters from the depression, but let's hope the country is never that bad off again.

"I do think it's a shame there are so few kids getting any boxing experience," Basilio continued. "I think boxing should be taught in the schools. I think boxing builds more genuine character than any sport there is.

"I don't know if I can say this right, but each boy is in there on his own. He doesn't have a substitute to look for on the bench. It gives him self-confidence, the ability to do things on his own. This is a great thing, to have boys able to think this way, to do things on their own without looking for help.

"You always feel fear going into a ring, but you learn to live with it, you learn to conquer it. This is where self-confidence comes in."

Carmen works out frequently and can still go a pretty good three or four rounds.

He trained his nephew, Billy Backus, to the welterweight championship, but he subsequently lost.

"Billy never liked to work with me in the ring," Carmen complained. "He said he couldn't bring himself to hit his uncle."

His adopted sons, Eddie and Freddie are now grown and married. Carmen has two grand-daughters, one from each.

Carmen Basilio, paragon of all the virile virtues of the squared circle: honest, dedicated, courageous and indefatiguable. He never presented anything but the totally trained boxer, and never gave less than all of himself in any fight.

BOBO OLSON

Born to Fight

THE YEARS HAVE mellowed Bobo Olson, even though they haven't been kind to him.

In his prime, as middleweight champion of the world, Olson was moody and abrasive, suspicious of others, and not an easy man to like. Today, he speaks with affection of his boxing career and what it meant to him. He feels he was badly used, financially, but displays no bitterness and, most of all, no regrets.

Bobo Olson was born on the 11th of July, 1928, in Honolulu, Hawaii. He displayed an early sensitivity, particular against any jocular reference to his impressive crop of freckles.

His response was physical; and he became a street fighter of some prominence. They had gangs even then, and though young Carl, which was Bobo's given name, was not the oldest member of his gang, his fighting ability made him the acknowledged leader.

By the time he was twelve years old, Bobo had discovered the boxing gym, and spent as much time as he could in its steamy confines polishing the raw skills of the streets.

Dado Marino, who was to become the world flyweight champion, was one of the first to see promise in the tough little youngster. Marino spent time with him, showing him the moves of the ring, and particularly bringing him to high proficiency in the art of feinting.

By the time he was 16, Bobo was beating some of the professionals who trained at the gym; and one Herbert Campos, a Honolulu dairyman with a side interest in boxing, decided this was a kid worth having.

Age 16 was too young to fight professionally, but Campos and Olson decided to circumvent this. To make him look older, Bobo went to a tatoo parlor and had tattoos applied to each arm. They forged an ID card which lied about his age, and Bobo Olson started his professional career. He had seven or eight fights before the ruse was discovered, and the authorities forced him to quit. He won them all.

Olson went back to the gym to keep training, and to pare his weight which had ballooned to 188 pounds. He had decided the middleweight division was his best area for success. It carried a 160-pound limit—a limit with which he was always to have trouble. Usually, he would steam off three or four pounds the morning of a fight, but in getting down to it he hardened his muscles and quickened his speed.

It was during this enforced period of gym-only activity that Bobo met his man of destiny.

Sid Flaherty was to become one of the most influential boxing managers in the United States. In boxing's television heyday of the 1950's and early 1960's, Flaherty's stable of boxers would grow to such numbers that he would supply as many as four or five main event fighters in any weight class simultaneously in arenas around the country.

Flaherty was in the United States Army at that time, stationed in Honolulu in charge of an Army physical education program.

When Flaherty was due to return to the mainland, he wanted Bobo to come along. With a fresh set of ID cards, Olson made the trip and renewed his professional boxing career in the San Francisco area. Again he put together a string of victories, and they were impressive. He knocked out 17 of the 18 opponents he met. But someone from the islands who knew the situation passed the word to the California Boxing Commission. Again they brought a stop to his under-aged career and sent him back to Honolulu.

But now he had a place to go and, in Sid Flaherty, a man who could move him along. Bobo maintained a steady training program in Hawaii, and finally reached his 18th birthday.

At that age, with written parental consent, he could enter the professional ring legitimately. The papers were signed and Olson was off once again to San Francisco.

Bobo picked up right where he left off. With Flaherty guiding him carefully through a steady upgrading of opponents, Bobo slammed his way through 24 consecutive victories.

They made their first grab for the brass ring.

It was far too early in his boxing life to meet the likes of Sugar Ray Robinson, but Bobo was impatient and Sugar Ray wore the crown. The challenge was issued and accepted, and the fight was made for Philadelphia.

As Bobo looks back on Robinson today he says: "There is no comparing this man. Pound for pound, he was the greatest fighter of any era. They talk of Mickey Walker and Harry Greb. Walker was tough, hard to hurt and could hit hard. Greb could take you out with one punch. Robinson could do this and box, too. He could weave and feint and beat you any way he had to. In his prime nobody could beat him. You made one mistake with Ray Robinson and you were out."

And out went Bobo Olson. Not as quickly as in some of his later meetings with Sugar Ray (he would fight him four times), but in a twelfth round ending to a bruising encounter.

After the kayo, Olson was kept out of action for six months before hitting the comeback trail.

Again he piled up an impressive string of consecutive triumphs, and again a chance at the middleweight championship opened for him. This time it would be a payday as well. In his abortive challenge of Sugar Ray, Robinson wound up keeping not only the crown, but most of the money as well. Olson had received just a little over $1,000.00 for the match.

But Robinson, feeling secure with his string of Harlem business investments, had retired. An elimination was set to fight for Sugar Ray's vacated crown. The final bout, the winner to be champion, brought Bobo Olson against Britain's Randy Turpin. The year was 1953.

"Of all my fights," says Bobo, "this is the one that stands out in my mind. It was a very tough fight. Turpin was an awkward fighter, and that made him very difficult to handle. He could hit hard with either hand; a very confusing style. I lost the first three or four rounds before I figured out the only way to fight him was to stay right on him. I knocked him down three times, but I couldn't keep him down and, finally, won it in a 15-round decision."

Bobo had made it. He was middleweight champion of the world. But already clouds were beginning to form.

Bobo had a quick eye for a pretty girl and found them readily available. His excursions brought on a tense relationship with his wife of that time, the former Helen Caveco. This was to lead to divorce, and a body blow to the financial well-being of this newly-crowned champion.

But, in the ring, 1954 was a high point. Bobo Olson was named "Fighter of the Year." His standout victories were an eleven-round TKO of France's Pierre Langlois and his impressive disposal of Kid Gavilan, a fast and skillful boxer.

In 1955, Olson and Flaherty accepted a match with the aging Archie Moore. Though the high riding Olson had no misgivings about stepping out of his weight class, it proved a mistake.

The fight was less than eight minutes old when Moore started a whistling left hook. Olson's hands were high, guarding either side of his face, but the punch slammed through that guard and crashed against his jaw. Moore landed a short right as Bobo started down, but it wasn't needed. Olson was counted out in the third round.

Bobo never seemed the same after that devastating hook, and the high point was to be proven by an unretired Ray Robinson. Sugar Ray had found his thinly-spread investments weren't all that solid, and he started a comeback.

It was not impressive. Robinson had shown nothing at all against Tiger Jones. Journeyman Rocky Castellani had knocked him down and Robinson had all he could do to last the distance.

It seemed to Olson an easy way to pick up a good payday from this once great fighter who now seemed so thoroughly over the hill. After Robinson's problems with Tiger Jones, Olson had whipped Jones easily. Robinson was accepted as a challenger and the fight was made for Chicago in mid-December of 1955.

Olson was installed a prohibitive favorite. The odds were laid at 17 to 5, and it was very close to an "out" match with the bookmakers. Robinson was now 35 years old, while Olson, at 27, was at his physical peak. The adage "they never come back" seemed in no danger of being disproved that night. Only one acknowledgeable voice, that of former champion Willie Pep, ventured to disagree.

"Don't forget, Robinson took him *two* out of *two,*" said Pep. "You got a big edge on a guy when you know you set him down twice. I give Ray a helluva chance."

The experts conceded Robinson might flash some of his old speed for a few rounds, but that the plodding Olson would blunt him, wear him down, and eventually put him away.

Olson never had the opportunity.

In the second round, Robinson swung into gear. A right—left —right combination delivered with smoking speed, the big hit a superb right uppercut, turned the lights out for Bobo Olson. Sugar Ray Robinson had brought off an incredible comeback! He was once again middleweight champion of the world.

Mrs. Olson, divorcing him, and now with four children to support, attached Bobo's purse.

Olson had been operating under the notion he was financially secure. It was rapidly becoming apparent to him that such was not the case, and a rift was developing between Olson and his mentor, Sid Flaherty.

Flaherty and Olson had been a perfect ring team. Sid was a master at analyzing an opponent and developing the overall strategy. He would flash hand signals to Bobo triggering the moment for the pre-determined moves. Olson had the capability of executing the strategy, and the implicit faith to follow it.

In the rematch, the figuring between them was how to keep it going so the age factor would work for Bobo. The game plan was to wear Robinson down in the early rounds by clinching, leaning on him, body-punching, and, above all, protecting the Olson jaw.

Sugar Ray waited to see how Olson would fight before deciding on his own strategy. The first rounds made it apparent Robinson had to find a way to open Olson up, and he decided the way was to beat him at his own game.

Robinson played possum in the third round. He deliberately slowed his punches. He began to act the weary fighter. He allowed Bobo to land punches he ordinarily could have blocked.

Olson took the bait. In the fourth round Bobo abandoned the clinching and leaning that had gone before and came out swinging away. Robinson found the opening he had waited for. He slammed a sickening right into the pit of the stomach. A left hook that couldn't have traveled more than eight inches was on its way as Olson's guard came down. It splattered against his jaw and Bobo was kayoed again.

By all logic, Bobo Olson was through. It was time to hang 'em up. But he found he couldn't afford it. His financial problems were now acute. He was to come to a final parting with Sid Flaherty in 1957, and fight another ten long years to try and pay off a staggering bill for back taxes.

"Sid Flaherty was like a father to me," says Bobo. "And I trusted him completely. When I was making a little money he said he was going to put it in a trust fund for me and start some annuities. When I got to making big money, I found out he had formed this corporation, and he had charge of all the money. Then I found out I had no trust fund, no annuities, nothing. He never even paid the taxes on it. I got hit for back taxes all at once; about $115,000 in back taxes.

"I left him in 1957 and made a comeback to pay off my taxes. I was 39 years old when I finally quit. My last fight was in 1967 when I lost a split decision to Don Fullmer. We opened up the Oakland Coliseum with that fight."

Bobo's second wife, Judy, chimed in: "It was a case of bad management. Sid formed the corporation and controlled it. They invested and spent money, and Bobo had no say in it. They didn't even require his signature."

Sid Flaherty recalled those trying times a bit differently.

"Yes, we formed a corporation," Flaherty recalls. "We were all in it, and we set aside a portion of our income in a trust fund. But the Internal Revenue Service disallowed it as a trust, and that was the end of it."

It was an effort on Flaherty's part to defer income, to have it taxed at a later date and, of course, at a lower rate.

Recently, laws have been passed enabling people with high earnings in a short period of time to average their income over a five-year period and thus reduce their tax burden. This is of particular value to the professional athlete.

But in Olson's time that relief wasn't available and Flaherty hired the best legal minds he could find. "We fought it for almost three years," said Flaherty, "and that cost a great deal of money. When it was over, they disallowed it and we lost the case. That's all there was to it.

"He wasn't the only one who was in the trust. All of us were in it, and we all had the same fate. We were taxed back to the years of earnings, retroactive, so he wasn't the only one who was unhappy about the outcome of the case.

"I think we had the best lawyers there were and they fought the case for a long time. But it just ran into a monstrous amount of money, and we lost. We just blew it, that's all."

Referring to Olson's comments, Sid went on: "He gets that way every now and then, I suppose, but that legal fight wasn't the only drain. When you're keeping two wives and two homes and buy cars like they're confetti, you use up a lot of money.

"When you buy a Cadillac for $7,000, in the bracket he was in, it costs him $11,000. But these are things he didn't understand and never could understand.

"But as far as the trust is concerned, that was just something that was fought out in court and lost."

WHERE IS HE NOW?

Bobo Olson and his second wife, Judy, live in Santa Rosa, California, some fifty miles from San Francisco. He went back to Honolulu upon the recent passing of his father, but he has no desire to stay there to live. "It's gotten too commercialized."

Now 43 years old, Bobo still works hard at conditioning. His home is close to a golf course, and there he maintains a steady regimen of roadwork, running two to two-and-a-half miles every day. He keeps his punching sharp on a speed bag set up in his garage.

He gets occasional assignments as a security guard. He gets additional income from a fairly busy schedule of personal appearances, to which he brings memories in the form of some four or five fight films he managed to gather together.

He holds no bitterness, whatever happened to his money.

"I boxed for 24 years," he says, "and boxing was good to me.

I have no regrets. That trust fund business is water under the bridge. I got the one thing I wanted: to be champion of the world, and that's paying off for me in the personal appearances I'm able to make.

"I've got my health, I'm still in good shape, and I've got a wonderful wife in Judy."

Does he see many fights? "No, I rarely go. I think it's a shame the way boxing has gone down. I guess there aren't enough hungry kids these days.

"I love boxing and I think it is one of the best of sports. I think boxing should be taught in the schools. With the headgear and the big gloves a kid can't get hurt and it gives them something they can't get anywhere else. Every boxer I've known was a real gentleman."

OLLIE MATSON

A Most Extraordinary Trade

ON MARCH 1, 1959, the Los Angeles Rams made one of the most unusual trades in the history of the National Football League.

For one player, they traded the following:

(1) Four starting linemen: Frank Fuller and Art Hauser, defensive tackles; Ken Panfil, offensive tackle; and Glen Holtzman, defensive end and offensive tackle.

(2) The Rams' second, third and fourth draft choices from the 1959 draft: Don Brown, Houston halfback; Larry Hickman, Baylor fullback; and John Tracey, Texas A & M end.

(3) One player to be picked prior to the 1959 season.

(4) A high 1960 draft choice.

And what did the Rams receive in return? His name was Ollie Matson, and he was six feet, two inches tall, and weighed about 210 pounds. He was 28 years old at the time, and if he had lost any of the speed that earned him a place on the 1952 Olympic team, it wasn't apparent at the time.

But speed wasn't all Matson had in his private arsenal of offensive football weapons. He also had power and strength, and he was what Notre Dame coach Ara Parseghian describes as "goal oriented."

Green Bay's Paul Hornung had it, too. Something deep in his psyche manifested itself when the shadows of the goalposts fell upon a football field.

It all started in his prep days in San Francisco, but Ollie Matson really burst upon the national scene when he entered the University of San Francisco. Former Notre Dame star and coach

Ed McKeever recruited him, but it was Joe Kuharich who reaped the benefits of his ability. Ollie, along with Gino Marchetti, led the San Franciscans to an undefeated season in 1951, and the following winter the Chicago Cardinals (before they moved to St. Louis) made Matson their No. 1 draft choice. And no wonder!

In the Dons' undefeated season, Matson gained 1,566 yards, more than all their opponents combined. What's more, he scored 126 points to lead the nation's collegians in scoring, including the University of Washington's great running back Hugh McElhenny.

His future as a pro player seemed assured; and actually it was. But before he went into the pros, Ollie Matson wanted to prove something to himself. He wanted to make the U.S. Olympic team and compete in the 1952 games in Helsinki, Finland.

A couple of years before, in a National Amateur Athletic Union track meet in Berkeley, California, Matson ran against the great Jamaican sprinter Herb McKenley in a 440-yard dash. McKenley won the race and set a world record of 46 seconds, but at the finish Matson was only 1.7 seconds behind.

"Dink Templeton, the track coach at Stanford thought I should stick to track," Ollie recalls, "but, even though I had always dreamed of running in the Olympics, I made up my mind to play football."

So it was on to the University of San Francisco and national fame. But the Olympic dream had never left him and after the Cardinals had drafted him, he sought out the Stanford coach who then was in charge of the American track squad for the Olympics.

Templeton was sympathetic, but also apprehensive. "Ollie, you laid off track too long," he told him. Yet when the plane took off for Helsinki Ollie was on it. He placed third in the 400 meters behind Jamaica's George Rhoden and McKenley and ran on the U.S. 1,600-meter relay team which finished second, thus winning a bronze and silver medal competing against the finest sprinters in the world.

Ollie returned from Helsinki in time to get his football legs in condition for the annual College All-Star Game at Soldier Field in Chicago. The collegians lost 10-7 to the Rams, but Ollie played well enough to learn that there was a career out there for him. All he had to do was try it. He couldn't miss and he didn't.

Matson was well on his way to rewriting the record book until he broke his wrist in the fifth game of the season. He played anyway, gained 1,240 yards, scored 54 points including touchdown runs of 100 and 79 yards, and was named Rookie of the Year. And he was something to behold.

Matson was a runner whose style was difficult to forget. Coupled with his speed was an almost awesome power, and when he ran over defenders at the line of scrimmage, he had the quickness to bolt by the secondary. In addition, he was almost impossible to ride out of bounds. Like Jim Taylor was to do later for the Packers, Matson simply would lower his shoulder and punish the defender.

So, on the first day of March, in 1959, when the Cardinals decided they needed a new football team, and that Matson would be the price, he left behind him a legacy that Cardinal fans hardly can forget. In six seasons with the club, before it moved to St. Louis, Matson carried the ball 761 times for 3,381 yards. His six-year mark with the Cardinals almost surpasses the 3,511 yards the great Charlie Trippi gained in *nine* seasons with the club. He also caught 130 passes for 2,150 yards and he scored 300 points. He also picked up 2,553 yards on kick returns.

When informed of the trade, after three days of dealing between coach Frank Ivy and managing director Walter Wolfner of the Cardinals and coach Sid Gillman and general manager Pete Rozelle of the Rams, Matson was not exactly ecstatic. "I wanted to finish my career with the Cardinals," he said forlornly. But later, when the Rams went to camp at Redlands, California, Matson was resigned to his fate. He didn't bad-mouth the club that had drafted him No. 1, but he gave the impression that he was happy to be back on the West Coast.

"The Cardinals were a fine bunch of fellows," he said, "but this is a fine team." And he meant it, because he had reported a week early with the rookies so he could familiarize himself with the Los Angeles system employed by perfectionist Gillman.

There were many more games, yards gained and other teams. And before his 14-year National League career ended he was third on the all-time rushing list with 12,844 yards. Los Angeles sent him to Detroit, and later he joined Joe Kuharich, his coach at the University of San Francisco and St. Louis, at Philadelphia. Kuharich, who is not given to dispensing superlatives, calls Matson the "finest player I have ever seen or coached."

After his playing career ended, Matson became a scout for the Eagles, but when they wanted to put him on a part-time basis, he gave it up and went into youth work. In the back of his mind was the desire to be a teacher and coach. That ambition has been realized, but the memory of Ollie Matson as a player in the National Football League will be preserved, not only in the minds of football fans, but in the Pro Football Hall of Fame at Canton, Ohio.

He and Marchetti were enshrined the first year they were eligible, in February of 1972. Marchetti became the prototype for today's defensive ends. Matson, although he played flanker, tight end and defensive back, as well as fullback and halfback, will always be remembered as a running back.

And that is as it should be, because that is what he did best, maybe better than anyone else in the history of the National Football League.

WHERE IS HE NOW?

Ollie Matson and his wife, Mary, live in Los Angeles with their four children, Lisa, Ollie III, Bruce and Barbara, and Ollie is back in football at the high school level.

He was handpicked by Dr. Norman Schachter, a supervisor in the Los Angeles school system. He is the same Norm Schachter was was an official in the National Football League during most of Matson's career.

It was in February of 1971 that he was signed at football coach, assistant track coach and physical education teacher at Los Angeles High. And a few days later, he awakened a moment or two before 6 A.M. to run his customary mile before breakfast. But there was a certain stillness about things; and something inside him, probably stemming from his years in San Francisco, told him Los Angeles was going to have an earthquake.

"I got the kids up and told them to go into the hallway and showed them how to brace themselves," he recalled. "Then I woke my wife very gently and told her 'we're having an earthquake.' None of us was alarmed and we were very lucky. The quake was devastating downtown, but we just had a few cracks in the ceiling of our home."

Los Angeles High was not so fortunate. Before Ollie could put his first football team into competition, the school had to be torn down because the earthquake damage weakened it structurally. It survives only on video tape as "Walt Whitman High" on the A.B.C. television series, "Room 222."

Quonset huts were erected while a new school was being built and Matson put his first team on the field in the fall of 1971. He won two and lost six. He was not too unhappy with that record. "I've always hated to lose," he said. ". . . I encourage my players to be No. 1, good sportsmen. I stress that I want them always thinking in terms of sportsmanship, good discipline and respect for their fellow man."

It took a while, but the kids at L.A. High are beginning to realize that there is a superstar on the athletic staff. At first, they didn't know that Ollie had won a bronze in the 440 at Helsinki or helped the 1,600-meter relay team win a silver medal.

"They're beginning to know," he said. "They go to the library and look me up and they say, 'Coach, why didn't you tell us that you did this thing or that thing?'

"And I tell them, 'What I did isn't important now. What I am interested in is you doing it.' "

A year later, Matson received bad and good news on two consecutive days. First the bad. On Monday, February 7, 1972 the University of San Francisco, like so many other Jesuit schools, announced that it was dropping football. Only an exhilarating bit of news the next day rose Ollie's spirit: the pro football Hall of Fame announced that Ollie Matson, along with Gino Marchetti, Lamar Hunt and Clarence (Ace) Parker were elected to join 70 others in that exclusive society.

"When I read that the school had dropped football, I was just shocked," Ollie said. "I was hurt. There can be no program at a university unless you have athletics. Young people need a sense of identification and if you don't have an athletic program, what do they have to identify with?"

He is grateful, of course, for the chance to join the professional greats in Canton, but right now he is concentrating on his teaching and coaching duties at Los Angeles High.

He thinks that today's athletes are much different from the way he was as a star at George Washington High in San Francisco. "They have a lot more than we had," he said. "You have to be a little careful how you approach things. You have to take into consideration that we were more dedicated.

"Young people today have to really be motivated or they don't care for this game (football)." He uses film a lot, a carryover from his professional days, and shows the kids what they are doing wrong after each game. "If you're going to teach, you have to have some means of showing the youngsters what they're doing," he says.

He also realizes that because he was such a great athlete himself, there always is the danger that he is asking too much of his players.

But then he adds: "All I ask is that they do their best. That's all any person can do."

And Ollie Matson ought to know. That's what he always did.

DON LARSEN

The Instant Hero

IT WAS A MONDAY NIGHT in New York, and the late Joe E. Lewis was appearing at the Copacabana. Joe E. was dispensing his unique brand of humor: "You only go around once," he said, drink in hand, "but if you do it right, once is enough."

Just about that time, there was a flurry of activity at ringside where a table was being hastily set up and a large party took their places—ordering champagne for all.

Dominating the scene was a tall, athletically constructed man with a modified crew-cut. The date was Monday, October 8, 1956. The six-foot, four-inch, 228-pounder hoisted his glass and the ring-siders broke into spontaneous applause. They recognized him all right. He was Don Larsen of the New York Yankees, and that afternoon he had pitched the first and only perfect game in World Series history, beating the Brooklyn Dodgers 2-0.

Not one Dodger reached base as Larsen struck out seven. He threw three balls to only one batter, Pee Wee Reese in the first inning. In all he threw only 97 pitches at the Brooks, and the last one was a called strike on pinch-hitter Dale Mitchell who batted for Dodger starter Sal Maglie. It was belt high and cut the outside corner.

Don Larsen was in his element that night at the Copa—well, almost. He usually spent his evenings at a place called McAvoy's, because the draught beer was good and the pretzels plentiful. And for an insomniac like Larsen, there was always someone to talk with until closing time.

There have been hundreds of fun-loving characters who have roamed through the major leagues in the past century, guys who have had as much fun off the field as they did on it. These days we call them "flakes" or "hot dogs," but it's all the same, only the names have changed from generation to generation. And of all these characters, one of the most colorful was Larsen, a right-handed pitcher, who thought like a left-hander. He wandered through his career, never really distinguishing himself, yet always showing enough potential to hang on in the big tent.

Larsen broke in with the old St. Louis Browns, but when they moved to Baltimore, it didn't sit well with the big right-hander. He had a 3-21 record and that, of course, didn't make manager Paul Richards too happy either, so he decided to rebuild the club. For starters, he traded Larsen, pitcher Bob Turley and shortstop Billy Hunter to the Yankees for nine rostered players and three from the farm system. Manager Casey Stengel wanted the hard-throwing Turley and Richards had eyes for outfielder Gene Woodling, catcher Gus Triandos and pitcher Harry Byrd. Larsen was practically a throw-in, but he was happy to get out of Baltimore. Everything closed down so early there.

But when the 1955 season rolled around, Stengel shipped Larsen to New York's farthest outpost in its minor league chain. Don went to Denver. His exile lasted only two months because he won nine of ten games there and hit a dozen home runs. The Yankees rescued him in July and he came to New York and won nine and lost two helping the Yankees to the 1955 pennant.

The following spring, Larsen was up to his old wanderings again. The Yankees were training at St. Petersburg, and Stengel thought his young right-hander was safely tucked away at the midnight curfew. But at 5 A.M. one April morning, while driving his new convertible through a residential area, Larsen either fell asleep, or the rising sun clouded his vision, and he smacked into utility pole, shearing it in half.

Naturally, the local constabulary was called, and Larsen was charged with failure to reduce speed and driving with an improper license. A couple of days later he was fined $15 though he suffered nothing more than a broken cap on his front tooth and a bad case of the jitters. Stengel was angry. "It's too bad," old Case said, "because he has been obeying the curfew and attending to business. Now he has to go and spoil it all." When Stengel demanded an explanation, Larsen told him exactly what happened and Casey conferred absolution on the spot. "Why shouldn't I?" Casey rasped. "He told the truth, didn't he?"

Stengel was right, of course, because Larsen usually told it like it was. Once when he wanted to report late for Baltimore's spring training he was refused permission. So he reported late anyway. He read comic books instead of joining the rest of the boys in workouts, and he balked every time he was called upon to pitch batting practice. One of Richards' first orders was to get rid of him first chance that came along.

Larsen's reputation as a happy wanderer began when the Orioles were the Browns in St. Louis. Marty Marion was managing the club and Larsen endeared himself to the former shortstop great by setting a record for pitchers—by getting seven straight hits.

Marion, of course, immediately caught the importance of such a feat considering the way things were going, or not going, in St. Louis. So one day in Boston, he kept Larsen shagging flies for a couple of hours after the game. Why not get that bat in the lineup every day, Marion thought.

Larsen apparently had other ideas, as he weighed the advantages of pitching every fourth or fifth day, and standing in the broiling summer sun every day of the week. So when Marion actually put him in the lineup, as an outfielder, Larsen's batting prowess suddenly deserted him, and his opinion of Marion the slave-driver was proven beyond a reasonable doubt.

So the trade to the Yankees opened the swinging doors of all New York to Larsen. And he met the challenge. He didn't need the Copa or Joe E. Louis to savor the perfect game that October night. Don Larsen already had more friends in more cities than any ball player before or since. He was happiest when he could stop in at McAvoy's or Taylor's in New York, have a few quiet beers and enjoy himself.

And that's what he did on Sunday night, October 7, 1956, because he knew he had to pitch the fifth game of the Series, which was tied at two games each for the Yankees and the Dodgers. His only concession to such an assignment was to leave the place at midnight. When he got to the Stadium the next morning, he remarked casually: "I've got to win today. I've already spent the losers' share."

Surrounding the making of such folk-heroes as Larsen are tales, fairly attributed and otherwise, and one of them had Larsen asking Bill McCorry, the Yankees' traveling secretary, for a $200 advance on his Series check. "I've got to get home to California, and I don't have a nickel," it was said he said. "Win today," McCorry replied, "and I'll see that you get the money." So when Larsen pitched his masterpiece, McCorry fought his way through a hundred writers and broadcasters, and offered him the check. "I don't need it now," Larsen said above the clubhouse din. "I've already made $2,000 since the game ended."

Larsen doesn't recall the story, but he'll never forget what he now calls *the* game. And this is the Brooklyn batting order he faced. Jim Gilliam, second base; Pee Wee Reese, shortstop; Duke Snider, centerfield; Jackie Robinson, third base; Gil Hodges, first base; Sandy Amoros, left field; Carl Furillo, right field; Roy Campanella, catching and Sal Maglie pitching.

Despite his seemingly nonchalant attitude, Larsen was well prepared for his historic start. He had developed a new style a couple of weeks previously, much to the chagrin of Jim Turner, the martinet who coached the Yankee pitchers. Larsen decided, on his own, that batting as well as pitching was a matter of rhythm, a continuous flowing motion.

So he reasoned that if he pitched without a wind-up the batter would have less time to set and follow the flight of the ball. And he was right, to a point. He won a couple of late season games with his newly-found method, but in the second game of the Series, the Brooks bombed him, reaching him for one hit and four runs in one and two-thirds innings.

But Stengel knew his man. From the beginning, Casey figured that while Larsen may not win games in large numbers, he would win important games. And the fifth game was that, to say the least.

Larsen had no control problems as he methodically wiped out Dodger after Dodger, but almost each inning was fraught with danger. In the first, Hank Bauer made a knee high catch of a sinking liner by Duke Snider and in the second Jackie Robinson smashed a ball off third baseman Andy Carey's glove that Gil McDougald fielded nipping the speedy Robinson by half a step. In the fifth, Mickey Mantle made the play of the game, and Larsen got his biggest fright. Here is the official play-by-play from Associated Press:

> Robinson flied to Bauer. Mantle made a spectacular catch of Hodges' drive to deep left-center. Amoros drove a long foul that barely missed being a home run, the ball landing in the right-field stands, just on the foul side of the pole. Martin threw out Amoros, who became the 15th consecutive Dodger to be retired. No runs, no hits, no errors.

And so it went, as the correspondent dictated the play-by-play to the AP operator who flashed it to hundreds of newspapers throughout the civilized world. And when the last pitch to pinch hitter Dale Mitchell was a strike, Don Larsen became the most celebrated baseball player of the century because he accomplished what no other man has done in the history of the game.

An instant after the ball plopped into the glove of Yankee catcher Yogi Berra, the little fire-plug plunged toward the mound and, in full view of millions watching on television, he grabbed Larsen around the head and put a leg-scissors around the big pitcher's middle. Their joy was unbounded.

Becoming an instant hero is not an easy thing and it was particularly difficult for Larsen, because it interrupted his routine. For the next few weeks he found it impossible to enjoy his favorite pastime of dropping in at his old haunts for a quiet beer.

His agent, Frank Scott, lined up personal appearances for him and the biggest was a guest shot on Bob Hope's television program.

Hope stole Larsen from under the noses of New York's Ed Sullivan and Steve Allen, the reigning geniuses of the tube at the time. Larsen got $5,000 for that one, and for a month he did what heroes are supposed to do. He appeared at banquets, supermarkets and such, and in 30 days he picked up $25,000. Essentially a loner, although he liked the company of others, Larsen simply turned his back on further appearances and went home to San Diego. And when he did, he gave up a small fortune.

But he had other problems. His marriage had gone sour and his wife was demanding support payments for their daughter. A day after *the* game, he caught up on those, and later a divorce was granted.

After that, it was all downhill. He kicked around with Kansas City, the White Sox, the Giants, the Orioles, the Astros, and the Cubs, and bounced up and down from the minors before finishing his career in 1968. During his wanderings, Larsen found himself another bride, Corrine Audrey Bruess, an airline stewardess he met on a flight to San Diego in 1956. They were married in Benson, Minnesota, Corrine's home town, in December of 1957.

WHERE IS HE NOW?

Don and Corrine, along with Don Scott, born in 1963, live in Morgan Hill, California in the Salinas Valley. Larsen is a salesman for a paper company, and calls on farmers in that area, sitting on lettuce crates talking baseball as he goes about selling the product of the San Francisco firm.

Larsen had a difficult time adjusting to the rigors of business life after 21 years in professional baseball. He wanted a front office job in baseball, but nobody wanted him. Then he tried a desk job with a trust company, but that didn't work either. His problem got worse when two liquor firms told him that they were not interested in a 40-year-old beginning salesman. But, finally, the sales job with Blake-Moffit & Towne opened up and he's been happy with it.

Larsen didn't appreciate the 1972 players' strike. "I think the players owe the fans something," he said. "I know what they did affects fellows like me who are about to start collecting on the pension, but I think it was a little unfair to the fans," he said.

Larsen has no plans to start collecting his pension at 45. "That might change if I need the money," he said. He admitted that he had saved nothing from his two decades in the game, and he has no regrets about it.

"I'll tell you truthfully," he said. "I've had a good time."

So it looks as though Joe E. Lewis was right. All things considered, once around is enough.

WES SANTEE

He Took the AAU to Court

WHEN KARL SCHRANZ of Austria was singled out for expulsion from the 1972 Winter Olympic Games by President Avery Brundage and his Olympic Committee, it awoke memories of a strikingly similar Avery Brundage "example" of eighteen years earlier. The 1954 pariah, drummed out of the corps for violation of the spirit and letter of the amateur code was a young man from Kansas named Wes Santee.

Schranz was the world's premier downhill skier. Santee was the world's premier mile runner.

Schranz has been credited with achieving a $50,000 income as an "amateur" skier. Santee was demanding a thousand dollars per appearance in the lucrative, big-city, indoor track tour.

Despite cries, and evidence, that "everybody was doing it," Schranz was singled out because his violations were the most blatant. Ditto Santee.

Santee may have been the greatest mile runner who ever lived! Long before they discovered the training regimen that was able to bring several runners to the sub-four-minute mile, Santee came within a half-second of breaking that supposedly insurmountable barrier.

He grew up on a farm at Ashland, Kansas, just 50 miles due south of Dodge City—that historic hotbed of frontier life.

Those were depression times, and farm work was hard and unrewarding. The wonder is that young Wes emerged at all in the field of competitive athletics. The future miler's father was typical of the Kansas farmer of his time, immersed in the struggle for survival, scantily educated, accepting a life of hard work and limited horizons. The elder Santee's notion of the proper time for a boy to play boy's games was when the chores were done. And the chores stretched out from dawn to dark.

As Wes Santee looks back upon his boyhood his guess is that had the time to play been available to him, his best sport would have been baseball. Muscle-hardened by the physical labors of farm work, Wes could throw a baseball very hard. He secured a copy of Bob Feller's *Handbook for Pitching* to learn how to pitch and throw the curve.

But there just wasn't time to get involved in baseball activity beyond an occasional pick-up game, and the effort was reluctantly abandoned. It was in the effort to pry out some time that he could call his own that Santee began to run. To and from school; to and from his chores; to and from anything, Wes went through his boyhood at a gallop.

The high school coaches of that community doubled as physical education instructors in the junior high school. This gave them the opportunity to survey the gym class youngsters and single out those with athletic talent. These were given special attention to prepare them for competition on the high school teams.

It is rare that a boy becomes a mile runner at the outset, but such was the case with Wes Santee. The coaches quickly discovered this junior high school youngster could run faster and farther than anyone else. The mile was the longest distance run in high school competition, and the coach decided Wes should begin his concentrated effort to compete at that distance.

Twenty years before Wes Santee, another Kansan named Glenn Cunningham had made the mile run the glamor event at any track meet. He was the first of the mile superstars. He had set world records indoors and out and beome a Kansas legend. Twenty years after he ran, Cunningham still held virtually all the mile high school records in the state.

Santee competed as a freshman, and finished seventh in his first state championship run. He would lose only one other race through the entire remainder of his high school career. In every stadium in which he ran, Santee would find the program noting the meet or stadium record for the mile was held by Glenn Cunningham.

Santee's ambition was immediate, to break all of Cunningham's records. His success was also immediate. He surpassed every Cunningham mark before the end of his sophomore year. He knocked a second and a half off Glenn's all-time best high school mark.

In Santee's junior year another avenue of opportunity opened up. Bill Easton, renowned track coach at Kansas University, had succeeded in getting a cross-country program added to the Kansas high school event structure. Wes became a cross-country champion as well.

"Cross-country was really my most enjoyable track experience," says Santee. "That hard, physical life on the farm had given me tremendous endurance, and I just felt I could run all day. It was really a great deal of fun." Almost lost in the glamor of his achievements at the mile is the fact that Santee was the national collegiate cross-country champion in his senior year at Kansas.

As one travels his trail of memories with Wes Santee, it is apparent his rebellion against the morés of the sport, which was to climax with his stormy departure from competition, was beginning to ferment in high school. As he explains his relish of cross-country competition, the key reason for it seeps to the surface. The hill and dale course was away from the crowd of spectators, and the important thing was winning the race, not the time of it. When Santee erased all the Cunningham records in his second year of high school competition, he discovered a truism about the mile run. Winning the race is secondary to the time.

"This is one of the great problems to the miler," Santee opined. "That of trying to win the race and at the same time live up to your image as a public figure. Winning alone is not enough, the public demands you must also have an excellent time.

"I quickly ran out of competition in high school, and while I might win a race by as much as a half a lap, if the time wasn't spectacular, I had achieved nothing in the eyes of the crowd. It is very difficult to record a fast mile without competition, yet I discovered early this is what I had to do."

Santee's resentments were further crystallized—this time against the over-bearing bureaucracy of the track and field hierarchy—in the 1952 Olympic competition.

Wes had moved on to the University of Kansas, and already at 19 years of age was established as the best mile runner in the country, a predictable gold medal winner in the 1500 meters, the metric mile, of the '52 Olympic Games. Santee had also done well in the 5000 meters. Indeed, he had beaten everyone in the country except Curt Stone, who competed for the New York Athletic Club.

As Wes and his KU coach, Bill Easton, arrived on the west coast for the Olympic trials, they checked the program and discovered the 5,000 meter trials were to be run on a Friday with the 1500 set for the following day. The two agreed Santee should try in both, and, if he was a qualifier in each, he could pick the one in which his performance would indicate he had the best chance.

On Friday, Wes ran the 5000 meters and again finished second to the one man who could beat him at the distance, Curt Stone. But in finishing second, he had made the U.S. Olympic team in the 5000, since the first three finishers qualified.

On Saturday, Wes reached the stadium early to run a few warmup laps before the 1500 meter trials. He was on the training table getting a final rub-down when Coach Easton came in and said he could forget it. He was not going to be allowed to run in the 1500. The Olympic Committee felt he would not be physically able to compete in both events and since Santee had already qualified at 5000 meters, that was to be his event.

Santee still feels frustration as he thinks of it. "I was in complete agreement that I could not handle both events, but it was our thinking to try and qualify for both, then pick the one which I would have the best chance of winning. Since Stone had proven best at 5000 meters, it was obvious that my best contribution to the team would be at 1500. Rounding out the three-man squad for the 5000 would be a simple matter of moving up the fourth man. It made sense then and it still makes sense today."

But the cloudy reasoning of the committee prevailed and the best man at the distance was barred from the metric mile.

The 5000 meter run proved a disaster for Wes. The European distance runners held a lock on the event. Where Santee was a beginning collegian at 19 years old, the Europeans were mature men ranging in age from 28 to 33. Santee never placed as the Europeans ran to a new Olympic record.

"I was over-matched," says Santee bitterly. "They put me in an event that was out of my league, when I could have won the 1500 meters."

Santee can support this claim. Two weeks later, in a meet at London, England, he defeated the Olympic milers in a field that included Greg Landy, Roger Bannister and Bobby McMillan. McMillan, of Occidental, California, had finished second at Helsinki.

Embittered by the experience, Santee began to get what he could from his ability. The indoor track season, contested in the big arenas of the major cities of the United States, had become big business. The glamor event was the mile and Santee was the best of the milers. Virtually every track star demanded, and got, excess "expense money" of a few hundred dollars for their appearance at a meet. It was all done very surreptitiously, and in these modest amounts, until Santee came on the scene.

The athletes, in all justice, were bound by antiquated rules on allowable expense money that were honored in the breach rather than the observance. At the time, reimbursement could not exceed railroad fare and a twelve-dollar per day living allowance. In order to compete, the athletes had to fly to the cities, and air fare was much more expensive than rail. It was impossible to subsist on twelve dollars a day in the hotels of a major city.

"I guess the biggest problem was one I still have today," says Santee. "I am very outspoken, very forthright. I'm on top of the table. I don't beat around the bush, and I suppose sometimes I push a little too hard."

Where the others were content with a few hundred dollars, Santee was determined to be rewarded for the people he brought to the arena.

"You know," Santee argues, "they themselves took sports out of a pure amateur status when they started charging admissions. This was one of my arguments when I was suspended. It is conceited, perhaps, but many a stadium was filled at three to five dollars a seat because I was running there. The fact that I got a thousand dollars was, percentage-wise, chicken-feed compared to what the promoters were making."

Chicken-feed it was not, to the AAU. They came down on him hard, suspending him for accepting excess expense money in three California meets in the spring of 1955. Had Santee accepted the suspension in quiet and penitence, there is little doubt he would have been returned to competition for the 1956 Olympic Games. Indeed, the Kansas AAU lifted his suspension at the local level three weeks after it was imposed. But the national body would not agree to this local lenience and insisted the suspension remain in force. Santee went for broke. He took the AAU to court.

The die was now cast. If he won the case he would be free to run again, but if he lost, the ban would be for life.

He lost.

New York Supreme Court Justice Walter A. Lynch, in handing down the decision that he found against Santee, nevertheless conceded there was merit in some of the counter-charges brought by the runner.

Justice Lynch droned through the basis of his ruling: "His engagement of a booking agent, his demand for monies for the attendance of his wife at various meets, and the collection of said monies without the attendance of his wife, the excessive expense accounts, the check of $400 to his father-in-law from the promoter of a certain meet, these and other matters foreclose any serious consideration of his plea that he was harshly or unfairly dealt with.

"He agreed to abide by the rules of the Union. He has not only failed to do so, but makes no pretense of having done so."

Justice Lynch had some words to say to the other side, however: "From this unfortunate incident, some good may come to amateur athletics in the United States. Promoters of amateur athletic meets should realize the fault lies in no small part with them as a class. Plaintiff has eliminated himself as an amateur athlete, but not without an assist from some of the 'guardians' of amateur athletics."

Did it do any good? "I like to think so," Santee responds. "I was the fall guy, in my opinion, but I know that right in the middle of the trial the AAU changed their rules to allow for reimbursement of airplane fare, and upped the per diem allowance from twelve to twenty-five dollars a day."

WHERE IS HE NOW?

Wes Santee is back at the scene of his college triumphs, Lawrence, Kansas. He heads up his own insurance agency and is enthusiastically active in the Marine Corps Reserve. When he completed his required two years of service with the Marines, Wes was caught up in the traditions and camaraderie of the service and determined to stay with it in the reserve organization. He is now the commanding officer of MATCU-72, an air traffic control unit operating out of Olathe, Kansas, near Kansas City.

This devotion and enthusiasm for the military brought him to divorce. His wife was caught up in the peace movement and became equally active in the marches and sign-carrying. There was no compatible middle ground.

His second wife is Tony, short for Antonia, and the family rounds out with the children of his first marriage: two teen-age sons, Spike and Bob, and their little sister, Susie.

His running skills are being harnessed once again. Wes is the running instructor for the Kansas City Royals baseball team, working with both the professionals and the youngsters at the Royals' quickly famous baseball academy.

Santee looks upon the Royals' owner, Ewing Kauffman, as the most progressive man in baseball.

"He's going to revolutionize player development," Santee declares. "He took a bunch of kids who mostly had little or no baseball development, put them through an intense period of high level instruction at his baseball academy and they went out and beat the pants off everybody in the Florida Rookie League. That's some testimonial when you realize those other teams were made up of youngsters hand-picked by the major league teams as big league prospects. I'll predict that there will be ten or twelve kids from that academy class who will make Kansas City minor league teams right out of the school."

Santee is appalled at the lack of coaching, the ignorance of proper diet, the lack of intelligent weight training, and the absence of any thought to the techniques of running that prevails in what he calls the "tradition-bound" game of baseball.

Santee discovered practically every baseball player runs with his toes pointed out, instead of straight ahead. He proved the value of the latter simply by measuring the stride of the player with toes fanning out, again with them pointed straight ahead. They discovered they could gain an inch just by straightening out their feet.

"It takes about 18 strides for an average size guy to get from home to first," says Santee. "So it's easy to see he can arrive at first base eighteen inches ahead of the other way, with the same number of steps. It's the difference between out and safe on a close play.

"When a batter hits the ball, he becomes a sprinter, pure and simple. When you add instruction on getting up on the balls of the feet along with the proper arm motion . . . well, I found I could improve those kids two to four-tenths of a second on their time from home to first. That's a big improvement when you consider it is only 30 yards and realize how tough it is to shave just a tenth of a second off the time of a 100-yard dash."

As he looks back on his abruptly-ended track career, the perspective of time has erased the bitterness. "Even though I didn't win the Olympics, I got to go," he says. "Track was a fantastic experience. It took me all over the Far East when I was a freshman, and all over Europe the following year. I've been in almost every country of the world as a result of athletic trips. These things they can't take away no matter what they do."

Santee has remained active in the track and field program in his home area of Kansas and is enthused over the ascendancy of Jack Kelly to the presidency of the National AAU.

"He is already moving to get rid of antiquated and stupid rules that restrict our athletic development in this country, and our ability to compete on even terms with others."

It is obvious Wes Santee would like to help him.

PETE RADEMACHER

The Impossible Fight

IN ALL THE ANNALS of boxing, there is one match which must be labeled "the impossible fight."

A man fought his first professional fight for the heavyweight championship of the world. He fought for a corporation of which he was vice-president and, as such, received a salary rather than a share of the gate. The whole purpose of the fight was to create a market for a BB gun.

The hero of this quixotic attempt to wrest the heavyweight crown from its holder in a single professional attempt was Pete Rademacher.

Pete was born in a tiny town named Tieton, snuggled in the Yakima Valley of the state of Washington. His first experience with boxing came with attendance at the Castle Heights Military Academy, a prep school in Lebanon, Tennessee. In a tournament among the Tennessee military academies, Pete emerged the light-heavyweight champion.

He returned home for college, at Washington State. He lettered as a guard on the football team, got his degree in animal husbandry, and continued his boxing as a successful amateur. Rademacher became the Northwest Golden Gloves heavyweight champion in 1949, 1951, 1952 and 1953. He was also the winner of the National AAU championship in 1953.

This figured to end his boxing career, for in the same year he married Margaret Sutton, and a clearly understood part of the deal was that he quit boxing. The bride was unalterably opposed.

Pete and Margaret set up residence at Ft. Benning, Georgia, in 1954, where Rademacher was to begin his ROTC requirement of a two-year service hitch.

The Army, then as now, was an image-conscious organization and the Ft. Benning brass felt they had, in Rademacher, a likely representative for the 1956 Olympic boxing team. Pete was reluctant at first, what with his wife's feelings clearly stated on the subject, but he finally began training in secret.

Some three months later, Margaret heard another of the Army wives talking about it at a cocktail party, and hit the roof. "It was about two months of combat," says Pete, "but she finally agreed to let me pursue it."

It was along in here that the germ of the preposterous idea hit him. He knew there would be no marital peace if he embarked on a professional career in the customary manner. But what if he could win the Olympic championship and have just one professional fight . . . for the heavyweight championship of the world?

Pete began to quietly bounce the idea off people he would meet who were associated in various ways with the professional game. He once had a chance to suggest it to Rocky Marciano, who stared at him without comment for a full thirty seconds, then walked off shaking his head. Rocky clearly felt Pete had had a few too many fights already.

Floyd Patterson had succeeded the retired Marciano as champion when Rademacher dropped his idea on Joe Gannon, who was an inspector for the Washington, D. C. Boxing Commission. Joe had been the opponent in Patterson's first professional fight at Madison Square Garden, an eight-rounder, and had lost on a decision. He was one of the few to go the distance with Floyd, which may have made the suggestion seem not quite impossible in his eyes.

Gannon got to Patterson's manager, Cus D'Amato, and at least got him intrigued. Meanwhile, in Georgia, Rademacher chanced upon the proposition's most important ingredient, the man who could put up the money.

Near Ft. Benning, in Columbus, Georgia, was a youngish World War II Navy veteran namel Melchior "Mike" Jennings. Mike had come upon considerable wealth as an heir to a Pittsburgh family oil fortune, but was disenchanted with keeping it in the oil business, or Pittsburgh. Jennings felt the nation was suffering for lack of challenge to its youth, and had visions of forming an enterprise that would provide such challenges. While contemplating this, he had left Pittsburgh for the environs of Columbus, where a man can stroll through the piney woods and think deep thoughts. It was his wife's hometown, and for openers he set himself up in business with a sporting goods store. It was a low pressure sort of place, where the hunting and fishing set gathered to talk as much as to buy. It was here that Jennings happened upon a remarkable shot, with a remarkable manner of shooting, named Lucky McDaniel.

Lucky was a Georgian who had received local fame by downing a quail the first time he ever fired a shot. And he hadn't missed anything he had shot at since. This included such remarkable feats as knocking out tinfoil plugged into the center of a washer tossed into the air; or spattering a fly crawling on a wall. Almost as easy was hitting dimes spun into the air. Beyond this, Lucky could teach anyone how to do it in a matter of an hour or so, using a BB gun.

This was an attractively achievable challenge in the Jennings' vision, and he promptly made BB guns and the McDaniel instruction a lead item in his project, which had come to be named Youth Unlimited.

When Jennings' friendship with Pete unearthed Rademacher's dream of a one-shot challenge for the heavyweight championship, they were in business. The Jennings premise in his Youth Unlimited was trying for the impossible and Pete's ambition easily qualified. He made Pete a vice-president.

Meanwhile, Patterson's manager, Cus D'Amato, was mulling the idea which had been presented him by Joe Gannon. D'Amato has had a few off-beat ideas in his own career. He finally sent word that the notion would not seem all that ridiculous if someone would put up a $250,000 guarantee for Patterson. Of course, to bring it off, Rademacher had to win the Olympic championship, but with his impossible dream now at least a possibility, there was no stopping him. He disposed of his first opponent in two rounds. A third-round TKO victory in his second bout got him to the finals.

The fight for the heavyweight gold medal matched Pete against the Russian, Lev Moukhine. Things being what they are, any time an American and a Russian are matched in a contact sport, it it draws attention. Rademacher annihilated Moukhine. The Russian had a string of more than 200 victories, yet Rademacher had him from the first punch. He slammed the Russian into a state of helplessness in moments, the referee stopping the fight in the first round with Moukhine draped over the ropes.

Pete was the Olympic headline.

Rademacher was discharged from the Army the following March and the aforementioned maneuvering meshed. Pete was officially named vice-president of Youth Unlimited. Jennings and his friends got up the quarter-million guarantee.

It seemed only logical that the most remarkable promoter of his time, the legendary Jack Hurley, should be given custody of the match. The stage was set for Seattle, Washington, taking full advantage of the native son hero that was Rademacher.

Rademacher and Patterson met in August of 1957, accompanied

by an editorial hue and cry against the fact the match was even permitted. A rank amateur, not just against a seasoned professional, but the heavyweight champion of the world! Rademacher had never fought more than three rounds at one time in his life, and those only two-minute rounds.

Patterson won a knockout victory, but Rademacher stayed with him far longer than anyone imagined he could. Pete looked the winner of the first two rounds. Indeed, scored a knockdown with a right to Patterson's head.

The tide swung quickly in the third round as Rademacher began, as expected, to tire and Patterson opened up. The string of knockdowns began in the third and piled up to a total of seven trips to the canvas for Pete. But it was not until the sixth round and that seventh knockdown that the count of ten was tolled by referee Tommy Loughran, the former light heavyweight champion.

In defeat, it remained a splendid achievement, an impressive display of courage. Rademacher was untarnished as a hero.

It was a perfect moment to leave the boxing ring behind him, but Rademacher's taste of the ultimate glory had given him an appetite. He took a shot at Zora Folley (rhymes with holy) in July of 1958 with depressing results. Folley, not a noted puncher, knocked him down four times in four rounds.

Rademacher had made this match to provide needed funds for Youth Unlimited, which had now changed its name to Unlimited Enterprises. Shortly after this, frustrated with the lack of progress in the company, Pete decided to bow out of the association and take one serious fling at boxing.

He went on to some 22 additional professional fights and, while he won most of them, Margaret continued to object to this as a career. So, after beating George Chuvalo in Toronto, in 1961, losing a split decision to Karl Mildenburger in Germany and defeating the aging Bobo Olson in Honolulu in April of 1962, Pete turned to Margaret and said: "Okay honey, I'll find something else to do."

WHERE IS HE NOW?

Pete Rademacher is Executive Vice-President of the Kiefer-McNeil Corporation, based in Akron, Ohio. The Kiefer represents Adolph Kiefer, famed Olympic swimming champion. The company has four main product lines. From the Kiefer end of the endeavor come swimming pool chemicals and competitive supplies (lane markers, clocks, etc). In addition, the company packages windshield-washer fluids and anti-freezes for various oil and tire companies as well as the packaging and distribution of point-of-sale items for these firms.

Pete is involved in both product development and sales promotion. The product development traces back to a small amount of mechanical engineering study in college, plus a good amount of practical experience at his home on a cattle ranch.

"I got my degree in Animal Husbandry at Washington State, but the engineering turned out to be the useful area to me. We had a complete machine shop at the ranch: lathes, welding equipment, everything you need to make or repair equipment on the ranch. All this basic stuff came back to me when I got into product development at Kiefer-McNeil."

As a matter of fact, it was this ability that got them together. When Rademacher gave up boxing, he first went to work for a firm specializing in country club community development. His area was in marketing a cost-analysis book-keeping system for use by builders.

The shooting techniques of Lucky McDaniel were still with him, for Pete traveled with McDaniel for some five years in Youth Unlimited, mastering the art of instinct shooting and becoming a proficient teacher of it. While marketing his book-keeping system, Pete messed around in the shop, and designed and patented a couple of training devices to be safely used at home for practising this type of marksmanship. One was an indoor range, the other a trap-shooting setup for use with a BB gun. He took these to a stamping company and embarked on the production and marketing of them, an activity which led him to the Kiefer-McNeil firm and his present position.

Pete can dazzle an audience with his shooting, and will give an exhibition from time to time at public appearances. As Pete tells it: "I still teach and use instinct shooting practices for entertainment at customer gatherings which I find gives me an opportunity to get to know people with whom we deal on a level other than straight business communication."

He and Lucky McDaniel almost got baseball intrigued with it as a means of developing hitters. "We went to the Cincinnati Reds training camp in 1959. Our theory was, if we could teach batters the concentration on the target that is the secret of instinct shooting, they could transfer that to the pitched ball and greatly improve their ability to meet it squarely.

"The ball club went along as far as the shooting went. What we do is start the shooter concentrating on a rather large target, like a clay pigeon, some three or four inches in diameter. Then we gradually narrow their successful concentration down to a minute area until we have them hitting consistently a $\frac{3}{8}$ inch washer tossed into the air. We even had them hitting another BB, tossed into the air, about three times out of ten. But when we wanted to move them into the batting cage to start applying that concentration to a baseball, the batting coach said no. He was afraid we would louse up their swing."

Thus thwarted, the pair turned their attention to young Charles Comiskey, president of the Chicago White Sox. Comiskey agreed to let them give it a try and parceled out four or five players for them to work with, among whom was Jim Rivera.

To what degree the instruction helped is hard to say, but that year of 1959 saw Jim Rivera have an outstanding season, and the White Sox win the pennant. Two years later they got another chance with Cincinnati, in 1961. And Cincinnati won the pennant.

Why didn't the idea catch on? "Batting coaches did us in," says Pete. "They are afraid we will interfere with the batter's hitting style. Actually, we don't care how he swings. We feel he can hit the ball standing on his head when he learns the concentration.

"By developing their concentration to the point of being able to shoot an aspirin tablet tossed into the air, we develop a confidence in that concentration that can be transferred to a baseball.

"We found that the vast majority of batters miss a ball underneath. By developing an ability to concentrate on a spot on the ball, and setting that spot at the middle of the ball or above it, depending on the hitter, we got them to meeting the ball squarely as the pitch came in."

Pete still maintains an interest in boxing as his time permits. He referees Golden Gloves boxing and some professional matches around the Akron area and still looks upon his own exposure to boxing as the most rewarding experience of his life.

"It peeled off a shell of insecurity that I had, really, as a kid. The exposure of a boxer to crowds, making decisions and competing in front of people, is a tremendous experience not only in boxing, but in any sport. But in boxing, because you are so alone in there, if you can master the fear just a little bit you gain an inner strength that brings you all kinds of moral support.

"I think from that standpoint alone, a good high school program would be a valuable thing to kids growing up—under the supervision of people who know something about it and who won't just put gloves on the kids and say 'sic 'em.'"

Pete and Margaret have three teen-age daughters, so there isn't a budding boxer in the family. Susan is the oldest, then Helen and Margo.

He looks back on his boxing experience as "the greatest postgraduate course in public relations and sales promotion I could ever have."

Certainly no one could ever dredge up a greater example of the two skills than Pete's achievement of fighting for the heavyweight championship of the world in his first professional fight.

BILLY JOE PATTON

Mr. Unpredictable

AN OCCASIONAL 19TH HOLE discussion gets itself involved with singling out the man who has meant the most to golf. The bar historian will trumpet loudly for the man who first convinced Americans they could play this game, that being Frances Ouimet, who defeated the Britishers, Vardon and Ray, in an early Open.

More impressive vote totals, however, will come in for Arnold Palmer, who made the game a hit on television . . . or President Eisenhower, who came closest to making it the national pastime.

The ladies locker room will give a mention to Doug Sanders, but that is walking to the beat of another drum.

If, however, you tend to bracket these heroes into time periods, there can be little argument the man who had the greatest impact on the game and its galleries during his brief walk in the sun was the master of the shot from the jungle, Billy Joe Patton.

There is reason to suspect that Bobbie Gentry's clutching ballad, "Ode to Billy Joe," can lay part of its success to the mistaken notion among golfers that it was a song about the unsinkable Billy Joe Patton.

Billy Joe golfed and studied at Wake Forest College as World War II burst upon the scene. When college ended, he got into the action with three years in the Navy and didn't pick up a golf club until he had come back home to Morganton, North Carolina, found a job, and had settled back into the civilian pursuit of making a living.

He was a good player, readily capable of carving out a 67 or 68 in a Nassau match around home. Inexplicably, he would run some ten shots above that in any serious tournament competition and, thus, was always an early exit in things like the National Amateur.

The passing of time has obscured the reasons, but whatever the thinking, Billy Joe Patton found himself one day possessed of an invitation to compete as an amateur in the 1954 Masters Tournament at Augusta, Georgia.

It was more than just a chance to play in the prestigious tournament. For Billy Joe, it was a chance to meet his idol, Bobby Jones, whose grand slam performance of winning both the amateur and open championships of the United States and Great Britain stands to this day as the greatest feat in all of golf.

Patton came into the Masters a virtual unknown and came out a national celebrity.

Billy Joe could hit the ball a long way . . . and in any of several directions. It was his astonishing ability to hit out of trouble with some recovery shots that have grown to legends. It is this ability that captured the cheers of the Augusta galleries that year.

The plain truth of the matter is, Billy Joe Patton almost won it.

He didn't know the meaning of playing a safe shot. If the pin was within the range of any club in his bag, he used that club and went for it.

To find Billy Joe on the course, one only had to wait to hear the wild shouts of *fore!* and see the gallery scattering for cover.

And along his meandering trail he chatted happily with the spectators, went hell-bent for the pin, and endeared himself to the clustering fans as no one was to do until the arrival of Lee Trevino.

Patton charged along in the lead over the best golfers in the world until he finally dropped behind going into the final round. On that concluding day it appeared a battle between Snead and Hogan until a mighty roar erupted from the crowd around the par-three twelfth hole. As Bobby Jones described it: "The china started rattling. The walls trembled. I had to go out on to the porch to see what Billy Joe had done now."

What he had done was make a hole in one!

Now he was back in the race with Hogan and Snead, only to have his gambler's soul do him in on the next hole.

Patton tried for a birdie on the par-five 13th. Going for the pin on his second shot, he put it in the creek in front of the green and wound up making seven. He was out of it and Sam Snead came home the winner.

As he moved to the 14th tee, he had lost none of his ebullience. Surveying his glum gallery he smiled: "This is no funeral, let's smile again."

Looking back on it, Patton says: "I was cheering myself up as much as them, I still had five holes to play."

Billy Joe finished third behind Snead and Hogan, top amateur in the Masters. Much was made of his engaging camaraderie throughout the tournament. Considering his scant success, and tense preoccupation in previous tournament play, it was hailed as a remarkable change in attitude.

Patton disagrees. "When I got invited early in January, I really went to work on my game. I figured I'd never be invited again, and I wanted to do well. I spent hours hitting practice balls. Sometimes I would take part of my lunch hour to practice.

"When I got to Augusta I thought I was nearer ready than I had ever been before. That I was hitting the ball as well as I could.

"And you can have a little more fun when you're playing better. You can't really loosen yourself up. You can't kid yourself. You've got to be ready and you've got to know it better than anybody else. If you are ready, maybe you are a little bit looser and maybe you give a little different impression.

"I didn't win, but I played well, so I kind of enjoyed the thing. I didn't feel it was all that much a catastrophe that I didn't win it."

The near miss in the Masters sent Patton to new highs. He won the North-South Amateur, then finished sixth in the field to be high amateur in the U.S. Open.

The first round in the Open was a true Patton production. Under, over and through the trees, he put his tee shot in the fairway only seven times on the round, yet shot a 69 to lead the field.

It was inevitable that Dwight Eisenhower would invite Billy Joe to play and he held back not at all with the President.

Patton recalls: "On the 18th I went into the rough. From there I hit it behind a garage where they kept the tractors, and then through a parking lot."

When Billy Joe finally rejoined the group on the green, President Eisenhower asked: "Billy Joe, is that your first or second ball?"

"I'm playing only one ball," responded Billy, "but I'm hitting it a lot."

In 1957 the British sent over a truly fine team of golfers to meet the United States in one of the best of all Walker Cup matches. The pivotal match turned out to be that between Billy Joe and the then reigning British Amateur champion, Reid Jack.

The match was played over 36 holes. Eighteen holes in the morning, and the final round in the afternoon. Billy Joe was five down at lunch. He came back to win it in the afternoon, in his typically spectacular manner, pulling off shots that no sane golfer would even contemplate.

Billy Joe launched his afternoon attack immediately by winning

Eddie Arcaro at Washington Park.

Mickey Owen—there was more to his career than just that dropped third strike.

Sheriff Mickey Owen.

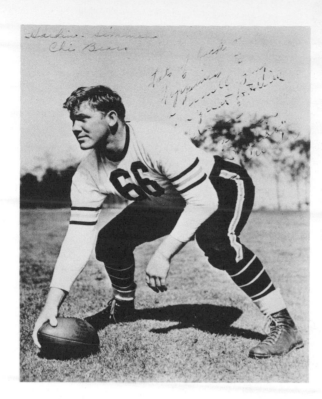

Clyde (Bulldog)
Turner—The Kid from
Sweetwater, Texas.

Ewell (The Whip)
Blackwell as he looked
with the Cincinnati
Reds in 1950.

Jim Mello—one of Notre Dame's best.

Jim Mello, below, now physical education director at the State Training School for Retarded Children in Mansfield, Conn.

Bobby Thomson, now a
paper sales executive.

Bobby Thomson, as a
New York Giant in the
1950's.

Bobby Layne, barking signals against the New York Giants.

Jack Fleck, today, with his wife Lynn.

Jack Fleck, blasting out
of a sand trap.

Tony Trabert today.
Left to right: son Mike,
Tony, wife Emeryl and
Brooke.

Tony Trabert as a U.S.
Davis Cupper in the
1950's.

Ollie Matson as a Los Angeles Ram running back.

Ollie Matson, today a Hall of Famer.

Larson, toward the end
of his career, with the
Chicago Cubs.

Don Larson as a
Yankee.

Wes Santee as a University of Kansas trackman.

Wes Santee, today an insurance salesman.

A recent picture of Pete Rademacher.

Pete Rademacher,
right, in the ring.

Tom Gola, now a
Philadelphia politician.

Parry O'Brien, today a
mortgage banking
executive.

Roy Harris in his ring days.

Roy Harris, wife Jean, and the rest of their brood.

Howard "Hopalong" Cassady, today a Columbus, Ohio businessman.

Tad Weed and (left to right) Stephen, Michael and wife Susan.

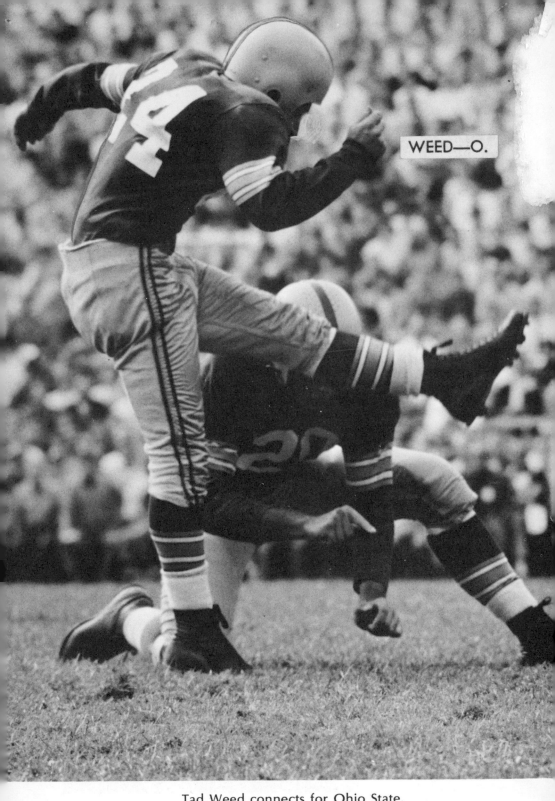

WEED—O.

Tad Weed connects for Ohio State.

the first three holes with what, for him, was more or less routine golf.

Patton got back another with a birdie on the par three sixth and was now only one down.

The match was being contested at the Minikahda Club in Minneapolis, where the seventh hole is a 432-yard dog-leg, bending to the right. On it, Billy Joe pulled off the shot of the year.

Reid Jack placed his tee shot in the heart of the fairway. Billy Joe put his in a stand of trees at the bend of the dog-leg. Jack, hitting first, struck a gorgeous five iron that braked the ball hole high, just fifteen feet to the right of the pin.

Patton looked to be out of the hole. Two large trees stood on his line to the hole, one about six feet away, the other some twenty feet in front of the ball. The ball itself had snuggled down in the rought.

As Billy Joe surveyed it, there was a miracle shot available. There *was* an opening between the two trees, but at its widest it was only about a foot. The odds were 100-1 against hitting a golf ball out of the rough given the limits of the situation. Naturally, it was the shot Billy Joe was going to try.

"Now you folks just stand where you are," Patton spoke cheerily to the gallery. "Everything's under control. Have confidence in me."

In that hushed gallery, the sound of the club striking the ball seemed over-loud, but Billy Joe had shot the gap.

It was a low liner dead through that skinny opening that buzzed onto and just over the green.

Billy had a little left to show the folks, for he promptly flubbed his chip shot, and followed that by sinking a 20-foot putt. Reid Jack took two from 15 feet and there it was; matching fours on the scoreboard.

Not how, but how many, the saying goes.

Patton now had that confidence that he had in the Masters. He had it rolling. He could hit any shot.

He stormed the ninth hole, 510 yards uphill, with two booming woods that set up his birdie and squared the match.

Patton had toured the front nine in 32 strokes, had come from five holes down to even the match after 27 holes.

On the 30th hole, Jack hit a fine drive, dropped his second shot eight feet from the hole, just missed the putt, tapped in for his par. Patton pushed his drive into the trees, hit his second into the rough alongside the green, chipped to four feet and sunk it. Also a four.

Next hole. Reid Jack hit two great woods to be ten feet away from the green on the 536-yard par five. Billy Joe hadn't hit the fairway yet on two shots. He pulled his drive, then knocked a long iron across the fairway on the other side. It came to rest in a tough, downhill lie 40 yards away from the green.

Billy Joe elected a running pitch from the tricky lie and the ball snaked across the green to stop 18 inches from the cup.

Jack took three to get down from off the green for his par. Patton dropped his putt for a birdie. Patton had the lead, one up, and when the match ended, that was his margin of victory.

"I'll remember that match as long as I have a mind," says Billy Joe. "You don't win many matches when you're five down at lunch."

Reminded that writers credited his comeback victory with lifting up the whole U.S. team, Billy could only reply: "It lifted the hell out of me, I'll tell you that."

WHERE IS HE NOW?

Billy Joe Patton is the most famous citizen of Morganton, North Carolina. He is in the lumber business now with his own Patton & Company, a hardwood broker representing some 30 mills.

His wife is Betsy, and they were married in 1948. The two oldest children, son Joe and daughter Betts, are both in college. Chuck, as of this writing, is an 18-year-old high school senior, who won the club championship at 16.

Joe shoots to a four handicap, Chuck is a five, and father is a one. ("It should be a two.")

While he will occasionally get into a father and son tournament with his sons, Billy Joe Patton is pretty much a weekend golfer now.

"The boys and I will jump into a cart on a Sunday and take off down the fairway. Argue like hell and play hard. Afterwards, the boys are old enough to have a beer now, and the old man has his scotch. We'll put a couple of steaks on and it's just a great day. I think that's what life is all about."

"Golf has been good to me," Patton went on. "To meet folks like Bob Jones and the General [Eisenhower] and a lot of great golfers I wouldn't have ever met.

You know, if it hadn't been for the game of golf, a fellow sittin' down in North Carolina, he wouldn't get to meet many Presidents.

"I reckon that was about the highlight of any experience I ever had, to be asked to play with President Eisenhower. He was a great competitor. Loved to hit a good shot.

"I remember a match once at Burning Tree in Washington. The General and Sam Snead were playing Charlie Halleck of Indiana and myself. Halleck at that time was minority leader in the House.

"Ike had two or three good holes in a row and they beat Charlie and me one up that day. He got a great kick out of that.

"I saw him break eighty a time or two. He wasn't a good putter, but he hit the ball a pretty good distance."

Billy Joe had not known Bob Jones personally until he played in the 1954 Masters, having missed an opportunity to meet Jones some 14 years before that epochal performance.

"I was invited to play golf with him one time in 1940 and had to turn it down. I had just returned from playing in an amateur tournament and I didn't feel I could ask my parents to foot the bill to send me over to Pinehurst to play with Mr. Jones. I always regretted it.

"Bob was the captain of the first golf team I ever played on, the first Eisenhower Cup team, and I got to know him a little better that way.

"When I was a member at Augusta I was with him often. We used to play a lot of bridge and talk a lot of golf. I think he was a great credit to the game," Billy Joe said softly . . . then added: "I think he was a great credit to humanity."

Another strong Patton memory is his Walker Cup competition. Asked if there was any special feeling to the golfer when he was representing his country, the Carolina drawl came back: "There was to Billy Joe Patton. I mean there's something about it when they hoist Old Glory and the Marine or Army band plans the Star Spangled Banner. If you can't get a feeling then, there's something wrong with you. It kind of made chills run over my whole body.

"I got a great thrill out of playing golf as a representative of the United States. I thought that was the greatest compliment I ever had."

TOM GOLA

The Biggest Quarter of an Inch

HOW DO YOU LOSE a quarter of an inch in height in one week? A Philadelphia draft board worked this bit of tape measure legerdemain, and to Tom Gola it became the biggest quarter of an inch in the world.

It was by that last-minute margin that the board got Gola under the height limit and was able to classify him 1-A. By so doing, it cut short one of the most auspicious beginnings the world of professional basketball had yet witnessed. Tom Gola's explosive rookie season had lifted the Philadelphia Warriors from the NBA cellar to the 1956 championship. His second professional season would come three years later. It was a shattering interruption to an uncommonly promising career.

At Philadelphia's La Salle High School, Tom was labeled the best high school player in the country. A high school All-American, he was picked to play in the North-South High School All-Star Game, and was voted the game's outstanding player.

He journeyed no further than across the street for college, made the varsity in his freshman year, and promptly delivered La Salle College to the NIT championship. Two years later, in Gola's junior year, La Salle became the NCAA champion. He was the only player to be a unanimous choice for the all-tourney team. Tom concluded his college career as one of basketball's rarities, a three-year All-American.

Born in Philadelphia, Tom Gola and the city were a love affair. High school, college and professional, he never left its environs of his own volition. He is easily the most popular athlete the city ever claimed. He is almost painfully honest, completely self-effacing, embarrassed by the honors constantly heaped upon him.

Tom was one of seven children, the son of a Philadelphia policeman. His gaudy success as a high school phenom brought him, by actual count, scholarship offers from 62 colleges and universities. It was sifting through these that brought Philadelphia as close as it would ever come to losing him.

"Like all kids," says Tom, "I was interested in the good basketball schools, and I narrowed it down to three of them. I visited Kentucky, St. John's in New York, and North Carolina twice."

Gola pretty much settled on North Carolina after his first trip there, accompanied by his high school coach. They discussed the scholarship, and what it and the university had to offer, and liked that they heard.

The second visit, however, brought some disturbing departures from that original conversation. Tom returned to Philadelphia and related what he termed the double-talk to his coach. They decided Tom might well be better off staying right in Philadelphia and, with that, La Salle College got Tom Gola.

Tom had achieved his height of 6'6" when he arrived at La Salle for his freshman year, and he had uncommon mobility for his size. He moved immediately and easily to the varsity, for freshmen were eligible at the school at the time. His instant stardom was so pronounced that Joe Lapchick, famed center on the original Celtics professional team said, after seeing Tom in just one game, "He could move directly into any one of the professional league's starting lineups."

His coach, Ken Loeffler, abandoned the traditional pivot-man offense to take advantage of the uncommon mobility and finesse of his rangy newcomer. Instead he set up a flowing pattern using a five-man weave and since the opposition tended to assign their big man to the job of guarding Gola, the matchups were almost no contest.

In his college years, Tom was chosen the outstanding player of the year many times: in New York's Madison Square Garden, Buffalo's Memorial Auditorium, Philadelphia's Convention Hall, Kansas City's Municipal Auditorium and the Cow Palace in San Francisco.

La Salle College's campus newspaper had a custom of selecting one of the school's athletes as "Explorer of the Week." Gola was given the honor so often the editors, with the blessing of the administration, ruled him ineligible so that some of the others might have a chance. Predictably, Tom applauded the move.

But of all the impressive performances and experiences, Tom looks back on that freshman year at LaSalle, and the winning of the NIT championship, as the greatest thrill of them all. It stands ahead of the subsequent NCAA title and the pro championship of his rookie year in the NBA.

"You see, it was the dream of every kid to play a game in the

Garden," Gola explains. "And there I was, playing there my freshman year. Of all my years in basketball, the best year I ever had was that freshman year in 1951. And the number one game is still that game when we won the NIT in the Garden."

In the course of moving through college, the game programs began to add a bit to Gola's height. By the time he reached his senior year he was listed as six feet, seven and three-quarter inches. This is sometimes helpful in intimidating the opposition, and when Tom was drafted by the Philadelphia Warriors, they continued the inch and three-quarters fib.

Thus it was with considerable surprise, after his championship rookie debut with the pros, that the citizens awoke one morning to discover their beloved son had been drafted.

Gola had exceeded the fondest dreams of the Warrior fans. He had poured in a season total of 732 points, had been superb on defense and rebounding, and had set up plays like a veteran of many seasons.

Attendance at Warrior games tripled. The Philadelphia club appeared on the threshold of one of those dynasties. They had a competent array of seasoned veterans dramatized by this young, new talent—a genuine superstar. Best of all, they thought, Gola wouldn't have to worry about being drafted into the Army. He is too tall.

But the Selective Service doesn't go by program measurements. Tom's draft board called him in for a physical. He measured out a shade over 6-6, just barely, but still too tall.

They called him in again for another physical, this time with that magic tape measure. This time the numbers echoed through the corridors like the weigh-in announcements at a championship fight.

"Six feet, five and three-quarters inches!"

That made Tom Gola just under the height limit, and Ft. Jackson in South Carolina was the next stop.

"I guarantee you I could stand up with some others in the NBA who were made 4-F," Gola recalls. "But it just happened to be one of those bad times for an athlete. The Army was very reluctant to let anyone in sports get away because of the bad time they were getting on their experiences with Billy Martin and I think Whitey Ford of the Yankees.

"Two years later, when I was discharged, a captain told me there was no way I was going to get out of the draft. He was there when I got that physical. So it was just one of those things."

One of those things or no, the two years of Army duty destroyed the finely honed precision that was Tom Gola the basketball player. Not completely, of course, for Tom came out to renew his professional career for several more years. But the superstar status was no longer his to obtain.

"I couldn't play at all in the Army," says Tom. "They just were too sensitive about giving any sports figure any kind of a break. I was an enlisted man and had all the duties; K.P. and everything else as it came up. I tried to play with the post team at first, but we would get back to the Fort around two in the morning, and I would have to get up at five to work in the kitchen and just couldn't handle it."

Gola came back to the Warriors two years later considerably overweight and pretty much out of touch. Tom explains: "As it turned out, my second year in the league was three years later. I was up against different personnel and of course things had changed a lot. You can see it today. In just a couple of years a man can change and a system can change."

Life got even more complicated when the team was sold and went clear across the country to become the San Francisco Warriors.

Gola was clearly unhappy with the distance between himself and Philadelphia. The Warriors did the best they could for him, trading him to the New York Knicks, just 90 miles from home.

But it was a burdensome 90 miles—four years of commuting between New York and Philadelphia—and it severely dampened his zeal for the game.

Tom Gola retired from professional basketball in 1966.

He established an insurance business in Philadelphia, and in the fall of 1966, ran for the State Legislature. Predictably, he was elected. He was elected again in 1968 and in the same year accepted the position of basketball coach at his alma mater, LaSalle.

His coaching career was to last only two seasons, for in 1969 Tom ran for the office of Philadelphia City Comptroller and won.

He resigned as LaSalle coach after the 1969 season to devote full time to his new office.

WHERE IS HE NOW?

Tom Gola is still the city comptroller and will seek re-election in 1973. He has turned his insurance business over to a management firm. His thoughts beyond the local political level are not firm. Asked about the possibility of moving to the national scene, Gola responded: "You have to take one step at a time in politics. You have to be the right guy at the right place. Right now I'm only concerned with re-election to this office."

Tom met his wife, Caroline Norris, on a summer vacation in New Jersey. They were married in 1955. Their only child is a son, Thomas Christopher. "If that formula of doubling the height of a two-year-old works out, I figure he will grow to about six feet four," says Tom.

Tom's athletic pace has slowed, and he is now into golf and fishing. He golfs in the high 80's, carrying a 12 handicap.

"I've seen just one pro game in two years. I used to get involved with an occasional old-timers' game, but I've cut that out too. Last year I got banged up pretty good, jammed a tendon in my hand, and I figure it's not worth it."

With so much being made lately about the recruiting excesses of colleges searching for a top basketball team, the question was asked of his own experiences at La Salle as a coach.

"When I recruited at La Salle, we could offer a boy room, books, tuition and fifteen, I think now its twenty dollars a month. This is basic. That is all that any coach offered me when I was recruited and as far as the school is concerned, every coach at every school offers every boy the same thing.

"But then the alumni come in, in conjunction with some of the coaches or the university, and tells the boy how easy they will make it for him while he's at that school. This is the basis of recruiting.

"Now the Ivy League—they have a system of proving financial need. But their tuition is so high that almost everybody can prove it. What they do is come around and say, 'We'll give you a summer job for $5,000—$3,000 for your tuition and such, and $2,000 for yourself.' "

Tom's ideas for correcting abuses are simple: "It has to be straightened out by the schools themselves. The same people that make the rules are the ones who break them. I think the way it is now you can't control it . . . you can't police it. So let's just forget all the hypocrisy and let the schools go out and do what they want to do. That's what is being done today, even with the rules."

PARRY O'BRIEN

The Man Who Revolutionalized
Shot Putting

A WEEK IN MAY of 1954 will remain forever historic in the annals of track and field competition. In a span of days, the two most stubborn barriers in sports were broken: four minutes in the mile run, 60 feet in the shot put.

In Oxford, England, Roger Bannister made the mile breakthrough with a run of 3:59.4. Halfway around the world, in Los Angeles, the unlikely combination of the ancient science of yoga and a new technique burst the bonds of the shot put's mystical barrier as Parry O'Brien recorded a shattering heave of 60 feet, five and one-quarter inches.

A gifted athlete with an intellectual bent, O'Brien was one of the most sought-after prep athletes upon graduation from high school in Santa Monica. Six feet, three inches and well over 200 pounds, he was a superb football end, a high school champion in the shot and discus, and with all his size, an excellent sprinter.

He enrolled at the University of Southern California with the intention of competing in both football and track. But when Parry, as a freshman, steadily reached 54 feet with the shot while none of the varsity could even do 50 feet, it was time for a decision. Though only a freshman, it was evident that O'Brien was ready for world-class competition. There was an immediate opportunity for a tour of Europe with a United States team, but he would miss spring football practice if he went.

At that time, USC football was at a low ebb. It was evident the best opportunity to gain lasting fame, both for Parry and the university, was in concentration on track and field and the abandonment of football. The decision was made and with it Southern Cal quite probably lost an All-America end.

As mentioned, O'Brien had remarkable speed despite his size. The European tour had him competing in three events; the shot, the discus, and as a sprinter on the relay team. He could point to an official 10.7 seconds in the 100 meters.

It was this plethora of events that started Parry toward revising the technique of putting the shot. "I was looking for an easier way to throw the shot," the reminiscing O'Brien said, "simply because I was involved in so many events each week."

The shot-put circle is seven feet in diameter, with a toe board in front. Traditionally, shot putters had moved from a side stance, a long hop from the back of the circle to gain momentum, then the body turning 90 degrees with the arm action launching the shot.

O'Brien began to increase the body turn. "Little by little, almost degree by degree, I increased the turn by altering my stance at the beginning point until my back was turned completely from the intended line of flight."

Now, instead of the sideways hop, O'Brien started with a hard backward jump that landed him on his right foot in the center of the circle. Retaining this momentum, he would bounce off the right foot, spinning his body a full 180 degrees as the arm thrust out to start the 16-pound ball on its way, landing at the toe board in the follow-through.

It was on a European tour, in Germany, that Parry first tried the new technique in competition. The results were not spectacular, but the promise was obviously there. "I got so much whip with the 180-degree turn," says Parry, "and while I was only achieving about the same distance, I was doing it so much easier."

With the Olympic Games coming up in 1952, O'Brien began an intensive, two-pronged program. At 19, he was not yet fully developed. To accelerate that development, he embarked on an exhaustive program of working with weights—daily workouts with 60-pound dumbbells and a 320-pound barbell.

The shot put technique itself needed much more practice and polish. There was no one to coach him, for the 180-degree turn was his own invention. The timing of the arm-thrust with the body turn required an almost exquisite coordination, and the greatest problem O'Brien encountered was achieving the high degree of total concentration needed to execute it properly.

It was here that yoga rendered a notable assist.

O'Brien's study major at USC was commercial aviation, but it was not a serious major. He was to eventually get his degree in business and finance. But the Korean situation still weighed heavily upon the United States, and young men in college had military requirements to fulfill. O'Brien satisfied the armed services by enrolling in the Air Force ROTC and taking the commercial aviation major.

His intellectual leanings drew him to many interesting side studies, one of which was a class in Eastern Religions. Here he was exposed to the study of yoga, the ancient Hindu discipline aimed at training the consciousness for a state of perfect spiritual insight.

The degree of concentration available with some mastery of yoga intrigued O'Brien. The university had a strong international attraction and its cadre of foreign students included a goodly number from India.

With them, O'Brien became a serious student of yoga. "With my heavy body-building program, I wasn't able to accomplish any of the contortive exercises that are an important part of the yoga discipline," said Parry, "but it helped me tremendously in concentration. With yoga, I was able to concentrate completely—almost in a trance-like state that shut out all outside influences and distractions."

Now the twin paths of build-up and technique were beginning to mesh and Parry O'Brien was on the threshold of revolutionizing the art of putting the shot. His inventive style was to become forever known as the "O'Brien Technique" and is universally used in the sport today.

Parry had never reached 56 feet with the old method, but now in the spring of 1952 he was going over 57 feet and he won a place on the Olympic team.

The games of that year were held in Helsinki, Finland. O'Brien presented a strange sight to the coterie of behemoths who made up the shot put contingent. He was still but 20 years old, and by their standards slight at a mere 230 pounds. He would sit off by himself in a trance-like state. He would speak to no one as he readied for his try. Then he would rise and trot easily up and down the field, occasionally pausing to bend nearly double. He would clench his fists and rotate them swiftly, all the while emitting a ferocious series of animal-like "woofs."

Then he stepped into that seven-foot circle and won the gold medal with an Olympic record heave of 57 feet, one and one-half inches.

It was in 1953 that Parry first became aware that breaking the 60-foot barrier was within the realm of possibility.

Another winter of weight-lifting was steadily increasing his bulk and musculature in a program that was to eventually bring him to 260 pounds.

The world record at the time O'Brien poised in the circle at the 1953 Fresno Relays was 58 feet, ten and a half inches, held by Jim Fuchs of Yale. Parry had been flirting with it in preceding meets with puts in the low and middle 58's.

Now he crouched, found his balance, and exploded into the

thrust. The 16-pound ball bounced to the ground to leave its tell-tale dent 59 feet and three-quarters of an inch from the toe board for a new world record.

The tantalizing 60-foot goal remained out of reach through the rest of 1953, but in May of 1954 the moment came.

It was in Los Angeles, in a dual meet between USC and UCLA. The actual break-through was something of an anti-climax, for Parry surpassed the distance in his final warm-up.

Still in his sweat clothes, O'Brien launched a practice toss that traveled 60 feet, four inches.

"It surprised me," O'Brien recalls. "I never threw very far in practice. I just tried to maintain an even pace and work on technique. I would generally run two to three feet less than in competition."

But that practice effort left no question the moment was at hand. The crowd exploded as O'Brien let go the one that counted. The barrier had been broken with something to spare. The distance was measured at 60 feet, five and one-quarter inches.

In June, Parry broke his own record with a put of 60 feet, ten inches. As happens, once the mental block of a seemingly insurmountable barrier is broken, the move beyond it is dramatic. Parry had been the first to pass 59 feet, and the first past 60. He went on to record firsts past 61, 62 and 63 feet.

O'Brien competed in four Olympiads. He won the gold medal in 1952 at Helsinki, and won another gold in 1956 at Melbourne, Australia. It was a silver medal in Rome, Italy, in 1960 and his Olympic competition ended in 1964 with the Tokyo, Japan games in which he finished fourth.

World records are no longer his, save one: the combined left and right hand shot put. "It's an odd-ball event," O'Brien admits, "but it is still competed in some European meets. Many attempt it and can do well right handed, but they have a devil of a time getting past 20 or 30 feet with the left."

Parry recorded 61 feet, three-fourths of an inch right handed and a remarkable 45 feet, nine and a half inches left handed for a total of 106 feet, ten and a quarter inches.

WHERE IS HE NOW?

Parry O'Brien is vice-president of the Colwell Company in Los Angeles, a mortgage banking concern. He reached his 40th birthday in 1972.

His family includes his wife, Arden, whom he married in 1960, and his four-year-old daughter Erin.

His weight has been pared from 260 pounds down to 235. There was a drastic cutdown on the enormous amounts of food he consumed while competing, but otherwise the reducing process was not all that difficult.

"When I stopped the weight program, I lost about 20 pounds almost at once," he said. "Muscle tissue is much denser than ordinary tissue and when I stopped maintaining them through weight-lifting, the weight just dropped off.

"I still keep myself in good shape, however. I still do some work with light weights to keep up my muscle tone and I run at least two miles a day. My main sports activities now are handball and bicycling."

With the present attention being given to the unwise use of drugs in athletics, the question arose about the use of steroids, drugs that can produce dramatic gains in weight and bulk.

"I never used them," O'Brien responded. "They were just becoming known when I was active. You know the Los Angeles area is probably the weight-lifting capital of the world. The muscle boys were trying them but no one knew very much about them at the time. I looked into them, but I felt there were just too many unknown factors. There was kidney and liver inflammation that some of the weight-lifters were experiencing and I didn't feel there was enough research on them to risk a try."

That Parry keeps in shape was evidenced at the Senior Sports International competition in the Los Angeles Coliseum in June of 1971. He won both the shot put and the discus throw in the 35 to 39 year-old category.

He stays close to the sport as a special commentator for the American Broadcasting Company in their Wide World of Sports coverage of meets as well as their coverage of the Olympic Games. And when the shot put comes on the screen, Parry O'Brien delivers a rare expertise.

You could say he invented it.

HOWARD "HOPALONG" CASSADY

The Brilliant Buckeye

THE SEASON FINALE of 1955 would have been an easy game for Ohio State to lose. The Buckeyes couldn't return to the Rose Bowl under the Big Ten "no repeat" rule. A victory for Michigan in this game would send the Wolverines to the Bowl.

But Ohio State coach, Woody Hayes, regarded the Big Ten championship as the most important thing—whether or not it resulted in a trip to the Rose Bowl. Woody's insatiable hunger for that title, together with a young man named Howard Cassady playing his last game in the scarlet and gray of Ohio State, combined for a lop-sided wipe-out of Michigan that was awesome to behold.

Ohio State had swept through the conference the previous year, spearheaded by the brilliant running of Cassady, to achieve not only the Big Ten championship, but the nation's number one ranking as well.

Hayes had installed the then new split-T option offense invented by Missouri's Don Faurot. With a runner like Cassady, and a gifted quarterback named Dave Leggett, there was no stopping it.

The Rose Bowl of January 1, 1955 matched them against Southern California.

Ohio State and Southern Cal met in fog and rain . . . and mud. It was that kind of rain that if Noah had been around, he would have built another ark.

It was a day designed for fumbles, but Ohio State was not to commit a single miscue. Cassady slashed through the line on quick-openers, and trailed Leggett to skirt the ends on his pitchouts. The only time they switched from their overpowering ground attack in the first half, Leggett threw a running pass, for a touchdown.

The Rose Bowl victory was 20 to 7, Ohio State.

Now it was almost a year later. While Ohio State could win the Big Ten championship again, the emotional edge had to go to Michigan. If Michigan won, they would go to the Rose Bowl. If the Wolverines lost, Michigan State would drop in behind Ohio State as runner-up, and the Rose Bowl trip would be theirs.

It was the final game in the illustrious career of Ohio State's Cassady. Dubbed "Hopalong" after the hero of the then current TV western series, Cassady had come onto the Ohio State scene at a time when freshmen were permitted to play varsity football. His four years of stardom were closing out, and this was to turn out to be Hopalong's "day" at Ann Arbor.

Cassady led a 70-yard drive that ended in a field goal. He led another of 52 yards and scored the game's first touchdown.

Ohio State trapped Michigan for a safety, then added another touchdown. They shut out Michigan 17-0.

Hopalong had a total rushing yardage of 146. This was 37 yards more than the entire Michigan team could gain all afternoon.

Over a span of nine games that season, Cassady had amassed 958 yards on the ground, a rushing average of well over 100 yards per game, an all-time Ohio State record. His career total of 2466 yards rushing was another.

These had been glory years. Cassady had exploded for three touchdowns in the first college game he had ever played, as a 177-pound freshman against Indiana.

In his junior and senior years he was a unanimous choice for All-American. At the conclusion of his senior season he was named the winner of both the Heisman and Maxwell Trophy awards. More recently, Hopalong has been honored as "The Outstanding Player" on the all-time Buckeye football team.

Strangely, it was a basketball game that sold Ohio State coach Woody Hayes on the Cassady of Columbus' Central High. The youngster had made All-City in football, baseball and basketball as well as All-State in football. But he didn't have too much size, and Hayes deliberated about bringing him in. The famed coach had time to deliberate, for Ohio State was the only university Cassady wanted.

When Hayes saw young Cassady score the last 17 points in a game in which Central High upset the defending state champion, he made up his mind.

"When I saw that basketball game, I decided to take him," Woody Hayes recalls. "He was a winner."

If there was one man who played a key role in the eventual fame of Hopalong Cassady, it was his high school coach, Dave Parks. When young Cassady enrolled at Central High School, it was with no thought at all of going to college. He came to Central from a very poor section of town, where the kids just didn't go to college. Not a slum, but, as Cassady puts it: "Just a neighborhood where nobody had any money.

"Neither of my parents finished high school, let alone go to college. My mother and father both worked, and when I went into high school it was to learn a trade. I signed up for all the manual training courses, woodworking, metalworking, things like that."

When coach Parks saw the blossoming athletic skills of his three-sport whiz, he knew that a college career was a distinct probabilty and proceeded to change young Cassady's academic life.

Parks convinced Hopalong to switch to courses that would qualify him for college admission, and Cassady found himself enmeshed in algebra and Spanish and chemistry.

Surprisingly, he also found his grade average shooting up.

"Those subjects really came easy to me," Cassady recalls. "In the trade courses you had to make a project just so and I was getting B's and C's. In the academic courses I was hitting A's and B's."

The concern of Coach Parks opened up the world to Cassady. Record-breaking runner, two-time All-American, Heisman Trophy winner, and the recipient of the biggest bonus professional football had paid to any player at that point in time.

In addition to football, Cassady was a considerable star in baseball. Hopalong played shortstop and centerfield on a team that also had the renowned slugger, Frank Howard. In two of Cassady's three years of competition, Ohio State won the Big Ten baseball championship, with Cassady hitting well above .300 in every year of his competition.

With college behind him, Hopalong had two major professional sports beckoning. The New York Yankees, Cleveland Indians, Detroit Tigers and Cincinnati Reds were making highly attractive offers, and he was the top draft choice of the Detroit Lions of the National Football League.

Cassady had married at the end of his freshman year and the family now included their first son. His wife, Betty, was the major influence in deciding which sport to pursue as a professional.

"Football looked at that time like a far better deal for me," Cassady recalled. "I'm not sure I would make the same decision if I had it to do over again, but with a wife and baby I just couldn't see spending a year or two in the minors, being away from home for most of the year between spring training and the season, just living out of a suitcase. Football was just six months long, you were always at home except for weekend travel to 'away' games."

Buckeye coach Woody Hayes took Cassady under his wing in the jousting for contract terms with the Detroit Lions, and Hayes negotiated a contract that produced a record bonus.

"I'd guess you'd smile at it today," says Cassady. "It was $15,000. But no one had gotten anything like that before then, and no one got that much after that until around 1960."

Winning the Heisman Trophy was no jinx for Hopalong Cassady as a professional. He played five years for Detroit without ever missing a game. His steady five and six yards per carry were instrumental in bringing the Lions to the National Football League Championship in 1957, his second year with the team. He was to be co-captain of the Lions for two years. and in all carve out an eight-year career with that team.

Prior to retiring, he would also see service with the Philadelphia Eagles and Cleveland Browns, but when the end of his active career was at hand, he was ready for a business career at home in Columbus, Ohio.

WHERE IS HE NOW?

Hopalong Cassady is an object of community pride in Columbus.

He and his wife, Betty, now have three children, two boys and a girl.

His oldest son, Craig, is bringing the Cassady name back to Ohio State. Craig is six feet tall, 155 pounds, and starred mainly as a defensive back (All-City) at Whetstone High School.

"He's little," Woody Hayes conceded, "but he's a real competitor. Has the same fire as his dad.

"We'll use him as a defensive back or a flanker. He has good speed and good hands. He ran a screen pass 80 yards against Lima."

Hopalong Cassady is now Marketing Director for the Evans Adhesives Corporation.

He wasn't long out of football when Cassady became involved with the Joseph Kennedy Foundation for retarded children. The Kennedy clan enlisted the aid of prominent athletes for their Retarded Children's Olympics program and, in Cassady, they got an unexpected bonus of deep personal involvement.

Hopalong did far more than simply lend his name and endorsement to the program. He toured the country helping local groups start the regional activities that would lead these unfortunate children to their own "Olympics" and the greatest adventure of their encumbered lives.

He still maintains that heavy travel schedule on behalf of the

Kennedy Foundation, for now their activities embrace every state and Mexico and Canada as well.

The first Retarded Children's Olympics was held in Chicago, and for Cassady, it is a warm memory. "Retarded kids had never had an athletic program before where they've ever competed. Some of these kids had never left home."

Then Hoppy warmed up to a particularly strong memory: "They talk about the Chicago Police. Hell, they had over 500 members of the Chicago Police Force donate their time to work with these kids . . . to handle them in the hotels, security, to transport them back and forth and the watching over them at the games.

"With retarded kids you know you just can't leave them out in the big city. They're so unaware of what's going on."

He has merged a successful business career with a tremendous national community effort in behalf of the most luckless of our children.

Hopalong Cassady. Still an All-American.

ROY HARRIS

The Heavyweight from Cut N' Shoot

IT WAS ONLY 40 miles from the cosmopolitan and oil-rich environs of Houston, Texas, but it was another world.

It was called the Big Thicket, a mysterious and sprawling tangle of palmetto swamp, dense pine, alligators and assorted snakes. The wild life peculiar to the area included its human inhabitants.

The law of the Big Thicket was the law of the fist, the knee, the knife, the axe handle. When a minor oil strike in the depression-ridden 1930's brought the drilling gangs to the Thicket, the resistance of the shadowy inhabitants was monumental. Unimpressed by the possibility of riches from the black gold, they fought to stop the ravaging of their domain caused by the rigs and the roads and the fences.

There were three or four killings a night. Every night.

If the Big Thicket had a capital, it was the community with the paperback name of Cut 'N Shoot. Not that it was the principal city. That was Conroe, the county seat. But if there was a wild and untamed epitome of life as it was lived there, it was Cut 'N Shoot. It was Al Capp's Dogpatch come to life, including a real L'il Abner.

His name was Roy Harris, a remarkably handsome young man with the build of a Greek statue. He became a professional boxer to pay his way through college, and he fought for the heavyweight championship of the world. Not surprisingly, he was named after a gangster.

The first Harris to arrive in Cut 'N Shoot was Roy's grandfather, John Wesley Harris, who populated the area to the extent of siring 16 children. Three of the sons, Bob, Jack and Henry, became storied brawlers in their time, still the heroes of the wildest legends of Cut 'N Shoot's epic mayhem.

Wielding an axe handle, Bob Harris is credited with flattening 16 men in ten minues flat. And there are plenty of other such stories too.

Like the time a vengeful bunch of toughs called his uncle out to the road with the offer of a drink of moonshine. As Bob tilted the jug, one of the party slugged him with a length of iron, and another leaped on him with a knife. The reeling victim suffered about a dozen stab wounds before he was able to draw his own knife. He spun on his tormentor and his whirling slash almost completely decapacitated his assailant.

"That's a true story," says Roy. "I'd guess the same sort of thing probably happened to my daddy maybe three or four times. When the oil crews came in, it was a pretty rough place. There'd be three or four killed a night."

Henry, the youngest of the formidable brothers, is Roy's father. He named Roy for Roy Tipton, a gangster associated with Machine Gun Kelly, who came into the Big Thicket on the lam from Chicago and struck up a warm friendship with Brother Jack.

About here, it should be pointed out that the Harris brothers were not animals, but simply proved out best at what was necessary to survive. Henry was a stern father, intent on raising a circumspect family. There are eight children in all, four sons, four daughters. Tobe is the oldest son, then Roy, then Henry. Jimmy was a late baby, only three months old when Roy climbed into the ring with Floyd Patterson for his shot at the heavyweight championship of the world.

Henry Harris was a bear of a man, nicknamed Big Henry in deference to the 240 pounds of muscle spread over his six foot, three-inch frame.

"If daddy had followed boxing, he'd of done much better than I did," said Roy. "He was much bigger than me and much faster. He could run the hundred in 9.7."

Big Henry was demanding in the education of his children. Poor grades were not tolerated. All his sons were to go through college. His ideas of education included learning how to fight, and, when Roy was only six and Tobe seven and a half, he brought home a set of boxing gloves and put up a make-shift ring.

The ring was on bare ground, set in the corner of a fenced-in yard, with the existing fencing making up two sides of it. That the existing fencing was of barbed wire was of little concern to Big Henry. It served to keep the youngsters in the center of the ring and hard at it. Years later, when Roy was fighting professionally, he still was not one to go against the ropes.

Both boys were to become good boxers, but Tobe's career was

cut short when he was thrown from a horse and wound up with a badly injured shoulder.

Roy became an exceptional amateur boxer, losing only ten of 83 amateur fights. He became the Texas Golden Gloves middleweight champion in 1952 and, subsequently, won the state light-heavyweight title three years running.

While he was still in high school, Roy wound up on a college boxing team. Nearby Sam Houston State Teachers College had trouble filling the welter and middleweight slots on their squad and frequently, on out-of-town matches, they would simply bring along Roy and turn him loose.

The experience made Roy determined to go to college and it was boxing that got him through. Not on a scholarship, but as a professional.

Benny King, a friend in Houston, told Roy he could get him $75.00 a fight if he wanted to turn professional, to which Roy responded: "Line 'em up."

"Boxing made college possible for me," Roy insists. "I couldn't have made it without it. I could make about $250 a month, and that was all it took."

Roy was not all that enamored with fighting. If it hadn't been a means of getting through school, he insists, he would never have turned professional. But as long as he was doing well at it, Roy stayed with boxing after getting his degree at Sam Houston and, as a local attraction, found himself in a match with the fancy and well-known Willie Pastrano.

The fight was set in Houston, promoted by Lou Viscusi. Viscusi owned the then lightweight champion Joe Brown and former featherweight champ Willie Pep. In addition to managing, Viscusi promoted fights in Houston and Tampa, with occasional stops in between.

Roy Harris, meanwhile, was getting discouraged with the alliance with Benny King. Benny was proving unable to get Roy the fights that could move him into the important money in boxing.

He looked upon the Viscusi promotion as an opportunity, and solidified it by beating the highly regarded Pastrano.

"I went to Lou and told him if he would manage me I would keep on fighting," Harris recounted. "If he didn't, I was going to quit."

Viscusi took him in, and put him under the tutelage of one of boxing's renowned trainers, Bill Gore. For all his fighting heritage, Roy was still unpolished. Because he retreated so seldom, he didn't know how to do it, and one of Gore's immediate projects was to teach the budding heavyweight the footwork of maneuvering. In short order, Roy was to need all the instructional help he could get.

The reigning monarch of boxing at the time was Jim Norris of Chicago. Norris headed the International Boxing Club. The IBC controlled virtually all the fighters of any consequence and the matchmaking for the two national television fight shows each week. But to their consternation, the most important of all boxers, the heavyweight champion, eluded them.

The youthful Floyd Patterson had risen to the heavyweight throne. His manager, more guru than manager, was Cus D'Amato. Cus, using his control of the heavyweight championship as leverage, was determined to establish a boxing empire of his own in defiance of the IBC.

The two top-ranked challengers were Eddie Machen and Zora Folley, both controlled by the IBC. Attempting a freeze-out, the IBC refused to match either of them against Patterson under D'Amato's aegis.

Cus had to forage elsewhere to keep his champion active and in this quest came upon Viscusi's Roy Harris. The match was made for Wrigley Field in Los Angeles, to be fought on the 18th of August, 1958.

Unwittingly, the IBC gave the fight a notable assist. To show the world the superiority of its two contenders, the IBC made the mistake of matching Machen and Folley against each other.

While these two were both expert boxers, it was equally true that each was a counter-puncher. It was imperative they have an opponent who would bring the fight to them if they were to show their impressive skills.

The result of their meeting, on coast-to-coast television, was a monumental yawn. For twelve harmless rounds they stalked and circled, each waiting for the other to lead, bringing to the American ring what may have been boxing's only no-hitter.

The charade brought sudden substance to Roy Harris as a suitable opponent for Patterson and when the sporting press discovered the Cut 'N Shoot heritage of the challenger, the match rocketed in its public interest.

The Harris training site was the Arrowhead Springs Hotel in California's San Bernardino mountains. No matter how many reporters gathered, there were Cut 'N Shoot stories to go around. The Big Thicket achieved overnight fame. Coupled with the engaging personality of this totally handsome, unaffected and surprisingly educated young man, the fight became a press agent's dream.

It was somewhat of a nightmare to trainer Bill Gore, however.

Harris had nowhere near the skills of Patterson. Where Floyd's machine-gun combinations would rain three to five punches in scientific sequence, Harris was being painstakingly led through the rudiments of the simple one-two. Hope persisted largely through the fact that Roy had defeated the very clever Willie Pastrano. That, and the one truly impressive punch in the Harris arsenal, a sizzling right uppercut that just might find its way through the gloves of Patterson, who fought with them held high, on either side of his jaw.

While those hopes were to be dashed, the fight itself was one in the finest Big Thicket tradition.

Patterson, rusty from his sporadic competition, began slowly. A quick left hand and that right uppercut were scoring for the pride of Cut 'N Shoot. In the second round, the uppercut found Patterson's chin and dropped him for the count of four. Back on his feet, Floyd caught a left hook that almost dropped him again.

The crowd of 22,000 which had paid a California record gate of almost a quarter of a million dollars was in a frenzy. Patterson backed and filled, his superior skills keeping Harris under control. Finally, the sharpness that only fighting can bring began to return to the champion. He drew blood on Harris's heretofore unmarked face. A right hand dropped Roy in the seventh round. Patterson knocked him down twice more in the eighth, once with each hand.

The cuts multiplied and opened on the face of Roy Harris. At the same time, the cumulative effect of Floyd's combination were taking their deadly toll to the body.

The twelfth round saw a long right crash Harris to the canvas again. Roy wobbled up, fell back on one knee, finally staggered to his feet at the count of nine, and somehow lasted the round.

But Bill Gore had had enough. For all his awesome courage, to allow the fight to continue could have ruined the game young Texan. Gore signaled to the referee that the fight was over.

Though he had lost the fight, Roy had won the crowd. Half blinded, he drew a thundering ovation as Bill Gore gently led him back to his dressing room.

The odds on the fight had Harris a 7-1 underdog. He wasn't expected to last three rounds. Instead, he went twelve, fighting back even when hopelessly outclassed in a manner that gave Patterson his toughest fight since he had won the crown. His face was carved to a bloody pulp, but he wouldn't be knocked out.

It was a brief moment in the sun for Roy Harris and he cashed in on his new-found fame through a run of some ten more fights before he decided to call it a career.

WHERE IS HE NOW?

Roy Harris is still in Cut 'N Shoot. He is in his second term as county clerk, elected unopposed the last time around. Roy has become a man of modest wealth with extensive cattle and land holdings in Texas and Arkansas. The old, part log, part frame homestead in the Thicket has been supplanted with a sprawling manor. It houses, at the 1972 head count, wife Jean, eleven-year-old Connie, Robert at ten, Kevin, who is eight, and six-year-old Sabrina.

Roy has been involved in gathering real estate since an early age. "I've been buying land since I was 16 years old, in high school," he says. "Bought nine acres from my aunt, working in the summers to get the money."

From that point on, whatever money he could save, he invested in land. While he didn't make big money in boxing, what he did make followed this investment pattern. The growth of the Houston area did the rest.

"You wouldn't recognize the Thicket any more," Harris says somewhat ruefully. "The sub-dividers have torn it up. They staked out lots around Lake Livingston, a 90,000-acre lake, and they're all sold out. Now they're working on Lake Conroe, about five miles west of here. That'll all be built up soon.

"Houston is growing fast and moving this way, and I've been real lucky. Boxing was a big help to me. It got me well known to a lot of people who have helped me a good bit."

Roy was not averse to helping himself. When he finished boxing he went back to school and majored in history, then went back again and got a major in education. He taught school for a while but found he couldn't get by on the low pay and moved full time into the real estate business.

This inspired him to return to school again, this time to the University of Arkansas Law School. He could only spare the time to amass some 14 hours of credit, but it was the beginning of continuing study reading law in a local law office. He made one try at the Texas bar examination, coming away with a grade of 70.

"You need a grade of 75 to pass," Roy laughed, "so I'm about ready to take it again and see if I can't pick up those other five points."

Roy's land holdings in Arkansas consist of two large tracts, one in Lawrence County, the other in Randolph County. "My tract in Randolph County is just a great place," Roy enthused. "That's up near the Missouri border along Highway 93. It's 1,500 acres with three-quarters of a mile fronting along the highway and about a mile and a quarter frontage along the Eleven Point River.

"That's a famous river up there. It has real good fishing and is probably the cleanest river in the United States. It's about 200 feet wide at my property and runs around 25 feet deep and you can drink the water right out of it."

Roy's memories of boxing are warm ones, particularly his association with Lou Viscusi. "He was a real good man," says Roy. "He was one of the few men in the business who was really honest and tried to take care of his fighters. I think he's tops."

Big Henry is still living, but is no longer at the scene of his legends. This most impressive of fathers has moved to Arkansas with Tobe, Henry and Jimmy. Big Henry has bought land adjoining Roy's and looks after Roy's cattle along with his own.

Like his father before him, Roy has brought out a set of boxing gloves for his own sons, Robert and Kevin.

"I probably won't start them actually boxing for another year or so. I don't want to push them on it. But I definitely want them to learn how to fight.

"I don't care if they fight professionally, but I do want them to learn to fight well enough to protect themselves. A person who hasn't ever fought doesn't realize how helpless he is trying to fight when he runs into someone who knows what he is doing."

The dwindling Big Thicket is now suburbia. The raucous roughnecks who gave Cut 'N Shoot its name have long departed —some unexpectedly, some, like Big Henry, to other, less crowded soil. But the clan still has a worthy representative in Roy Harris, and as the gloves come out for the tiny fists of little Kevin and Robert, a tradition carries on.

TAD WEED

The PAT Man Who Started a
New Country

YOU WILL FIND THIS story hard to believe.

But then a lot about Thurlow "Tad" Weed is hard to believe. Five feet, five and one-half inches tall, 145 pounds, and a football player at Ohio State? For Woody Hayes?

Tad was a kicker, naturally. He was an integral part of Ohio State's 1954 undefeated team that went all the way to the Rose Bowl. Weed went through that year without missing a single extra point attempt—something that had never been done before that time.

Tad was small, even for a place kicker. He is three and one-half inches shorter, and played at 27 pounds lighter than even the Miami Dolphin's Garo Yapremian, the smallest of today's specialists. Since Tad Weed played for half a season with the Pittsburgh Steelers, on record he is the smallest man ever to play in the National Football League.

As if all the foregoing wasn't distinction enough, the diminutive ex-football hero is now in the process of starting his own country.

We'll get to that later.

"I just quit growing when I got to the ninth grade," says Tad, looking back.

He had been playing halfback and figured to continue as such until he realized he had attained about all the size he was going to.

He was born in Columbus, Ohio, and was raised almost literally in the shadow of Ohio State's mammoth stadium. Football was a big part of his life, and he turned to kicking as a way to stay in it. He had done a little kicking the year before and now he started practicing the art in earnest. From that ninth grade realization until he finished his college football, Tad practiced his place kicking the year around.

Tad's father was doing comfortably well in the oil business, so Tad could plan on going to college, even though there were no scholarships for five-foot, five-inch placekickers. Tad started making plans to attend Northwestern.

His freshman coach at Grand View High School was Bill Hess. When Bill learned Tad was planning to go out for football as a kicker, the coach had an earnest talk with him on the likely greater glories of playing right where he was.

"As I got to thinking about it," Tad says, "I began asking myself, 'What am I doing?'

"This is the football capital of the world. Eighty-five thousand people at every game.

"I changed my mind at the last minute and enrolled at Ohio State."

On the first day of practice, not knowing what he should do, Tad hung around the halfbacks. The next thing he knew, it was his turn to run a play.

Only one.

An assistant coach did a classic double-take at the sight of this mite of a boy trying to find some daylight in a forest of ponderous legs. He blew his whistle.

"Forget it, son," said the coach. "Here's a football. Just get off to one side and kick it."

As things turned out, Tad Weed was to kick it very well. Woody Hayes never did let him kick off. He always seemed to have someone about 6'4" and 240 to handle that. The thought of little Tad possibly having to tackle someone made him blanch.

They didn't have to get him a special uniform, but they did have to take the size "small" in pretty drastically.

"I didn't wear any pads on my hips or thighs, either," Weed volunteered. "I was so small that wearing full pads shortened my range, so I only wore the helmet and shoulder pads."

Two games stand out in the memory of Tad Weed. His final regular season game with Ohio State, and the Chicago College All-Star game the following year.

"The Rose Bowl game was a unique experience," says Tad, "but not the high point the other two were.

"That 1955 Rose Bowl game was the year of the rain. No one in California wanted to admit it could rain like that, but the water was pouring down the seats of the Rose Bowl like a waterfall.

"We had a punt *stick*. You know how much rain there has to be to have a ball come down and stick in the ground."

Ohio State had played Michigan in the last game of the season, for the Big Ten Championship and the Rose Bowl. It is a vivid memory to Weed.

"It was one of those wild football games, with so much confetti in the air it looked like snow.

"You realize you are playing your last game and a place kicker has to hold himself mentally taut and not really indulge, emotionally. You've only got a second to produce, and if you're thinking about something else, it's all over.

"So it wasn't really, I guess, until it *was* all over, standing there in the middle of the field, that it hit me that we had gone through the season undefeated, and I had realized my own ambition of going through a whole season without missing an extra point."

The 1955 College All-Star game was a reunion for Tad and Notre Dame quarterback Ralph Guglielmi. They had been teammates all through Grandview High School.

Guglielmi was named the game's outstanding player, but Tad Weed made the difference. Weed kicked three field goals as the All-Stars achieved one of their rare victories over the professionals, beating the Cleveland Browns, 30 to 27.

"I was pretty lucky, too," Weed says in retrospect. "Len Ford, the Browns' defensive end, was in fast enough to block two of them. I'll swear one went right past his ear and the other went right under his armpit."

Tad had a few more hours to compete for his degree at Ohio State, but the Los Angeles Rams drafted him.

As things turned out, this didn't interrupt his education at all. Weed was cut by the Rams at the end of the exhibition schedule, just in time to return to Ohio State and enroll for the fall term.

The professional season was half over when the Steelers ran into kicking troubles, and signed Weed for the last half of the campaign.

The Steelers never won a game with Tad and the little guy had started and ended his professional career in that brief span.

WHERE IS HE NOW?

Tad Weed is forming his own country! An honest-to-goodness, brand new nation that is rising out in the South Pacific some 380 miles south of the Fiji Islands.

As Damon Runyon used to say . . . a tale goes with it. And if you get the feeling this is something akin to a Woody Allen movie plot, please understand that this is a very serious and thoughtful venture by Tad Weed and his associates.

A book written by Michael Oliver, entitled *A New Constitution for a New Country,* is pretty much credited with triggering the movement. The book discourses on what it claims was the truly unique achievement of the birth of the United States, that of having its founding fathers create a constitution which limited the government to the same "live and let live" rules that the people had to live by.

Says Weed: "We believe that we have now flip-flopped the premise that really made America great. We have traded individual rights for group rights and we're going to have a lot of trouble as long as we proceed on that premise."

The book, and its philosophy of returning to a purely capitalistic laissez-faire government, one that attempts no regulation or interference in the market place, inspired the search for some remote piece of real estate upon which such a new country could be established.

Two groups of determined individualists merged into the common cause. They were the Caribbean Pacific Enterprises, Ltd. and the Ocean Life Research Foundation.

While Tad Weed disavows any role as spokesman for the group, it was Tad and Bob Marks of Los Angeles who took the first steps needed to establish the new country: that of making it visible.

The search for territory had failed to disclose any area of land anywhere that was not already claimed by, or within the sovereignty of, an existing nation. This discouraging investigation led to the thought of finding some unclaimed, submerged land. So it was they checked out, and decided upon, the Minerva Reefs in the South Pacific.

There are two sets of reefs, about 18 miles apart, each approximately 14 miles in circumference. They barely break the surface at low tide, are totally submerged at high tide, and they belong to no one.

The plan is to dredge up the sand from the shallow lagoons formed by the reefs and build up the surface above the high tide level in a manner that will withstand the ocean, the hurricanes, and the various forces of nature.

Late in 1971, Marks and Weed set out for the Fiji Islands. There they chartered a salvage vessel capable of modest dredging operations. Three nights and two days later they were at the reefs. At points along the periphery, Weed and Marks dredged up sand to build small islets above sea level on which to install navigational aids: lights and radar reflectors.

With international law thus satisfied, the main body of the group established a provisional government and notified the state departments of all nations that a new nation had come into being.

It was to be called the Republic of Minerva. The notification carried with it the declaration of territorial sovereignty and maps of the territorial area.

Official spokesman or no, Tad is vocal on the project.

"We wanted to make a demonstration, and we also wanted to live in the first truly laissez-faire atmosphere. We are all businessmen who would like to operate where the government, in principle and in the constitution, is prevented from interfering in the marketplace as a force institution.

"We think we can prove that a force institution cannot morally participate in the marketplace, which is essentially a series of voluntary agreements.

"This is really a tremendous test for the market of liberty, for freedom is probably our only product. We want to see if business will follow us into what is really a God-forsaken area of the Pacific. This has happened in similar situations like some islands in the Caribbean, or Hong Kong, or Lichtenstein, so-called tax haven countries.

"Those businesses which are conveniently carried on off-shore in the various tax havens of the world will probably be the first to develop in our country. Bermuda, for instance, has many corporations based there to take advantage of liberalized Bermudian law."

The question naturally arises: What does his family think of all this?

For background, let's look at what has been going on up until now.

Tad Weed has been in the oil business, an independent producer exploring and drilling largely in the east. Tad's father was in the business before him and when the elder Weed retired, Tad took over and began looking after the wells.

Inevitably, the younger Weed began drilling on his own, forming his own company, known as Thurlow Weed and Associates.

"As a little independent, you do the same thing the big oil companies do," says Tad. "The only thing is, you wear a lot of hats. You take off your geologist's hat and put on your lawyer's hat . . . the big difference is you do everything on a small scale."

Tad was a geology major for his first two years in college. Then he went into petroleum engineering, and finally graduated as a Bachelor of Philosophy.

"The philosophy prepared me for the dry holes and my study of geology prepared me to argue with consultants," Tad laughed.

Now he is closing up the business. He has two children, Michael and Stephen, ages six and eight.

"Surprisingly," says Tad, "my boys understand the call of freedom and understand my urge better than many adults. You can explain some abstract, philosophical ideas having to do with freedoms being necessary for human beings to function well, and the little six and eight year old kids can really understand this."

Tad's wife, Susan, is a ski instructress and actively involved in local politics. They were married in 1960.

"As for Susan, the jury is still out," said Tad. "She hasn't let me know whether she approves or not. Sometimes, what we have been trying to do comes across as a rejection of America, which doesn't sit too well with voters.

"We consider ourselves profoundly pro-American. Indeed, among the very few Americans who appreciate where all this abundance came from and how it got here. It hurts us to have some people misinterpret what we're doing as a rejection of America."

The eventual land size of the dredged-up Republic of Minerva is figured to be around 4,000 acres. There is enough risk capital among the group to make a considerable start on the operation, but not enough to proceed immediately to its eventual completion.

"Most of the group are like me," says Weed, "fugitives from over-regulated businesses who would like to operate in a truly laissez-faire capitalistic atmosphere. We are going to have to establish businesses that can get into a pay-as-you-go situation from the beginning."

For Tad Weed, this means a first notion of setting up a postal system. Also, "I'm certainly interested in banking and possibly providing some type of information service. Postal services and information I can see as a couple of very early needs in the country."

He might have to get himself into the airline business, too. There used to be some big old Sutherland flying boats in Fiji which serviced the area on an emergency basis. But as they became obsolete, it hasn't proved worthwhile to bring in any new amphibious equipment.

"It's about three days' run to Suva, the principal city of Fiji, with the ships we can afford," Tad went on. "Any time you are that far away from hospital service you have to be careful not to get appendicitis. Until we can afford to raise a hospital or afford an airline consisting of some amphibious aircraft, it's going to remain a frontier area.

"Everyone in this thing is an individualist, and it is sometimes hard to get such people working together and thinking along the same lines. But the individuals together possess enough so that we can get a very good test as to whether this will work or not. By that I mean bringing in dredging equipment and seeing how difficult it will be to create and maintain quite a number of acres of dry land.

"The big question is if the nations of the world will tolerate our presence. We've made quite a commitment and the people involved will be very upset if we are undermined politically, or stomped on. What we could do about it remains to be seen."

There is no timetable for the country. It will grow as they can get to it.

"It's a very exciting project," said Tad.

History may look back upon that as a considerable understatement.